AF608213

The Recipient of Extreme Unction

This dissertation was approved by the Right Reverend Clement V. Bastnagel, S.T.L., J.U.D., Dean of the School of Canon Law, as director, and by the Reverend John Rogg Schmidt, A.B., J.C.D., LL.B., and the Reverend Bernard F. Deutsch, J.C.D., I.C.D., as readers.

THE CATHOLIC UNIVERSITY OF AMERICA
CANON LAW STUDIES
No. 419

The Recipient of Extreme Unction

A DISSERTATION

Submitted to the Faculty of the School of Canon Law of The Catholic University of America in Partial Fulfillment of the Requirements for the Degree of Doctor of Canon Law

BY

CHARLES GEORGE RENATI, A.B., J.C.L.
Priest of the Archdiocese of San Francisco

THE CATHOLIC UNIVERSITY OF AMERICA PRESS
WASHINGTON, D. C.
1961

Nihil Obstat:

Clement V. Bastnagel, S.T.L., J.U.D.
Censor Deputatus

Washington, D. C., May 20, 1961

Imprimatur:

✠ John J. Mitty, D.D.
Archbishop of San Francisco

San Francisco, California, May 23, 1961

COPYRIGHT © 1961
THE CATHOLIC UNIVERSITY OF AMERICA PRESS, INC.

Printed by
The Wickersham Printing Company
Lancaster, Pennsylvania

"He took pity on them, and
healed those who were sick."

Matt. XIV:14.

To My Mother and Father

FOREWORD

Inasmuch as man is a psychophysical unity there exists a real interdependence between his physical well-being and the vigor of his mental and spiritual activity—between the strength of his body and the strength of his spiritual life. Even when possessing sound health, man does not find it easy to battle against the forces of the world, of the flesh, and of the devil; but when his body is weak and his strength is low, the impacts of those forces increase while his own resistance and vigilance decrease. To fortify a Christian in these particular exigencies of the spiritual life on earth, Christ, in His compassion and understanding of the trials of the sick, instituted a sacrament by which the spiritual debility of the sick is alleviated, namely Extreme Unction or the Sacred Anointing of the Sick.

"Is anyone sick among you? Let him call in the priests of the Church, and let them pray over him, anointing him with oil in the name of the Lord. And the prayer of faith will save the sick man, and the Lord will raise him up, and if he be in sins, they shall be forgiven him." [1]

The purpose of this study is to review the qualifications postulated by the law of the Church in canons 940-944 of the Code of Canon Law for the valid and lawful reception of this sacrament. Special attention will be paid to the condition of danger of death, which the Code stresses as a requirement in the recipient, for it seems to offer the most difficulty in determining whether a sick person is to be anointed or not, and whether he can be anointed again or not. The entire question of administering Extreme Unction to non-Catholics is outside the scope of this study, although the writer must treat of it incidentally when speaking of the requirements of baptism and intention in the recipient.

The writer here expresses his gratitude to his Archbishop, The

[1] St. James, V:14,15.

Most Reverend John J. Mitty, D.D., Archbishop of San Francisco, for the opportunity to have pursued postgraduate studies in Canon Law, to the Faculty of the School of Canon Law, and to all the priests with whom he has been associated at the Catholic University of America during the past three years, for their friendship and assistance.

TABLE OF CONTENTS

PAGE

CHAPTER IV

CHAPTER I

THE OBLIGATION TO RECEIVE EXTREME UNCTION

"Is anyone among you sick? Let him call in the priests of the Church and let them pray over him, anointing him with oil in the name of the Lord." [1] Cornelius a Lapide (1567-1637) saw in these words promulgating the sacrament of Extreme Unction not only a counsel but a precept.[2] Kern (1856-1908) held it probable that Extreme Unction is *per se* necessary for salvation to a sick person who is dying, and that it involves the consequent serious obligation on the part of the sick person approaching death to receive this sacrament.[3]

Bord, on the other hand, saw no strict command in the words of St. James,[4] and Lehmkuhl (1834-1918), following St. Thomas (1225-1274) and St. Alphonsus (1696-1787), wrote before the Code that no grave obligation is incumbent on a sick person to receive the sacrament.[5]

The Council of Trent (1545-1563) made it quite clear that no one could hold Extreme Unction in any contemptful regard without being guilty of sin, but did not define any particular obligation on the part of the faithful to receive it.[6] Canon 944 of the

[1] St. James, V:14.

[2] "... non tantum consilium sed praeceptum."—*Commentarium in Sacram Scripturam* (21 vols., Neapoli, 1859), X, ad Jacobum, V: 14.

[3] *De Sacramento Extremae Unctionis Tractatus Dogmaticus* (Ratisbonae: Sumptibus et Typis Friderici Pustet, 1907), p. 364 (hereafter cited *De Extrema Unctione*).

[4] *L'Extrême-Onction, d'après l'Epître de Saint Jacques, Examinée dans la Tradition* (Bruges: Charles Beyaert, 1923), p. 59.

[5] Lehmkuhl, *Theologia Moralis* (9. ed., 2 vols., Friburgi Brisgoviae: Herder, 1898), II, n. 578; St. Alphonsus Liguori, *Theologia Moralis* (editio nova, cura P. L. Gaudé, 4 vols., Romae: Typographia Vaticana, 1905-1912), Lib. VI, n. 733.

[6] Sess. XIV, can. 3, *de Extrema Unctione:* "Si quis dixerit Extremae Unctionis ritum et usum . . . posseque a Christianis absque peccato contemni, A.S."; cap. 3, *de Extrema Unctione:* "Neque vero tanti sacramenti

Code expressly declares that, although Extreme Unction is not *per se* a necessary means to salvation, it is not allowed to neglect this sacrament.[7]

A sick person would be guilty of neglecting Extreme Unction if he voluntarily declined to receive it when available to him, and this without any cause for doing so.[8] Such neglect would be contrary to the charity owed to oneself, but Cance believes the obligation to receive the sacrament could be considered as slight,[9] and this, says Conte a Coronata, is the common opinion.[10] This latter author distinguishes neglect from contempt. There is contempt for the sacrament when a person declines to receive it because he thinks it is useless or worthless. This contempt is certainly a serious sin.[11]

Though a person is not inherently under any grave obligation to receive Extreme Unction, a grave obligation could arise for incidental reasons. This would happen if by his neglect or refusal to be anointed he would foster a low regard for the sacrament among others, who in turn might be led to neglect this sacramental aid for salvation. This would result if a priest, or a religious, or a person looked upon as a good Catholic should

---

contemptus absque ingenti scelere et ipsius Spiritus Sancti iniuria esse posset."—Schroeder, *Canons and Decrees of the Council of Trent* (St. Louis: Herder, 1941), pp. 376, 379.

[7] "Quamvis hoc sacramentum per se non sit de necessitate medii ad salutem, nemini tamen licet illud negligere; et omni studio et diligentia curandum ut infirmi, dum sui compotes sunt, illud recipiant."

[8] Cf. Blat, *Commentarium Textus Codicis Iuris Canonici* (5 vols. in 6, Vol. III, Pars I, 2. ed., Romae: Ex Typographia Pontificia in Instituto Pii IX, 1924), III, n. 288.

[9] *Le Code de Droit Canonique* (3 vols., Vol. II, 8. ed., Paris: Librairie Lecoffre, 1951), II, n. 268.

[10] *Institutiones Iuris Canonici, De Sacramentis Tractatus Canonicus* (3 vols., Vol. I, editio altera emendata et aucta, Taurini: Marietti, 1951), I, n. 555 (hereafter cited *De Sacramentis*).

[11] Conte a Coronata, *loc. cit.;* Jone, *Commentarium in Codicem Iuris Canonici* (3 vols., Paderbornae: Officina Libraria F. Schöningh, 1950-1955), II, 171.

refuse to be anointed without any justifiable cause.[12] The grave scandal consequent on this neglect is what lends gravity to the obligation to receive it.

There could be a situation in which Extreme Unction becomes necessary as a means of salvation. This would be the case of one in mortal sin, with attrition only, who is unconscious. In such a condition, however, a person would hardly be in a position to be charged with any obligation. If he is conscious, other remedies are possible, such as the sacrament of Penance, or even perfect contrition. It does not seem that a serious obligation to receive Extreme Unction could ever arise in view simply of the personal needs of the subject.[13]

Although Extreme Unction is not absolutely necessary for salvation, it is one of the ordinary means instituted by Christ for achieving that salvation, and should not as such be ignored. True, there is no divine precept to receive this sacrament at any time during one's life, nor is there any ecclesiastical precept binding one to receive it even in danger of death, as there is for Viaticum, and for Penance in cases where there are mortal sins yet to be submitted directly to the power of the keys.[14] Nevertheless, the law states that *no one* can arbitrarily neglect this sacrament.[15]

The conclusion that there is some obligation for qualified subjects to receive Extreme Unction seems warranted. Christ instituted this sacrament not as a superfluous aid to the spiritual life, but as one immensely beneficial in a certain contingency of human life. And though some spiritual lives are weaker than others and therefore in more need of strength when that spiritual life is put under extraordinary stress, no one should feel that he is so confirmed in grace as to be able to do without Extreme Unc-

12 Conte a Coronata, *loc. cit.*, Koch, *A Handbook of Moral Theology* (adapted and edited by Arthur Preuss, 5 vols., St. Louis: Herder, 1918-1924), II, 193; Jone, *loc. cit.*

13 Lehmkuhl, *op. cit.*, II, n. 578.

14 Cf. canons 864 and 901.

15 ". . . *nemini* tamen licet illud negligere."—Canon 944.

tion when he finds himself in that particular trial of human life for which it was specifically instituted.

The obligation to receive it, however, does not seem in and of itself to be a grave one binding at any particular time in a Christian's life.[16] According to the doctrine of the Council of Trent, and of the Code, and in accord with the common opinion of the authors, the only neglect that intrinsically involves a serious sin is that which is born of contempt and disdain for the sacrament itself.

Canon 944, however, places an obligation on those who have charge of the sick that they "carefully and diligently" see to it that the sick receive Extreme Unction while they are conscious.[17] The Church greatly desires that the faithful avail themselves of all its spiritual treasures, and here expresses its strong desire that the sick receive Extreme Unction, despite the fact that no precept to do so is established.[18]

[16] Vermeersch-Creusen, *Epitome Iuris Canonici* (3 vols., Vol. II, 7. ed., Bruxellis: L'Edition Universelle, 1954), II, n. 228; Cappello, however, says that "taken speculatively the obligation is grave": "Sacramentum extremae unctionis per se non est de necessitate medii, sed nihilominus est per se necessarium vi suae institutionis ad salutem, quamvis non simpliciter et absolute. Quare obligatio suscipiendi hoc sacramentum *certa est,* et quidem probabilius—speculative loquendo, nisi causa iusta excuset—obligatio *gravis,* attenta ipsa rei natura."—*Tractatus Canonico-Moralis de Sacramentis* (5 vols., Vol. III, *De Extrema Unctione,* 4. ed., Taurini: Marietti, 1958), III, n. 272 (hereafter cited *De Extrema Unctione*). He derives this from the argument that a Christian in *danger of death* (the only occasion in which Extreme Unction is now *de facto* conferred) is bound to use the ordinary means available to insure his salvation. For the sick in danger of death Extreme Unction is such an ordinary means.—*Loc. cit.*

[17] ". . . et *omni studio et diligentia* curandum ut infirmi, dum sui plene compotes sunt, illud recipiant."

[18] "Extrema Unctio administretur etiam in casibus dubiis, scilicet sub conditione."—*Prima Romana Synodus MDCCCCLX* (Città del Vaticano: Typis Polyglottis Vaticanis, 1960), n. 461.

CHAPTER II

THE PHYSICAL REQUISITES IN THE RECIPIENT

Article I. Bodily Infirmity or Old Age

Each of the seven sacraments was instituted to supply a particular need in the Christian life. Extreme Unction has the specific purpose of counteracting and overcoming the spiritual ineptitude and debility occasioned by physical, bodily infirmity. Teaching his hearers the manner of Christian conduct in various circumstances of daily living, St. James exhorts them to pray in times of sadness and to sing in times of joy, and then, turning to a particular trial of human life, he says:

> Is any one among you sick? Let him call in the priests of the Church, and let them pray over him, anointing him with oil in the name of the Lord. And the prayer of faith will save the sick man and the Lord will raise him up, and if he be in sins, they shall be forgiven him.[1]

There is a special remedy against this common affliction that is physical sickness, a sacramental remedy. As it was "insinuated" in St. Mark, so now in this text of St. James the sacrament of the sick is explicitly "recommended and promulgated."[2]

The essential physical requisite set down clearly for the recipient of this anointing is bodily sickness.[3] "As to what the Blessed Apostle James wrote in his epistle," said Pope Innocent I in 416,

[1] St. James, V:14,15.

[2] Council of Trent, Session XIV, *On Extreme Unction,* Chapter 1—Schroeder, *The Canons and Decrees of the Council of Trent,* p. 99; St. Mark, VI:7,12,13: "And He sent them forth . . . and going forth they preached that all men should repent, and they cast out devils, and anointed with oil many sick people and healed them."

[3] A study of the word "sick" used by St. James will be made in the following section of this chapter.

"there is no doubt that it deals with the faithful who are sick." [4] The Profession of Faith of Michael Paleologus in the Second Council of Lyons in 1274 mentions Extreme Unction, "which according to the doctrine of Blessed James is applied to the sick." [5] "It is declared," says the Council of Trent, "that this anointing is to be given to the sick." [6] Pope Benedict XIV (1740-1758) emphasized the fact that the sick are the exclusive recipients of this sacrament: "Extreme Unction is to be administered only to the sick, not, however, to those who are physically well." [7] In his work *De Synodo Dioecesana,* the same pope mentioned the abuse that had crept into some parts of the Eastern Church of anointing with this sacrament those who were not sick. Citing both Arcudius (1562-1633) and Goar (1601-1653), who protested against such a practice, he agreed with Arcudius that it was simply an abuse, rather than with Goar who contended that, though the rite was identical with the sacramental rite, these anointings were not intended to be sacramental. Surprised that even a few Latin theologians believed that Extreme Unction conferred on the non-sick was valid, and describing their arguments in support of this opinion as "frivolous," Pope Benedict cited the Councils of Florence and of Trent, and pointed to the

[4] "Quod in beati Iacobi Apostoli Epistolis conscriptum est . . . non est dubium de fidelibus aegrotantibus accipi vel intelligi debere . . ."; Ep. *Si Instituta Ecclesiastica,* 19 mart. 416—J. P. Migne, *Patrologia Cursus Completus, Series Latina* (221 vols., Parisiis, 1844-1855), XX, 559 (hereafter cited *MPL*).

[5] ". . . Extrema Unctio, quae secundum doctrinam beati Iacobi infirmantibus adhibetur."—Ioannes Mansi, *Sacrorum Conciliorum Nova et Amplissima Collectio* (53 vols. in 60; Vols. I-XXXV, Florentiae, 1758-1798; Vols. XXXVI-LIII, Parisiis, 1901-1927), XXIV, 71.

[6] Session XIV, *On Extreme Unction,* Chapter III—"Declaratur etiam, esse hanc unctionem infirmis adhibendam. . . ."—Schroeder, *Canons and Decrees of the Council of Trent,* p. 376.

[7] Ep. Encycl. *Ex Quo,* 1 mart. 1756, § 44: ". . . solis infirmis administrandum, non autem benevalentibus. . . ."—*Codicis Iuris Canonici Fontes,* cura Emi Petri Card. Gasparri editi (9 vols., Romae [postea Civitate Vaticana]: Typis Polyglottis Vaticanis, 1923-1939, Vols. VII-IX, ed. cura et studio Emi Iustiniani Card. Serédi), n. 438 (hereafter cited *Fontes*).

consensus of theologians in general, as interpreting the words of St. James to mean that "only one who is sick" is capable of receiving Extreme Unction.[8]

Bodily illness is, without doubt, a requirement *"de necessitate sacramenti"* in the recipient of Extreme Unction.[9] Remove this condition and it is difficult to find a distinctive purpose for this sacrament. One who is healthy and in serious sin has the sacrament of Penance, as does also a sick person as long as he can manifest his sinfulness and sorrow. To sustain and strengthen their spiritual life of grace, the healthy and the sick as well have the Bread of Life in the Eucharist. For the Christian in danger of death there is the "last and indispensable" sacrament, Viaticum, which is the consummation of the whole Christian life, the sacrament that prepares man for his journey to Christ and the

[8] *De Synodo Dioecesana* (novissima editio auctior et castigatior, 3 vols., Romae: Ex Typographia J. Baptistae Cannetti, 1783), Lib. VIII, Cap. V. The reasoning behind the practice of anointing the non-sick was the fact that the sacrament was regarded as a remedy against all sickness, spiritual as well as physical. A person in sin was spiritually sick, and could therefore avail himself of it. Thus arose the practice, too, of anointing penitents. For a full treatment of this whole subject cf. Doronzo, *De Extrema Unctione* (2 vols., Milwaukee: Bruce, 1954-1955), II, pp. 533-561; Sainte-Beuve (1613-1677) was one of the few Latin theologians who thought that the Greeks were not in error in holding that the sacrament was instituted for the healthy as well as the sick, "nam neque Scripturae, neque Conc. Trid., neque Decretum Eugenii, nec denique nuncupatio materiae illius id postulat. Scriptura iubet ungi infirmos, non excludit sanos. . . ."—*Tractatus de Sacramentis Confirmationis et Extremae Unctionis* (Parisiis, 1686), Disp. VII, art. 1, p. 506.

[9] "Quod subiectum capax extremae unctionis sit solus *infirmus* ac propterea quod *morbus* sit de necessitate sacramenti, certum est."—Cappello, *De Extrema Unctione,* n. 230; Suarez, *Disputationes de sacramentis Confessionis et Extremae Unctionis, de Purgatorio, Suffragiis, et Indulgentiis,* Disp. XLII, *De subiecto cui dandum est hoc sacramentum* (*extrema unctio*), Sect. II, n. 2: ". . . eum tantum hominem qui corpore infirmus est . . . esse capacem huius sacramenti . . . est ergo haec conditio ex parte subiecti *de necessitate sacramenti;* nec in hoc est ulla difficultas,"—*Opera Omnia* (28 vols., Parisiis, 1856-1861), XXII, 851; Doronzo, *op. cit.,* II, 562; St. Alphonsus, *Theologia Moralis,* Lib. VI, 713, where the anointing of the non-sick is branded as *"omnino invalidum."*

vision of God. The sacrament for those in danger of death is not the Anointing, but Viaticum, as the I Council of Nicaea (325) taught over sixteen hundred years ago:

> Concerning the dying, the ancient canonical law is still to be followed; so that if any man be at the point of death, he must not be deprived of the last and most indispensable Viaticum.[10]

What in 325 the Council could call "the ancient canonical law" has always been the teaching of the Church, and it finds precise expression in the Code today. No one in danger of death is bound directly by precept to receive Extreme Unction, not even though he be dying from sickness, but every Catholic in danger of death from any cause whatever is obliged under precept to receive Viaticum.

> In periculo mortis, quavis ex causa procedat, fideles sacrae communionis recipiendae praecepto tenentur.[11]

So connected with the Christian's departure from this life is Viaticum that the second paragraph of canon 864 strongly recommends that one who has communicated earlier in the day but later finds himself in danger of death communicate again.[12]

The particular contingency in the Christian life for which Extreme Unction was instituted is not primarily that of dying or of death.[13] If it were, one would rightly expect it to be con-

[10] Canon 13: "De his qui ad exitum veniunt etiam nunc lex antiqua regularisque servabitur; ita ut si quis egreditur e corpore ultimo et maxime necessario viatico minime privetur."—Mansi, *Conciliorum Nova et Amplissima Collectio,* II, 682.

[11] Canon 864, § 1.

[12] "Etiamsi eadem die sacra communione fuerint refecti, valde tamen suadendum, ut in vitae discrimen adducti denuo communicent."

[13] ". . . se si guarda invece a tutta la tradizione liturgica e pastorale comminciare dal I Concilio de Nicea, il vero sacramento della Chiesa dei morenti è il Viatico."—Mario Righetti, *Manuale di Storia Liturgica* (4 vols., Milano: Ancora, 1950-1956), IV, 245. Cf. Charles Davis, "The Sacrament of the Sick," *The Clergy Review,* XLIII (1958), 726-746, and the fine study of the historical development of the administration of Exreme Unction by Paul F. Palmer, "The Purpose of Anointing the Sick; A Reappraisal," *Theological Studies,* XIX (1958), 309-344.

ferred on all who are in danger of death, no matter what the cause, whereas in fact it is refused to those who are in danger of death if they are not sick. Sickness is an indispensable condition for the anointing.

In man, body and soul are a psychophysical unity. The malfunctioning or weakness of one is certain to affect the activity of the other. A person who is physically tired, or sleepy, finds it more difficult to think quickly and clearly than one who is fresh and full of vigor. When a Christian is sick, his bodily strength dissipated by illness, he finds it more difficult to concentrate, to meditate, to pray, to unite actively his sufferings with those of the suffering Christ. His resistance to the forces of concupiscence and to temptations can be very low, and if he is worn out by illness he cannot watch and pray like one who enjoys health of body. To heal such a one of this spiritual weakness and ineptitude occasioned by the bodily infirmity, and to restore vigor to the spiritual life during the period of sickness, the sacramental help of the Unction is given." [14]

"Is any one among you sick?" Let him receive the anointing and "the prayer of faith will heal the sick man and the Lord will raise him up"—an unconditional guarantee. In this sense, that special help is bestowed by which the whole man, body and soul, can live the fullest and most profitable supernatural life despite the particular, added handicap of doing so when weakened by illness, the sick man is always healed—healed of spiritual debility and restored to spiritual vigor.[15] This is the "*conforta-*

[14] ". . . Ces personnes [the non-sick] sont encore, malgre la proximité du trépas, dans la vigeur de leur organisme et de leur âme; ils ne connaissent pas l'épuisement qu'une maladie grave produit dans les autres et qui les rend impuissants. C'est pour remedier cet épuisement et à cette faiblesse qu'a été instituée l'Extrême-Onction."—F. Cuttaz, *Remède Divin pour les Chrétiens Malades* (Paris: Desclée & Cie., 1950), p. 71.

[15] "Il defetto spirituale insito nella malattia è una manifestazione particolarmente grave della concupiscenza, compreso nel senso passivo e negativo, come impedimento della vita spirituale. La grazia sacramentale come rimedio contro questo difetto, restituisce all'uomo il vigore per vivere la vita soprannaturale. In altre parole, l'unzione restituisce all'infermo una parte della integrità . . . [estrema unzione è] un aiuto concesso alla persona intera per vivere intensamente la sua vita soprannaturale, nonostante la difficultà particolare dell'infermità."—A. Alszeghy, "L'effetto corporale

tio animae," singled out by the theologians as the principal effect of Extreme Unction.[16]

Treating of the effects of "this holy unction of the sick," the Council of Trent teaches that it

> wipes away sins, provided there are still some to be expiated, as well as the remnants of sin (*peccati reliquias*), and comforts and strengthens the soul of the sick person, by arousing in him great confidence in the divine mercy; encouraged thereby, the sick person bears more easily the difficulties and the trials *of his illness*, and resists more readily the temptations of the demon who lies in wait for the heel, and, when it is expedient for the health of the soul, he receives, at times, health of body.[17]

It is to help a person bear the "trials and burdens of his illness" that he is anointed.[18]

---

dell'Estrema Unzione," *Gregorianum,* XXXVIII (1957), 403-404. Sometimes the restoration of the sick person to spiritual vigor includes or is joined with a clinical cure of the body, when this is beneficial or necessary for the spiritual life.

16 " . . . hoc sacramentum . . . datur . . . contra illos defectus quibus homo spiritualiter infirmatur, ut non habeat perfectum vigorem ad actus vitae, gratiae, vel gloriae. . . . "—St. Thomas Aquinas, *Summa Theologica* (5 vols., Romae: Forzani, 1894), Pars Tertia Supp., Q. XXX, Art. I, *Respondeo;* "Ergo effectus principalis Extremae Unctionis est confortatio animi hominis infirmi, qua roboretur contra pericula debilitatis spiritualis, quae gravem morbum consequuntur."—Kern, *De Extrema Unctione,* p. 238; "Therefore, having excluded all others, we may conclude that the alleviation and the strengthening of the soul, the *confortatio animae* is the principal effect of Extreme Unction."—Henry S. Kryger, *The Doctrine of the Effects of Extreme Unction in Its Historical Development* (The Catholic University of America Studies in Sacred Theology, Second Series, No. 13, Washington, D. C.: The Catholic University of America Press, 1949), p. 87.

17 Session XIV, *On Extreme Unction,* Chapter 2—Schroeder, *Canons and Decrees of the Council of Trent,* p. 100, for English text, and p. 375, for Latin text (italics added).

18 The remains of sin which Exreme Unction removes from the sick person are the natural inclinations or passions adhering to the mind, the will, the imagination, the memory and the sensitive appetite in consequence of original sin, or as caused or augmented by actual sin, which remain even after the remission of sin and render the sinner spiritually weak.—Cf. Stanislaus J. Bryzana, *Remains of Sin and Extreme Unction according to*

Canon 940, § 1, states that only those who are in danger of death from sickness or old age can be anointed.[19] Evidently there is no particular exigency in the spiritual life of those who face death from causes other than internal physical causes. For them, even as they face death, the other sacraments prove sufficient for satisfying their spiritual needs.[20] For one who faces death without being sick is without a capacity for receiving Extreme Unction, says Cappello, and any administration to him would be invalid.[21] The sacrament can be given to only those who are near death because of illness, bodily wounds, childbirth, or old age, wrote La Croix (1652-1714) and St. Alphonsus (1696-1787), because only such people are sick.[22] Laymann (1574-1635) taught that the danger must arise from sickness, pestilence, wounds, poison, or some similar intrinsic cause.[23] The authors here spoke of the danger of death, but at the same time taught

Theologians after Trent (Rome: Catholic Book Agency, 1953), p. 97. The strength of these *"reliquiae"* is intensified during times of physical debility when man's resistance is lowered.—Cf. Alszeghy, *Gregorianum*, XXXVIII (1957), 402. Cognizant of this, the devil might well be expected to make extra personal attempts to secure the fall into sin of a friend of God in a weakened state.

19 "Extrema Unctio praeberi non potest nisi fideli, qui post adeptum usum rationis ob infirmitatem vel senium in periculo mortis versetur."

20 If Extreme Unction is in fact a sacrament for the dying; if its purpose is one *"immediate disponens ad gloriam," "proxime praeparans animam ad introitum in gloriam,"* if its purpose and essense is, as Kern teaches, to heal perfectly the soul of a dying Christian so that he may enter immediately into heaven when he dies (*De Extrema Unctione*, pp. 81-110) it is hard to see why such an immensely important sacrament of the dying should be denied to those Christians who are to die in consequence of a cause other than that of sickness.

21 "Huiusmodi homo, qui versatur in periculo mortis sine morbo, non est subiectum capax extremae unctionis, ideoque invalide administraretur."—Cappello, *De Extrema Unctione*, n. 232.

22 "Hoc Sacramentum tantum dandum est morti propinquis ex morbo, vulnere, partu vel senectute, *quia hi soli sunt infirmi.*"—LaCroix, *Theologia Moralis* (2 vols., Coloniae, 1719), II, 208; St. Alphonsus, *Theologia Moralis*, Lib. VI, n. 712.

23 ". . . vita periclitetur propter infirmitatem ex morbo, peste, vulnere, veneno, potato vel simili causa intrinseca."—Laymann, *Theologia Moralis* (2 vols., Bambergae, 1669), II, Lib. V, Tract. VIII, cap. IV, 4.

that sickness of the body is a prerequisite for anointing, no matter what agent brought on that infirmity. It makes no difference whether one has become sick by contracting a disease, by being exposed to the elements, by physiological complications of childbirth, by swallowing poison, by being burned, or beaten, or wounded, or by simply suffering the deteriorating effects of old age. As long as his bodily condition is one of sickness he is, at least on that account, capable of receiving Extreme Unction. It is the cause of the danger, and not the cause of the sickness, that needs to be intrinsic.[24]

Convicts about to be executed, soldiers ready to plunge into an odds-against-survival battle, passengers on a sinking ship, people trapped in a burning building, or persons about to risk their lives in an effort to save someone else from certain death—none of these can be anointed because they are not sick, and thus they do not fit into the class described by St. James as the beneficiaries of this sacrament—"Is any one among you sick?" [25]

The debilitating effects of sickness which create in man an exigency for a special sacramental aid are often produced, not by any specific illness or disease, but by the gradual and progressive deterioration of the body that accompanies old age. Old people whose physical forces have declined considerably say they cannot remember things very well, they cannot concentrate, or

24 "Sacramenti capax est qui propter venenum haustum vel vulnus acceptum aliamve similem causam in periculo mortis versatur. Nam hic homo est vere infirmus, undecumque infirmitas originem duxerit. Proinde iste aegrotans potest valide et licite recipere extremam unctionem, licet causa aegritudinis fuerit extrinseca et violenta."—Cappello, *De Extrema Unctione,* n. 232.

25 "Subiectum in mortis periculo *ex morbo* versari, ut ex Iacobi verbis liquet. . . . Ex hoc capite invalide inunguntur in periculo mortis versantes *ex causa extrinseca,* v. gr. capite damnati, milites instante bello, periculosam navigationem suscepturi, ii quibus mors imminet ob inundationem, incendium, hostium incursionem; item periculosam operationem chirurgicam subituri, nisi ex infirmitate iam periclitari videantur. E contra, valide inunguntur qui in mortis periculo versantur ex causa *intrinseca,* v. gr. morbo, venenosa potione, vulnere accepto, instante partu difficili et periculoso. Huc quoque revocantur *senio confecti;* ipsa enim senectus morbus est."—A. Piscetta-A. Gennaro, *Elementa Theologiae Moralis* (7 vols., Vol. V, 6. ed., Torino: Società Editrice Internazionale, 1938), V, n. 1027, III.

pray. The body is weak and does not serve the soul in its operations as it once did. If indeed old age does produce these effects in a person it is rightly equated to sickness, and should the old person be in danger of death because of that natural bodily deterioration (as canon 940 postulates) that person is a fit subject for Extreme Unction. He need not be ailing from any (other) particular illness.[26]

> Extrema Unctio praeberi non potest nisi fideli qui . . . ob infirmitatem *vel senium* in periculo mortis versetur.[27]

To be considered a fit subject for anointing, an old person must really show a decline in physical strength. Years alone do not constitute this *senium.* A person who is sixty, seventy or eighty years of age, but who is still vigorous and healthy, is by no means automatically a fit subject for Extreme Unction. Davis (1866-1952) and Augustine (1872-1943) held that some sign of waning vitality such as "continual attacks of fainting fits" should be present before Extreme Unction is conferred on the aged.[28] At any rate "old age" here must always be understood to mean the state of physical weakness and decrepitude that often overtakes people as they reach advanced years.

It is certain that one must be physically infirm in order to receive the sacrament of Extreme Unction; it now remains to be

[26] "Sicut si quis confectus senili aetate, moreretur ex ipsius naturae defectu absque alia aegritudine, nihilominus ungendus esset, quia illa est sufficiens infirmitas constituens hominem in necessitate huius sacramenti; . . ."—Suarez, Disp. XLII, Sec. II, n. 11—*Opera Omnia,* XXII, 855; ". . . et iis, qui prae senio deficiunt et in diem videntur morituri, etiam sine alia infirmitate."—*Roman Ritual* of Pope Paul V (1614), T. 5, *De Sacramento Extremae Unctionis,* Cap. I, n. 5; "Conceditur senibus, qui prae decrepita aetate, licet nulla alia speciali afficiantur aegritudine, in dies morituri creduntur; ipsa enim gravis et annosa senectus, infirmitas est quae interiora vitae organa labefactat, et mox ducit ad interitum."—Benedictus XIV, *De Synodo Dioecesana,* Lib. VIII, Cap. V, n. 2; the authors like to quote Cicero's statement, *"Senectus ipsa morbus est."*

[27] Canon 940.

[28] Henry Davis, *Moral and Pastoral Theology* (5. ed. revised and enlarged, 4 vols., New York: Sheed & Ward, 1946), IV, 7; Charles Augustine, *A Commentary on The New Code of Canon Law* (8 vols., St. Louis: Herder, 1918-1922), IV, 402.

seen whether it is necessary for that sickness to have reached any special degree or intensity before one is to be anointed.

Article II. Danger of Death

A. *The History of the Requirement*

1. *The Epistle of St. James*

The word *"asthenein"* used by St. James to describe the state of the recipient of the anointing means literally to be ill, sick, physically weak.[29] It is the common Greek word employed throughout the New Testament to designate bodily infirmity.[30] Standing alone it no more connotes a serious or dangerous illness than does the English word "sick" when used without any further qualification. St. James did not tell how sick the person referred to in the text actually was. Cornelius a Lapide, however, and many with him, held that this sickness was to be understood as one that brings with it the peril of death.[31]

Those who follow Cornelius a Lapide in this restricted meaning of the word cite several passages of the New Testament wherein the word is used of someone dying from sickness. But in all these instances it is the context and not the simple word "sick" that points to the seriousness of the sick person's condition. Only because the verse adds that he was "at the point of

[29] Cf. Arndt and Gingrich, *A Greek-English Lexicon of the New Testament and Other Early Christian Literature* (a translation and adaptation of Walter Bauer's *griechisch-deutsches Wörterbuch zu den Schriften des neuen Testaments und der übrigen urchristlichen Literatur,* 4th revised and augmented edition, London: Cambridge University Press, 1957), p. 115; Zorell, *Lexicon Graecum Novi Testamenti* (Paris: P. Lethielleux, 1931), p. 183.

[30] Acts, IV:9—used to describe the cripple cured by Peter and John; Luke, X:9—"But whatever town you shall enter . . . cure the *sick* who are there"; Matthew, XXV:43—"(I was) *sick* and you visited me"; Acts, V:15—"They carried the *sick* into the streets"; Mark, VI:56—"They laid the *sick* in the market places"; Luke IV:40—"All who had persons *sick* with various diseases brought them to Him"; II Timothy, IV:20—". . . but Trophimus I left *sick* at Miletus."

[31] "Intellige graviter et periculose ad mortem."—Cornelius a Lapide, *Commentarium in Sacram Scripturam,* X, *Commentarium in Epistolam Sancti Iacobi,* V: 14.—No proof for this limited interpretation is given.

death" is it clear that the ruler's son "lying sick at Capharnaum" was dangerously ill.[32] When Mary and Martha pleaded, "Lord, he whom Thou lovest is sick," who would conclude that Lazarus was near death if the account that followed did not in fact relate that he died from that illness?[33] The seriousness of Tabitha's illness is known, not from the phrase "she fell ill," but from the added words, "and died."[34] The perilous situation of Epaphroditus is not evident in the words, "he was sick," but in the further information that, "yes, he was sick, almost unto death."[35]

It does not seem correct to say that the word used by St. James "ordinarily indicates and presupposes a grave and dangerous illness" in New Testament usage,[36] nor that the restriction of its meaning to "those who are seriously sick"—if by seriously sick are meant only those who are in danger of death—"is undoubtably warrantable."[37]

The word *"kamnein"* used in the phrase, "and the prayer of faith will heal the *sick man*" means literally "to be weary or fatigued" with the secondary meaning "to be ill."[38] A very last possible meaning is "to be wasting away, hopelessly ill." There seems no justification, however, for forcing this last possible meaning into a context that otherwise neither describes the sick man's condition as desperate nor gives any indication of being a death-bed scene.[39] Had St. James had in mind one close to death from sickness he could so easily have made that clear. But he did not write, "is anyone dangerously ill, or sick unto

[32] St. John, IV:46-47.

[33] St. John, XI:11-16.

[34] Acts, IX:37.

[35] Philippians, II:27.

[36] Charles Pickar, "Is anyone sick among you," *The Catholic Biblical Quarterly*, VII (1945), 167.

[37] Kilker, *Extreme Unction* (The Catholic University of America Canon Law Studies, No. 32, Washington, D. C.: The Catholic University of America, 1926), p. 9.

[38] Cf. Arndt and Gingrich, *A Greek-English Lexicon of The New Testament*, pp. 402, 403.

[39] Cf. K. Condon, "Sacrament of Healing," *Scripture*, XI (1959), 35.

death, or dying from sickness," but simply, "is anyone sick among you?"

St. James did indicate, however, that the man was suffering more than a slight indisposition. His bodily strength was worn down; he could not go to the priests, so that he called for them to come to him.[40] When the priests arrived they prayed "over him"; he was apparently too weary to rise or to kneel, and so he lay prostrate.[41] His bodily vigor had been sapped. When an illness so debilitates a man, with or without any concomitant danger of death, it fits the physical condition described by St. James as a requisite for the reception of the sacrament of the sick. Insofar as an illness which renders a person at least temporarily weakened or helpless—such as high fever can—may be considered serious or grave, one might rightly say that the subject of the anointing according to St. James needs to be "seriously ill"; not, however, if by seriously ill is necessarily included the probability of dying.[42] This initial legislation concerning the recipient of Extreme Unction—legislation of the positive divine law—does not postulate a danger of death.

2. *The I to the IX Century*

In his minute and scholarly study of the administration of Extreme Unction during the first nine centuries of the Church's history, Chavasse concludes:

[40] This unusual summoning of a superior by an inferior, says Bord, is justified by the sick man's physical debility.—*L'Extrême-Onction d'après l'Epître de Saint Jacques*, p. 56.

[41] Bord, *op. cit.*, p. 57; Pickar, "art. cit.," p. 168.

[42] "Saint Jacques s'arrête spécialement à l'épreuve de la maladie. Le malade qu'il met en scène, sans être strictement un moribund est gravement atteint."—A. Charue, "Epître de S. Jacques," *La Sainte Bible,* Vol. XII (Paris: Letouzey et Ané, 1946), p. 380; "Car il s'agit d'un Chrêtien affaibli, épuissé par la maladie. Il ne s'agit ni d'un mourant, ni d'un agonisant."—P. Anciaux, "L'Onction des Malades," *Collectanea Mechliniensia,* Nova Series, XXIX (1959), 9. It is difficult to understand how Denis the Carthusian (1402-1472) could maintain that the recipient in St. James' account is one "so gravely sick as to be, in all probability, dying (graviter, ita ut probabiliter moriturus)—*Opera Omnia,* Vol. XIII, "Enarratio in Capitulum V Epistolae Catholicae Beati Iacobi" (Montreuil sur Mer, 1901), Art. VII.

> Never before the ninth century is there question of the anointing of the sick, in the texts that are extant, as a rite conferred *in extremis* with a view to preparing the sick person for death.[43]

There are two extant formularies for blessing the oil of the sick that date back to the first centuries, one in the ante-Nicene *Apostolic Tradition of Hippolytus,* the other in the fourth century *Prayer Book of Bishop Serapion.* Both indicate that the purpose of anointing is to "bring strength (comfort) and health to all who use it,"[44] and "for a throwing off of every sickness and every infirmity . . . for health and soundness of soul, body, spirit, for perfect strengthening."[45] Nothing in them hints that the anointing was reserved to the sick who were in danger of dying. The *"Emitte"* prayer for the blessing of the oil, as found in both the Gelasian and the Gregorian Sacramentaries and having its origin in the fifth century, regards the oil as a "safeguard of body, mind and spirit to drive out all pain, all infirmity, all sickness of mind and body."[46] Such expectations do not suggest that the anointing was to prepare the sick for death.

[43] A. Chavasse, *Étude sur l'Onction des Infirmes dans L'Eglise Latine du III au XIe Siècle,* Tome I, *De troisième Siècle à la Réforme Carolingienne* (Lyons, 1942), p. 196; also Paul F. Palmer, *Sources of Christian Theology* (2 vols., Westminster: The Newman Press, 1955-1959), II, p. 396, where basically the same conclusion is reached after an examination of the sources relating to the conferring of Extreme Unction.

[44] ". . . confortationem et sanitatem utentibus illud."—Chavasse, *op. cit.*, I, 34. This had reference to corporal effects, says Chavasse, *ibid.*, p. 39.

[45] Cf. full translation of prayer in P. Pourrat, *Theology of The Sacraments* (translated from the 3rd French Edition, St. Louis: Herder, 1910), pp. 325-326. The oil is called a "medicine of life and salvation," to expel "every demon and evil agent, every fever and chill . . . that they may depart from the inward and outward parts of these servants." The recurring references to demons and unclean spirits is appreciated when one keeps in mind the ancient belief that in many cases sickness was the result of or punishment for sin, or the work of the devil himself. It was for this reason, perhaps, that until the tenth century, the possessed were also anointed with the oil and rite of the sick (Chavasse, *op. cit.*, I, 160-162).

[46] ". . . tutamentum corporis, animae, et spiritus ad evacuandos omnes dolores, omnem infirmitatem, omnem aegritudinem mentis et corporis."—Ludovicus Antonius Muratori, *Liturgia Romana Vetus* (2 vols., Venetiis, 1748), I, 555 for the *Gelasian Sacramentary*; 55 for the *Gregorian Sacra-*

From several instances wherein the administration of the sacraments to dying Christians was discussed it is apparent that Extreme Unction was not considered "the Last Sacrament," or even numbered among the last sacraments.

> Concerning the dying, the ancient canonical law is still to be followed; so that if any man be at the point of death, he must not be deprived of the last and most indispensable Viaticum.

This canon of the I council of Nicaea[47] (325) did not mention the anointing for those who were dying. If it had already been given to the dying Christian, it was because of the bodily illness, and not because of the danger or proximity of death.

In his letter of 416 to Decentius, Bishop of Gubbio, Pope Innocent I wrote that the *poenitentes* could not be anointed since, as not yet absolved, they were denied the reception of the other sacraments, of which Extreme Unction was one. In the same letter he taught that these *poenitentes* were to be absolved on Holy Thursday, except in one case. If a *poenitens* became sick and was in danger of dying, the rule was to be waived, and he was to be absolved immediately, so that he might not leave this life without Communion.[48]

A distinction was made between the *poenitentes* who were sick and the *poenitentes* who were sick and in danger of dying. The pope had just explained that the faithful who were sick could be anointed, when he added his statement excluding the *poenitentes*,

---

mentary. This text resembles the text of the three prayers in the ritual following the anointings in Extreme Unction.

[47] Cf. *supra*, p. 8, footnote 10.

[48] Ep. *"Si instituta ecclesiastica,"* Cap. 8: "Nam poenitentibus istud infundi non potest quia genus est sacramenti. Nam quibus reliqua sacramenta negantur, quomodo unum genus putatur posse concedi?"—*MPL*, XX, 560; "De poenitentibus . . . quinta feria ante Pascha eis remittendum . . . Vel si quis aegritudinem incurrerit *atque usque ad desperationem devenerit* ei est ante tempus Paschae relaxandum ne de saeculo absque communione discedat."—*Ibid.*, 559. This Letter of Pope Innocent I is one of the chief sources for Extreme Unction, cited continually throughout the centuries by writers and ecclesiastical legislators. It receives mention in the annotation to canon 940.

meaning that those sick faithful who were still *poenitentes* could not be anointed. Once these sick *poenitentes* were in danger of death, however, they could be absolved without any further wait and could thereby be admitted to Communion and, following Innocent's principle, to the other sacraments.

Now, if danger of death had been regarded a requisite for the reception of Extreme Unction, Innocent's denial of the sacrament to penitents not yet absolved would have been meaningless since, as he himself allowed, a penitent in danger of death could always be absolved. The conclusion is that sick penitents who were not in danger of death, though they were capable of receiving the sacrament because of their bodily infirmity, were nevertheless denied it, as they were denied also the other sacraments that they were otherwise capable of receiving.

The reason for lifting the ban that barred absolution before Holy Thursday, said Innocent, was that the sick who were in danger of death might receive Communion, not Extreme Unction.

Writing to Bishop Exsuperius eleven years earlier, the same pontiff spoke of reconciling dying Christians. They were to be given the sacrament of Penance, he said, and with it "Last Communion," so that these men "in their last moments might be saved from eternal death." [49] Treating of the same subject, namely the reconciliation of dying Christians, Pope Saint Leo the Great in 452 repeated the identical rule to the Metropolitan Theodore: "Absolve them and administer Communion." [50] Where the administration of sacraments to be conferred in danger of death was explicitly dealt with, Extreme Unction did not receive mention.

Having carefully studied the accounts given by the historian Venerable Bede (673-735) describing the last moments of six great personages of the time, Chavasse finds no allusion in any

[49] Epistola 6: "Tribuetur ergo cum poenitentia extrema communio; ut huiusmodi homines vel in supremis suis, permittente Salvatore Nostro, a perpetuo exitio vindicentur."—*MPL,* XX, 498.

[50] Epistola 108: ". . . etiam talium necessitati ita auxiliandum est, ut et actio illis poenitentiae et communionis gratia, si eam, etiam amisso vocis officio, per indicia integri sensus postulant, non negatur."—*MPL,* LIV, 1012-1014.

of them to any last sacrament except Viaticum.[51] Nor does Chavasse hesitate to add that in no hagiography written before the ninth century is there to be found any mention of the administration of Extreme Unction to the dying saint.[52]

A hundred years after Pope Innocent had taught that the words of St. James refer to "the faithful who are sick" as recipients of the anointing, Saint Caesarius of Arles (470-542), in an attempt to extricate his people from the superstitious practice of resorting to the incantations of sorcerers and magicians in times of illness, exhorted them to make use of the "medicine of the Church," the anointing spoken of by St. James, whom he then quoted. Do this and you shall receive not only health of body but also health of soul, promised the bishop. When should they ask for this "medicine of the Church"? "Whenever any sickness comes on." [53]

And a hundred years after the time of Saint Caesarius, a similar exhortation that, "whenever any sickness comes on," the sick should trust in the Eucharist and the oil of the sick is heard from Saint Eligius (588-659), Bishop of Noyon. The sick Christian was to make use of this oil of the sick so that, in accord with the promise of the Apostle, "the prayer of faith will save the sick man and the Lord will raise him up." [54]

[51] *Op. cit.*, I, 135.

[52] If the account of an ante-ninth century saint contains such an account one can be sure it was written by a post-ninth century author.—Chavasse, *op. cit.*, I, 194-195.

[53] Sermo XIII, n. 3: "Quoties aliqua infirmitas supervenerit. . . ."—Germanus Morin, *Sancti Caesarii Arelatensis Sermones* (2 vols. [*Corpus Christianorum, Series Latina,* Vols. CIII-CIV], Turnholti: Typographia Brepols, 1953), I, 66; also Sermo L, n. 1; LII, n. 5—*ibid.*, pp. 224-225. Sickness, said St. Caesarius (in Sermo XIX, n. 5) is a special trial coming into the life of every man sooner or later. Sometimes it comes from God Himself, Who lets those whom He loves suffer in this world; often it comes as an opportunity for doing more penance and acquiring more grace. Sooner or later health will come again to the sick, because He (God) knows what is best for us, when it is fitting for us to be sick or to be well.—Morin, *op. cit.*, I, 90.

[54] Chavasse, *op. cit.*, I, 120; *MPL,* LXXXVII, 529.

In his commentary on the Epistle of Saint James, Venerable Bede (673-735) related that the Apostle's recommendation had been carried out in the Church from the time of the Apostles through the sacramental anointing that was administered to Christians when they had taken sick.[55] If Saint Caesarius or Saint Eligius or Venerable Bede believed that a danger of death was necessary for a valid anointing, it is not at all evident from the wide classes of "the sick" whom they included as coming within the scope of Saint James' Epistle.

3. *The X to the XVI Century*

The reform legislation that begins to appear at the beginning of the ninth century concerning the administration of the sacraments was occasioned by the rather general neglect of priests in this regard.[56] Jonas, Bishop of Orleans (818-843), bemoaned the fact that "because of ignorance or neglect and lack of interest," many were failing to make use of the sacrament of the sick. The Council of Aachen in 836 found it necessary to decree that the "blessing of the holy oils once a year is not to be neglected by the bishops throughout all the cities, as it has been neglected up until now." [57] And later the same Council continued:

> . . . If a subject shall be weighed down with sickness, let him not be deprived through the priest's carelessness of confession and the priestly prayer, and the anointing with consecrated oil. Then, if the end is seen to be near, he shall commend his Christian soul to his God with the reception of holy Communion.[58]

The recipient of the anointing here was simply one "who was weighed down with sickness." When that sickness brought him

[55] *MPL,* XCIII, 39.

[56] Cf. Righetti, *Manuale di Storia Liturgica,* IV, 237.

[57] Mansi, XIV, 678; Palmer, *Sources of Christian Theology,* II, 291.

[58] Hardouin, *Acta Conciliorum et Epistolae Decretales ac Constitutiones Summorum Pontificum* (11 vols. in 12, Parisiis, 1714-1715), IV, 1397 (hereafter cited Hardouin); Palmer, *op. cit.,* II, 291.

close to death, he was given the proper rites for the dying, the *commendatio animae* and last Communion.

The Council of Chalon in 813 reminded Christians that

> According to the document of the Apostle James, with which the documents of the Fathers are also in agreement, the sick ought to be anointed by priests with oil. . . . Accordingly, a remedy of this kind, which heals the weaknesses of soul and body, is not to be lightly regarded.[59]

The restoration of a conscientious administration of the sacraments to all the faithful was important, but especially so for those Christians who were near to death. To them were to be applied all the spiritual helps the Church could give. Thus as early as 769 a Capitulary of Charles the Great stated that "the dying should not pass out of this life without having been anointed and without reconciliation and Viaticum.[60] And another such Capitulary in 801 urged that all priests

> . . . mercifully bestow on all who are sick before the end of life Viaticum and Communion of the Body of Christ. In accordance with the decisions of the holy Fathers, if anyone is sick, let him be carefully anointed by priests with oil to the accompaniment of prayers.[61]

In these capitularies, states Palmer, the association of Extreme Unction with sacraments administered to the dying as such is first made.[62] Since most of the faithful in danger of death were dying from sickness, they were to be given the sacrament of the sick as well as Penance and Viaticum. And, although the sacrament thenceforth came more and more to be spoken of together with the "Last Sacraments," it cannot be concluded that it was given only to those sick who were in danger of death.

The sick who are in danger, said the Council of Mainz in 847, are to make their confession of sins so that "after they have been encouraged by the prayers and consolations of the Church, to-

[59] Hardouin, IV, 1040; Palmer, *op. cit.*, II, p. 291.

[60] *MPL,* XCVII, 124; Palmer, *op. cit.*, II, 290.

[61] *MPL,* XCVII, 220; Palmer *op. cit.*, II, 290.

[62] Palmer, *op. cit.*, II, 396.

gether with God's healing anointing," they can be refreshed with Viaticum.[63] The sick as here mentioned were unreconciled penitents who had not yet been anointed, not because they lacked being fit recipients for a valid anointing before a danger of death had developed, but because they were lawfully denied the sacraments as long as they remained unreconciled (as Pope Innocent had legislated in 416). In 850 the Council of Pavia reiterated the rule of Pope Innocent: "If a sick person is bound by public penance, he cannot receive the remedy of this mystery." [64] Again, if danger of death had been deemed necessary for a valid reception of Extreme Unction, and since in such danger unreconciled penitents could always have become reconciled before the termination of their public penance, such a rule would have been of no consequence.[65]

The practice of postponing Penance till the end of life was near, a practice that seems to have been common enough, excluded an otherwise fit recipient of Extreme Unction from receiving it before then, thereby making the danger of death the circumstance in which anointing *de facto* was usually received by the sick.[66] As the danger of death became the ordinary time at which it was received, the sacrament quite naturally began to be called the "last anointing," which in those circumstances it usually was. The term "Extreme Unction," though found now and again in the ninth and tenth centuries, did not become a common name for the sacrament until the twelfth century.[67] From the legislation of the Carolingian Reform Period it cannot be concluded that every anointing was a last anointing, or that the sacrament was reserved exclusively for the sick in danger of death.

The rituals for the visiting and the anointing of the sick, which

[63] Mansi, XIV, 910; Palmer, *op. cit.*, II, 292.

[64] Mansi, XIV, 932-933; Palmer, *op. cit.*, II, 292.

[65] Cf. *supra*, p. 19.

[66] "Through association with death-bed Penance the Anointing of the Sick is restricted first *de facto* and later *de iure* to those *in periculo mortis.*" —Placid Murray, "The Liturgical History of Extreme Unction," *The Furrow*, XI (1960), 583.

[67] Cf. Righetti, *Manuale di Storia Liturgica*, IV, 239.

first appeared at this time,[68] just as the ritual of today, contain nothing that would indicate that the sacrament was intended solely for the dying or for those who were in danger of death. The only description they give of the recipient is of one suffering bodily illness; the constant prayer in them is not for a happy death but for restoration and health. One of the ancient forms enshrined the prayer:

> Ungo te . . . ut fugatis omnibus doloribus vel incommoditatibus corporis tui, recuperetur in te virtus et salus quatenus per huius operationem mysterii et per hanc sacrati olei unctionem et nostram deprecationem, virtute Sanctae Trinitatis medicatus sive totus, pristinam et immelioratam recipere mereabis sanitatem.[69]

The three prayers of our present ritual, all of which date back to at least the tenth century, implore similar benefits:

> . . . cura . . . languores istius infirmi, eiusque sana vulnera atque dolores cunctos mentis et corporis ab eo expelle, plenamque interius et exterius sanitatem misericorditer redde, ut, ope misericordiae tuae restitutus, ad pristina reparetur officia.[70]

The recipient is one who is laboring under the burden of bodily infirmity, and the sacrament is conferred that he may be freed from the weakening effects of that illness. There is no hint of a preparation for death, no sign that the illness must have reached the state wherein it puts the man's life in danger.[71]

68 For a collection of these ancient rituals cf. Edmundus Martène, *De Antiquis Ecclesiae Ritibus* (nova ed., 3 vols., Venetiis, 1783), I, Chapter 7.

69 Martène, *op. cit.*, I, Chapter 7, Ordo V.

70 *Rituale Romanum* (1952 ed.), Tit. VI, Cap. 2, *"Domine Deus"*; the second prayer, *"Respice,"* describes the recipient as *"in infirmitate sui corporis fatiscentem,"* and asks that he be *"emendatus castigationibus"* and *"tua medicina salvatum"*; the third prayer, *"Domine Sancte,"* reads: ". . . ut famulum tuum ab aegritudine liberatum, et sanitate donatum, dextera tua erigas, virtute confirmes, potestate tuearis, atque Ecclesiae tuae sanctae cum omni desiderata prosperitate restituas."

71 If such prayers are to be applied only to the sick in danger of death, then it would seem that what is generally asked for—freedom from sickness and restoration of health—is a often miraculous recovery.

The association of the anointing with a death-bed sickness, however, and the consequently seldom-seen recovery of physical health worked to classify the sacrament gradually as a sacrament of the dying. The spiritual effects promised by Saint James, deliverance from sin, began to be considered of greater value than the corporal alleviation he had promised. "Faced with a 'new' sacrament of the dying, it is understandable," says Palmer, "that the great scholastic Doctors of the 13th century should readily agree that the purpose of the sacrament is to prepare the soul for immediate entrance into glory, and that they should also agree that the recipient of the sacrament should be one who is actually departing this life." [72]

Master Simon of Tournay († 1201) seems the first to have expressed the idea that the anointing was a preparation for death, and this doctrine was quickly developed by great Scholastic theologians.

The sacrament, said St. Thomas (1224-1274), is the last remedy which the Church can give, something, as it were, that immediately disposes one for glory. It should be given only to those of the sick who are actually dying, for this sacrament has for its chief effect to supply that assistance which is necessary to the dying on their way to heaven.[73]

[72] *Op. cit.*, II, 397.

[73] ". . . hoc sacramentum est ultimum remedium, quod Ecclesia potest conferre, quasi immediate disponens ad gloriam; et ideo illis tantum infirmantibus debet exhiberi . . . hoc sacramentum habet pro principali effectu illam sospitatem, quae exeuntibus, et iter ad gloriam agentibus est necessaria. . . ."—*Summa Theologica,* III Partis Supp., Q. XXXII, art. II. The question here could be raised: If this is the principal purpose of the sacrament, why cannot one who is not sick, but who nevertheless is about to die, receive it? St. Thomas answered that the spiritual cure effected by the sacrament is symbolized by the sign of corporal healing (the anointing). But since one who is not sick needs no physical healing, a symbol of healing applied to him is meaningless; therefore he is not a fit subject for anointing (Q. XXXII, art. 1). The writer believes the objection of Durantis (1237-1296) against this to be a valid one. Does a baby need to be physically unclean in order to furnish a sign of its interior state before validity can attach to the external sign of washing in Baptism? Must a dying Christian, in need of spiritual healing from the effects of sin, be physically sick in order to express outwardly his interior state?

St. Bonaventure, the Seraphic Doctor (1221-1274), a contemporary of St. Thomas, believed that the primary purpose of Extreme Unction was the complete deletion of all venial sin at the end of one's life. For him there was no questioning that the recipient of the sacrament was one who was about to die. No matter how sick a person might be, he was to be given the anointing only when he was at the very point of death.[74]

Duns Scotus (1266-1308) put it very eloquently. Extreme Unction, he wrote, is the last remedy, instituted by Christ, to heal from venial sin a soul about to leave its body, so that freed from all impediments it might enter without delay into its inheritance of heavenly glory.[75]

Extreme Unction has for its chief purpose the forgiveness of venial sin, taught Gerson (1363-1426). Its recipient, however, is only the Christian who is sick and so sick as to be actually dying.[76]

Although the scholastic theologians disagreed on the principal effects of the sacrament, St. Thomas holding that it was to delete the *"reliquias peccati,"* St. Bonaventure, that it was to wipe away venial sin, they were in accord that the sole recipient of this sacrament was a sick Christian in very imminent danger of death, if not actually breathing his last.

With such emphasis on the anointing as the "last or extreme anointing," it is not surprising to find also at this time a change in the ritual regarding the order in which the last sacraments were to be administered. The old rituals gave Penance followed

74 ". . . illud Sacramentum debet dari solis infirmis qui peccare potuerunt venialiter, et his, prout sunt in articulo mortis."—Lib. IV, Dist. 23, art. II, q. 2.—*Opera Omnia* (10 vols., Quaracchi [Florentiae], 1882-1902), IV, 598.

75 ". . . solumodo laborantibus in extremis, et in mortis articulo constitutis . . . cum enim sit ultimum remedium institutum a Christo ad curationem animae a venialibus proximae exiturae a corpore, ne sint ipsi impedimenta et iniiciatur mora adituris haereditatem gloriae coelestis."—Q. XXXII, art. II.—*Summa Theologica* (6 vols., Romae, 1903), VI, 368.

76 ". . . debent esse infirmi in statu exeuntium de hac vita; sanis enim non datur, quia habent aliud remedium, scilicet poenitentiam."—*Summa Theologica et Canonica in Sex Iibris Digesta* (Venetiis, 1587), Lib. IV, p. 289.

by Extreme Unction, and then (following the ancient canonical law) Viaticum. Now Extreme Unction, the *Sacramentum exeuntium,* was placed last, after Viaticum. In our own time concessions of the Holy See are allowing a reversion to the former use.[77]

In the thirteenth century, during which the Scholastic theologians were developing the doctrine that Extreme Unction prepared a Christian for death, and were thereby restricting its use to the dying, a dogmatic statement concerning the recipient of Extreme Unction emanated from the II General Council of Lyons (1274) in the Profession of Faith of Michael Paleologus.[78]

> The same holy Roman Church holds and teaches as well that there are seven sacraments of the Church; one is . . . another is extreme unction, which, according to the instruction of Blessed James, is used for the sick.[79]

Despite the prevailing opinion of theological thought at the time, no danger of death was alluded to as a requisite in the subject of Extreme Unction at this Council.

In the Bull *Exultate Deo* of Pope Eugene IV to the Armenians in 1439, however, there appears the since much-quoted sentence: "This sacrament ought (must) not be given except to those sick whose death is feared." [80] This Constitution is usually included in the acts of the Council of Florence, but it is seriously questionable that it ever received ecumenical approval, and most theologians do not regard the decree as a dogmatic definition. This is important to note, because those who seek to prove the necessity of a danger of death for a valid anointing inevitably cite this source, usually only as the "Council of Florence."

Exultate Deo itself was directed specifically to the Armenians, and bound them in matters relating to the discipline of the sacra-

[77] Cf. *Collectio Rituum* (Milwaukee: Bruce, 1954), Cap. IV, pp. 64-79.

[78] "This profession of faith in the seven sacraments never became the subject of debate either in the Council or between Catholic and dissident Christians subsequently."—Palmer, *op. cit.,* II, 219.

[79] " . . . extrema unctio, quae secundum doctrinam beati Iacobi infirmantibus adhibetur."—Mansi, XXIV, 71.

[80] *Fontes,* n. 52, § 14.

ments. When the Instruction declared for the Armenians that the form of Penance is *"Ego te absolvo . . . "* it did not define that this is the only valid form in the universal Church, for at the same time the deprecative form used in other Eastern Churches was and is yet recognized as valid. Similarly, the Instruction stated that the form of anointing is *"Per istam sanctam unctionem indulgeat . . . ,"* but this was not to say that the invocative forms used in the Oriental Churches are not equally valid. One must be careful in determining the binding force of disciplinary law not to extend particular law so that it becomes general law, or even dogmatic definition.

Furthermore it is not surprising to discover the qualification *"de cuius morte timetur"* in this decree, when it is known that this Instruction on the sacraments is taken almost verbatim from a small work of Saint Thomas entitled *"De articulis fidei et Ecclesiae sacramentis.*[81] It naturally mirrors his teaching that the sacrament is for the dying. It is not clear, however, from the phrase *"dari non* DEBET" that St. Thomas believed, or that the decree intended to say, that the anointing of a sick person whose death was *not* feared would be invalid, though St. Thomas certainly believed that the sacrament should in fact be administered only in the context of death.[82] Moreover, it cannot be held that in the clause *"de cuius morte timetur"* the decree postulated an objective and real danger for a lawful anointing. Fear that the subject would die or might die is all that is manifestly required.

[81] "Instructio haec fere ad litteram desumpta est ex S. Thomae opusculo *De articulis fidei et Ecclesiae sacramentis.*"—Henricus Denzinger, *Enchiridion Symbolorum Definitionum et Declarationum de Rebus Fidei et Morum,* quod post Clementem Bannwart et Ioannem B. Umberg denuo edidit Carolus Rahner (editio 30, Friburgi Brisgoviae: Herder, 1955), n. 695, only footnote (hereafter cited *Denz.*).

[82] Teaching that the fullest effect of the anointing comes when it is received with devotion by the subject and through the personal merit of those conferring the sacrament, and the general merit of the entire Church, Saint Thomas concluded: " . . . et ideo illis qui non possunt recognoscere, et cum devotione suscipere hoc sacramentum, *dari non debet. . . .*" This certainly is not necessary for validity (or even lawfulness). Cf. Saint Thomas, *Summa Theologica,* III Partis Supp., Q. XXXII, art. III.

4. *The Council of Trent*

> And now with regard to prescribing who ought to receive and administer this sacrament, this also was not obscurely expressed in the words cited above (James V:13-15). . . . *It is also declared that this anointing is to be applied to the sick, but especially to those who are in such danger as to appear to be at the end of life,* whence it is also called the sacrament of the dying.[83]

Here, in very definite and clear terms the Council stated who is a fit subject for this sacrament. A distinction is made between the sick in general and the sick who are in danger of death (between the *infirmi* and *illi qui tam periculose decumbunt, ut . . .*). From the wording and construction of the sentence the sick who are in danger of death form but a particularized group of the fit recipients, not the whole group or the exclusive group. The distinction, far from showing that a danger of death is required in the recipient, actually shows that it is not. The Council did not state that the sacrament is to be given the sick *qui tam periculose decumbunt ut in exitu vitae constituti videantur;* the sacrament was to be given simply to the sick, apart from any further qualification as to the degree of sickness, though thereupon specific mention was made of the sick who are in danger (*infirmis, illis vero praesertim qui periculose*).

Certainly if any sick person should be given this sacrament, it is especially that sick person who is close to dying, since, for him, the state of his spiritual life during that illness, which life this sacrament restores and strengthens against all spiritual weakness accruing from that sickness,[84] is of crucial and eternal

[83] "Iam vero, quod attinet ad praescriptionem eorum, qui et suscipere et ministrare hoc sacramentum debent, haud obscure fuit illud etiam in verbis praedictis traditum. Nam et ostenditur illic, proprios huius sacramenti ministros esse ecclesiae presbyteros. . . . *Declaratur etiam, esse hanc unctionem infirmis adhibendam, illis vero praesertim, qui tam periculose decumbunt, ut in exitu vitae constituti videantur, unde et sacramentum exeuntium nuncupatur.*"—Sess. XIV, *De Extrema Unctione,* Chapter III.—Schroeder, *Canons and Decrees of the Council of Trent,* p. 376, for Latin text, and p. 101 for the English text.

[84] ". . . unctio delicta, si quae sint adhuc expianda, ac peccati reliquias abstergit, et aegroti animam alleviat et confirmat, magnam in eo divinae

importance. In addition to other fit subjects the one sick and in danger ought to be fortified with this sacramental help just as he should be fortified with Viaticum also (though others besides the dying can receive Communion). And, inasmuch as it is given to one in his last illness, this anointing will literally be the "extreme" unction, and probably too, because the ritual of the times called for this anointing to be administered after Viaticum, it was "also" called the sacrament of the dying. The Council itself called it "Extreme Unction" and the "sacred unction of the sick" indiscriminately.[85] In the circumstance of death it is a sacrament of the dying.

It is true that the Council introduced the sacrament in the light of its salutary effects during the time of one's last illness.[86] But given at a time when imminence of death was *de facto* the ordinary, not to say exclusive, circumstance in which the anointing was conferred, such an introduction is understandable.[87] This

misericordiae fiduciam excitando, qui infirmus sublevatus et morbi incommoda ac labores levius fert, et tentationibus daemonis calcaneo insidiantis facilius resistit, et sanitatem corporis interdum, ubi saluti animae expederit, consequitur."—Council of Trent, Sess. XIV, Chapter II, *De effectu huius sacramenti* (Extremae Unctionis), Schroeder, *op. cit.*, p. 375. These effects can be realized in any real illness without danger of death; none of these *in se* suggest that anointing prepares one immediately for glory or that it totally wipes away all temporal punishment due to sin. For meaning of *reliquias peccati* cf. *supra*, p. 10, footnote 18.

[85] Cf. Canons on Extreme Unction, 1 and 2, Schroeder, *op. cit.*, p. 379. Communion given in view of death is fittingly called Viaticum, the anointing of the sick given to one in view of death is called the "Last (Extreme) Anointing"; it is not implied necessarily that neither Communion nor the anointing can be received outside the time of death. Extreme Unction is also used as a name for the sacrament, because in relation to the other sacraments conferred with an anointing, that is, Baptism and Confirmation, this is usually the last of the three received in the order of chronology.

[86] Cf. Sess. XIV, *Doctrina de Sacramento Extremae Unctionis*.—Schroeder, *op. cit.*, p. 374.

[87] Such an exposition of the salutary effects of the sacrament for the dying would also uphold the reasonableness of the practice of anointing them in the face of the Reformers' charge that such an anointing of "half-dead carcasses, whose life is quivering on the lips," was a violation of the text of St. James. Cf. Palmer, *Sources of Christian Theology*, II, 304-310, on the Writings of the Protestant Reformers.

fact, however, only points up the importance of the wording used by the Council to define the recipient of the sacrament. After having spoken about anointing at the time of death as it did, one might have expected the Council to define the recipients as "the sick who are in danger or whose life is feared for." But it is dogma the Council deals with here, and the words are chosen after much study and scrutiny. The phrase *"infirmis, illis vero praesertim qui . . . "* is not ambiguous. The words themselves say it, and the context of the chapter does not limit it,—the *valid* recipient of Extreme Unction is according to the Council of Trent simply one who is sick.

A brief glance at the discussions of the Tridentine theologians working on the formulation of the final dogmatic decrees will give an appreciation of how exacting they were as regards clarity and accuracy of expression. When the canons on Extreme Unction came up for review in 1547, a debate immediately evolved as a bishop moved that the name "Extreme Unction," or at least the word "Extreme," be deleted and that the sacrament be thenceforth called *"oleum infirmorum."* His reasons were that Extreme Unction was a *"novum vocabulum"* and that in the earlier Church the sacrament was given not only to the *"laborantes in extremis,"* but to anyone who was sick, as James attested. The bishops of Alife and Capri, among others, agreed that the word "extreme" should be deleted. The bishop of Verona wished the word retained in the first canon, since St. Thomas and the Council of Florence used the term, but asked for the use of the phrase *"sacramentum infirmorum unctionis"* in the second canon. The archbishop of Besançon objected to deleting the word since "this was a word used by the Church and one challenged by the Lutherans." The bishop of Minorca agreed, saying that the term "extreme unction" pleased him, "though it did not please some other Fathers, for it is the last anointing with regard to other anointings, and it is given *in extremis* (*quoad se datur morituro*)." With him the General of the Servites was in accord as was also the bishop of Motola who appealed to the practice of the Church of not giving it *"nisi laborantibus in extremis."* Others thought the name should be kept, because it was the one used by the Scholastics. Finally, the presiding Cardinal reminded the

Fathers that, in the section of the conciliar acts dealing with the sacraments in general, a section already ratified and published, this sacrament had been listed as Extreme Unction, and that it would consequently be difficult to drop the name completely now when the sacrament was treated *in specie.*[88]

In another meeting of the conciliar Fathers, the question arose as to how the fact ought accurately to be expressed that the sacramental anointing now employed by the sixteenth century Church had always been in use in the Church from the time of St. James. The archbishop of Besançon wanted it made clear that this continuous practice of the Church still in use was "that priests anoint the sick who are *laborantes in extremis.*" The bishop of Laval went further: he asked that the Council decree that "the words of Saint James are to be understood of the sick *in extremis laborantes.*"[89] He did not want it declared, however, that the *"consuetudo ecclesiae quae continuo sic usa est"* was an interpretation of James' words. Rather, he contended that "it is superfluous to interpret that custom now, *granted* that perhaps the primitive Church did give this sacrament to the sick, other than the ones *in extremis laborantes.*" The Fathers were not all in accord with his narrow interpretation of Saint James. If the Church did not always limit the use of anointing to the ones *in extremis laborantes,* answered the bishop of Acci, then the word "extreme" cannot stand. "Neither Mark nor James speak of the

[88] *Concilium Tridentinum, Diariorum, Actorum, Epistolarum Tractatuum* (*Nova Collectio,* edidit Societas Goerresiana, Vol. VI, Actorum Pars III, Volumen I ex collectionibus Sebastiani Merkle, auxit, edidit, illustravit Theobaldus Freudenberger, Friburgi Brisgoviae: Herder, 1950), pp. 311, 314, 315, 316, 317, 318, 328, 329, 330, 341 (hereafter cited *Conc. Trid. Acta*); both "extreme unction" and "sacred unction of the sick" were used in the final wording of the Council.

[89] "Bituntinus placet quod dicatur *usum;* sed addatur *qui nunc est in ecclesia, videlicet, quod sacerdos inungat infirmos in extremis laborantibus."* —*Conc. Trid. Acta,* VI, 353: "Lavellanus . . . item cuperet decidi quod verba Iacobi intelliguntur de in extremis laborantibus, ut *interpretatur* ecclesia."—*Ibid.,* p. 353. It should be remembered that the Reformers ridiculed the idea that the rite of St. James was ever intended to be given the dying *in extremis* which was *de facto* the only use of the Sacrament made by the Church generally at this time and for some time before.

practice as a *last* anointing, and it is to be believed that the primitive Church did in fact anoint the sick not *laborantes in extremis*."[90] The archbishop of Besançon admitted that "perhaps sometimes" the anointing was given in the early Church to the non-dying sick, but at the same time, so he contended, "it was also given to the ones *in extremis*, and there was never a time in the Church when the sacrament was not given to the ones *in extremis*."[91]

The bishops of Laval and Minorca employed the same argument. Their explanation why the sacrament was once given also to the non-dying sick (as they granted) is interesting. In the early days of the Church, they said, when it sought expansion through the conversion of infidels, it needed to look to miracles for facilitating its mission, and so at that time the sacrament was employed for its corporal effects. But since such miracles are no longer necessary, the sacrament is conferred only for its spiritual effects.[92]

The presiding Cardinal remarked that it would be "dangerous" to say that none of the sick except the ones *in extremis* were ever anointed, and equally dangerous to say that the sick *laborantes in extremis* were always anointed even in the primitive Church, even though only the *laborantes* are anointed today; and it cannot be denied that James and Mark spoke in a general manner (of the sick).[93]

[90] "Si usus, qui nunc est, i.e., quod detur in extremis, non semper fuit in ecclesia, prout credit, non potest stare verbum 'extrema' cum eius neque Marcus neque Iacobus meminerit; et ita est credendum, quod in primitiva ecclesia ungerent etiam non laborantes in extremis."—*Conc. Trid. Acta*, VI, 354.

[91] *Loc. cit.*—Accordingly the archibshop of Besançon justified the retention of the word "*extrema*" in connection with *unctio*.

[92] ". . . quia in ecclesia etiam primitiva semper data est haec unctio laborantibus in extremis, licet et non laborantibus aliquando data fuerit, ut sanitas corporis sequeretur propter infideles ad fidem convertendos, quibus miraculis nunc ecclesia non indiget."—*Conc. Trid. Acta*, VI, 354.

[93] ". . . iste usus ungendi laborantes fuerit semper in ecclesia adeo ut numquam nisi laborantes in extremis inungerentur et hoc esse maximi ponderis cum probari facile non possit, periculosumque videatur dicere quod numquam aliqui infirmi inuncti fuerunt non laborantes in extremis,

It was the burden of the Fathers to justify the Church's practice of using this sacrament for the dying, which the Reformers charged was a perversion of the rite for the sick as given by St. James. No one seems to have really doubted that the sacrament was in fact given to the sick generally in the past, nor that it could be given validly to the sick *non laborantes* now. The bishop of Laval himself said: "Today, if a sick person who is not *laborans in extremis* is anointed, he receives the true sacrament, but the priest who confers it sins, for he anoints one who is not to be anointed." [94] The practice restricting the administration of Extreme Unction to the sick who were in danger of dying was viewed and discussed, it seems, as a purely disciplinary norm established by the Church, not as a requisite in the recipient *de necessitate sacramenti* for validity.

The fact that the Fathers discussed the question "whether a real injury was inflicted on the sick by not giving them this sacrament except when their death was feared" presupposes the belief that the sick even without danger of death were fit recipients of Extreme Unction.[95] The General of the Friars Minor, who sided with those who desired to retain the name "Extreme" Unction, and to limit the sacrament to the sick near to death, said: "I do not like it to be said that it is erroneous to give this sacrament only to those in danger of death, for this does not impede the sacrament." [96] The question was not whether the

---

etiam quod laborantes in extremis semper etiam primitiva unxerit, licet hodie nonnisi laborantes in extremis inungantur, et negari non potest quod Iacobus (5:14) et Marcus (6:13) loquantur generaliter."—*Conc. Trid. Acta,* VI, 359.

[94] "Et hodie si infirmus non laborans in extremis ungeretur, reciperet verum sacramentum, licet sacerdos peccaret quia ungeret non ungendum."—*Conc. Trid. Acta,* VI, 354.

[95] A proposed canon, approved by all the Fathers read: "Si quis dixerit . . . in iniuriam infirmorum cedere, quod eis nonnisi, cum de eorum morte timetur, conferatur (Extrema Unctio) . . . anathema sit."—*Conc. Trid. Acta,* VI, 364.

[96] "Non placet quod dicitur erroneum esse dare hoc sacramentum in extremis tantum laborantibus, quia hoc non impedit sacramentum. . . ."—*Conc. Trid. Acta,* VI, 610. He also objected to changing the name to "oil

sacrament could be given to the sick without a concomitant danger of death, but whether it was justified to give it only to the sick *in extremis laborantibus,* as the Church had now been doing. If anything, the acceptance of anyone truly sick as a fit recipient of the anointing is manifested by the reading of these acts preparatory to the conciliar definitions of Trent. The point at issue as far as the recipient was concerned was the ecclesiastical practice in the administration of the sacrament, which practice delineated as lawful subjects simply those of the sick whose life was in danger.[97]

With these considerations in mind, one may well look once again at the deliberately chosen words employed by the Council of Trent in its definition of the recipient of Extreme Unction.

> Declaratur etiam, esse hanc unctionem infirmis adhibendam, illis vero praesertim, qui tam periculose decumbunt, ut in exitu vitae constituti videantur.[98]

If the Council had intended to teach that only the sick who are in danger are fit subjects for anointing, it knew very well how to express that doctrine in unmistakable words, as a proposed first draft of this sentence in 1551 proved. It read:

> Declaratur etiam, non esse hanc unctionem nisi infirmis adhibendam, *nec illis quidem omnibus,* ut ecclesiae traditio nos edocet, sed illis dumtaxat, qui tam periculose decumbunt, ut in exitu vitae constituti videantur. Quare merito et extrema unctio, et exeuntium sacramentum nuncupatur, quod

of the sick" because then it would follow that it would be given also to those sick persons who were not close to death.—*Loc. cit.*

[97] As for the Church doing this, the bishop of Acci remarked at the Council: ". . . quod non est inconveniens quod unum uno tempore uno modo observaverit ecclesia, aliud alio tempore, inspirante divino spiritu."—*Conc. Trid. Acta,* VI, 354.

[98] The Council repeated with Saint James that the sick in general are the recipients of this sacrament. The Council likewise (against the Reformers) stressed the fact that not only may this sacrament be given the sick *in extremis,* but that it should be given *especially* to them in their extreme need, as in fact was done. This declaration is really the same as that of the II Council of Lyons (1274): ". . . extrema unctio secundum doctrinam beati Iacobi infirmantibus adhibetur."—Mansi, XXIV, 71.

> *nonnisi* extreme laborantibus, et cum morte congredientibus, atque hinc ad Dominum migrantibus salubriter adhibeatur.[99]

This was rejected by the Council. Its final dogmatic form did not decree that "this anointing is to be used only for the sick, not indeed for all the sick, but only for the dangerously sick"; rather it decreed that "it is to be used *for the sick*, especially for the dangerously sick." Had it believed that not all the sick were fit recipients of extreme unction, it could easily have inserted the phrase, *nec illis quidem omnibus*, as proposed in the first draft.

It cannot be held that the Council of Trent demanded any danger of death as a requisite necessary for validity in the recipient of the Sacrament of Exreme Unction.

The Catechism of the Council faithfully repeats the infallible decree of that body when it states:

> Since, therefore, only the sick are in need of a cure, on that account those *too*, who seem so dangerously sick as to cause fear that the last day of life is near, should be given this sacrament.[100]

The essential physical condition is sickness. It is only because those who are dying from illness fulfill this condition, and not

[99] *Acta Genuina SS. Oecumenici Concilii Tridentini* (edita ab Augustino Theiner, 2 vols., Zagrabiae [in Croatia], Typis et sumptibus Societatis Bibliophilae, 1874), I, 590.

[100] "Cum igitur illi tantum, qui morbo laborant, curatione indigeant, *idcirco iis etiam*, qui adeo periculose aegrotare videntur, ut ne supremus illis vitae dies instet, metuendum sit, hoc sacramentum praeberi debet."—*Catechismus Concilii Tridentini ex decreto Concilii Tridentini ad Parochos Pii V Pontifici Maximi iussu editus* (editio quarta, Ratisbonae: Pustėt, 1907), p. 248. As long as they are sick, the dying come under the class of fit recipients. It is difficult to see how the following translation of this passage of the Catechism could possibly be justified: "Now only the sick need a remedy, *and therefore* this sacrament is to be administered *to those only* whose malady is such as to excite apprehension of approaching death." —*The Catechism of The Council of Trent for Parish Priests*, translated into English with notes by John A. McHugh and Charles J. Callan (13. ed., New York: Joseph F. Wagner, 1954), p. 311 (italics added). One reading this rendering without consulting the Latin Text would draw an inevitably erroneous conclusion as to what the Catechism taught and the Council infallibly defined.

because they are dying or in danger of dying, that they too are fit subjects for the reception of Extreme Unction.

5. *From the Council of Trent to the Code of Canon Law*

From about the tenth century the sacrament of anointing began to be associated with the last sacraments given at the time of imminent death. By the thirteenth century, aided immeasurably by Scholastic opinions about the tremendous effects offered by the sacrament at the time of departure from this life, the practice of anointing those only who were at the point of death had become well and exclusively established in the Western Church.[101] It remained so until the time of the Reformation and the Council of Trent. After the Council of Trent the pendulum began to swing in the other direction. The law of particular synods began to urge pastors to anoint the sick in good time rather than wait until the last moments as had once been thought most opportune. To do this deprives the sick of the full benefits of the sacrament, the Council of Trent had taught. The circumstances of impending death still remained the adiminstrative norm by which the sick were considered to warrant a lawful anointing, but the notion of that requirement would become wider and wider through the ensuing centuries, gradually allowing for a greater number of the sick to be anointed, or at least to be anointed earlier.[102]

[101] "Et ideo illis tantum infirmantibus debet exhiberi, qui sunt in statu exeuntium."—St. Thomas, *Summa Theologica,* Pars III Suppl., Q. XXXII, art. 2; ". . . debet dari solis infirmis, qui . . . sunt in articulo mortis."—St. Bonaventure, Dist. XXIII, art. II, Q. II—*Omnia Opera,* IV, 598; ". . . solumodo laborantibus in extremis, et in mortis articulo constitutis."—Duns Scotus, Q. XXXII, art. 2—*Summa Theologica,* VI, 368; ". . . debent esse infirmi in statu exeuntium de hac vita. . . ."—Jean Gerson, *Summa Theologica et Canonica,* Lib. IV, p. 280.

[102] Council of Avignon (1594): "Caveat parochus, ne in administranda extrema unctione neglegentiam, ullamque morae culpam contrahat; alioque si ad illius administrationem accersitus ire neglexerit, tum rationem Deo reddet, tum graviter ab episcopo poena plectitur."—Hardouin, X, 1848. ". . . omni studio ac diligentia periculose aegrotantibus adhibendum est (sacramentum); et eo quidem tempore, si fieri possit, cum illis adhuc integra mens et ratio viget; ut ad uberiorem Sacramenti gratiam percipiendam, . . ."—*Roman Ritual* of 1614, *De Extrema Unctione,* Tit. V, Cap. I, n. 1.

The Ritual of 1614 laid down the obligation that priests should give Extreme Unction to those who are so sick that a danger of death seems to be drawing close: "Debet autem hoc sacramentum infirmis praeberi, qui . . . tam graviter laborant, ut mortis periculum imminere videatur." [103] The IV Provincial Council of Milan (1576), under St. Charles Borromeo, reiterated the same obligation, " . . . ministrare debet adultis scilicet, periculose aegrotantibus, propeque moribundis." [104] The recipient of Extreme Unction was no longer to be *"laborans in extremis"* or in *"articulo mortis"* before he could be anointed. It sufficed that he be in danger of death. Soon theologians and canonists were to hold that even the danger need not be imminent or proximate, but that a remote danger suffices. Then it would further be allowed that this remote danger need not be certain but only probable, and more than that, the probability itself would not have to be certain but only "prudently judged" to be present. This in turn would raise the question whether a danger of death need be objectively present or merely subjectively judged to exist, and this eventually would lead to the question whether any danger of death is necessary for the valid administration and reception of the sacrament, even if only by positive ecclesiastical law.

What the Council of Trent said, and, perhaps more, what it did not say has resulted in a change of direction in both the theology and the discipline of the administration of Extreme Unction.

For Suarez (1548-1617) the wording of the definition in the Council of Trent raised a *magnum dubium* as to the necessity of any danger. He admitted that by inserting the particle *praesertim* the Council seemed to signify that the second state (danger of death) "is not absolutely necessary, or at least not as necessary as the first condition (sickness)." He said too that the text of James left some doubt, but citing the Decree to the Armenians (Florence) he concluded "that therefore this state

[103] *Roman Ritual* of 1614, Tit. V, Cap. I, n. 5.

[104] *Acta Ecclesiae Mediolanensis* (Mediolani, 1599), Pars I, p. 140. The use of *"ministrare"* instead of *"praebere"* seems to make this a bit more forceful than the ritual; The Council of Avignon (1594) had: "Parochus extremae unctionis sacramentum sicut his ministrare debet, adultis scilicet periculose aegrotantibus, propeque moribundis."—Hardouin, X, 1848.

(danger) seems to be required." Furthermore, he believed "because of the statement of the Council of Florence and the words of St. James it is at least necessary by precept and more *probably* necessary *de necessitate sacramenti.* "In practice," he added, "the sickness must not only be serious of its very nature, but must have advanced to such a state in the subject as to place him in a danger of death." This was the circumstance and condition in which Extreme Unction should ordinarily, in practice, be administered. To know with certitude that such conditions really are present, however, is not always possible, and much depends on one's judgment in the matter. The condition, then, "is not so substantial as to invalidate the sacrament should one be anointed a little prematurely"—that is, if it is not yet fully realized—"as long as the sickness is in itself dangerous and serious the sacrament is valid even if one does not wait for it to reach that stage." [105]

Speaking of anointing in a time of pestilence, Suarez felt that the sacrament could be conferred immediately, as soon as one became infected, before the disease has spread much, for since this sickness was in and of itself lethal and contagious, there was no need to wait for it to advance to any certain stage. The sacrament could furthermore be conferred (conditionally) to one not certainly infected with the disease if there was at least a probable opinion that he was infected.[106] Suarez had originally

[105] "Imprimis oportet ut infirmitas ex sua specie, vel in hoc individuo iudicio prudentum sit gravis, et quae infirmum in periculo vitae constituere valeat. Hoc constat ex usu Ecclesiae. Unde non dubito quin hoc saltem sit ex praecepto, ut convincit Concilium Florentinum. Et probabilius existimo esse etiam hoc de necessitate sacramenti, propter idem Concilium et propter verba Iacobi. . . . Ulterius addo, in usu servandum esse, ut non solum morbus ex se gravis sit sed etiam status talis sit, qui infirmum in gravi periculo mortis constituat. . . . Quia vero hic status non potest habere tantum certitudinem, multumque ex arbitrio pendet, ideo non videtur haec condito ita substantialis, ut si forte aliquantulum praemature ungatur infirmus, sacramentum propterea sit nullum existimandum; quin potius morbus ex se fuerit periculosus et gravis, existimo secramentum esse validum, etiamsi ad statum morbi vel non satis vel etiam nihil attendatur."—Disp. XLII, Sec. II, n. 4, 5, also n. 3—*Opera Omnia,* XXII, 852.

[106] "Partim anticipando collationem huius sacramenti statim in principio talis aegritudinis, priusquam multum inficere possit, quia, cum haec aegri-

stated that the *subiectum capax* is solely a man sick of body and in such a condition that his life is in danger.[107] Now it is sufficient that the sickness itself be a dangerous one, even though it has not yet brought on the actual danger. But if such is enough for the valid reception of Extreme Unction, then a real, objective danger could hardly be necessary *de necessitate sacramenti,* since here it exists not at all except *in causa,* and *in causa* every illness carries a danger of death which will develop if the illness is not checked. The recipient of a sacrament must be a fit subject at the time he receives the sacrament. If a real danger is necessary, it must really be present at that time; if a certain state of danger is necessary, it must have been reached by that time. But according to Suarez, if that danger or degree of danger was misjudged the sacrament was nevertheless valid; if it existed only remotely, *in causa,* there was a valid sacrament. In effect Suarez taught that only one who was sick and really in danger was to be anointed, but it sufficed that that danger be remote, or even only putative.[108]

tudo sit per se lethalis, et alias sit adeo noxia et contagiosa non oportet aliquem terminum eius expectare ut hoc Sacramentum detur sed statim a principio dari potest."—Disp. XLIV, Sec. III, n. 20—Suarez, *Opera Omnia,* XXII, 877.

107 ". . . eum tantum hominem qui corpore infirmus est, et in eo statu, ut vita eius periclitetur, esse capacem huius sacramenti."—Disp. XLII, Sec. II, n. 2—*op. cit.,* XXII, 851. Compare this with the wording in the Council of Trent, ". . . hanc unctionem infirmis adhibendam, illis vero praesertim, qui tam periculose decumbunt. . . ."—Cf. *supra,* p. 29.

108 "Suaresii verba . . . explicari possunt sive in sensu sufficientiae periculi mortis existentis virtualiter et in causa, . . . sive et ut minimum in sensu sufficientiae periculi putativi."—Doronzo, *De Extrema Unctione,* II, 592. Suarez, too, faced the dilemma of those who believed that Extreme Unction is chiefly a sacrament for the dying. When he was asked why one should wait for the illness to develop and become more serious, and the danger of death to increase and to become more certain, he answered that *"effectus et auxilium huius sacramenti ad illum articulum sunt maxime accommodata."* Then, if asked why such a sacrament which he said purifies the soul for entry into glory is not available to the non-sick who face death, he answered that the sacrament is instituted *"ad roborandum hominem deficientem ob aegritudinem."* But if the non-sick have their own natural strength, is this accidental circumstance enough to deprive them of the reception of the sacrament?

Coninck (1571-1633), a contemporary of Suarez, thought that when Extreme Unction was given to people seriously sick but not in a real danger of death, it was administered validly.[109] Lessius (1554-1623) believed that, if an illness was serious but not apparently dangerous, then the sacrament conferred would probably be valid, but those who knowingly conferred and received it under these circumstances would be guilty of sin.[110] Any sinfulness must certainly lie in the violation of a precept restricting the use of the sacrament to such sick persons who are in at least an apparent danger. It will be remembered, too, that the bishop of Laval, a theologian at the Council of Trent and a hardy proponent for defining that the anointing is only for the *laborantes in extremis,* had unreservedly stated: "Today, if a sick person who is not *laborans in extremis* is anointed, he receives the true sacrament, but the priest who confers it sins, for he anoints one who is not to be anointed." [111] The point is that these men considered it sinful, not because it could not be done validly, but because it should not be done according to the current discipline for the administration of the sacrament.[112]

Holding that Extreme Unction is to be given to those whose life is brought in danger by sickness, Laymann (1574-1635) hastened to add that it is expedient to give the sacrament when the danger is probable, and not to wait for it to become certain.[113] Even though it was foreseen that an illness would be protracted for a long time before it ended in death, Extreme Unction could be administered at the very first appearance of the sickness, at

[109] "Non tamen videtur invalidum si detur graviter quidem aegrotanti, tamen sine vero periculo mortis."—in Doronzo, *De Extrema Unctione,* II, 588.

[110] *Ibid.,* p. 589.

[111] *Conc. Trid. Acta,* VI, 354.

[112] Today it would be sinful for a priest of the Latin Rite to offer Holy Communion to his people in the species of wine, but it certainly would be a valid reception of the Eucharist. It would be sinful to baptize the child of infidels secretly against their will, but such a baptism would certainly be valid.

[113] *Theologia Moralis,* II, Lib. V, Tract. VIII, Cap. IV, n. 4.—". . . expedit dare cum periculum est probabile (non omnino certum)."

least if there was some supporting reason for doing this. Two of the reasons he suggested were the possibility that the illness be more serious than it appeared, and the fact that if one waited it might become dangerously contagious.[114]

What led such theologians as Laymann and Suarez to search so far for a danger of death in an illness was the fact that they clung to the Scholastic belief that the primary purpose of the sacrament was that of preparing the dying for death. This sacrament, said Laymann, was instituted for those who according to the common observation of men are probably dying.[115] Suarez taught that the sacrament's chief purpose was to serve as "a remedy for sick and dying men by which they were helped in the most serious danger of death, and disposed insofar as possible to enter into glory." [116] With such convictions, the only natural measure of what sick person could be anointed was, not the physical debility of his body, but the presence or absence of any danger of death in view of which the primary effect could be realized. It is amazing, indeed, that in spite of the preponderance of theological opinion espousing this view both before and after, the divinely guided Council of Trent in telling of the effects of this sacrament never gave this as even one, not to say the primary, purpose of Extreme Unction.

LaCroix (1652-1714), though holding that the principal effect was the "strengthening of the soul against the temptations of the devil at death," taught that if a man received the anointing while suffering a "common illness," but not a serious or a dangerous

[114] "Sed etsi diurnior morbus videatur, si tamen salus desperata sit, *posse statim in principio* morbi sacramentum Extremae Unctionis ministrare, saltem si aliqua causa exigat, ut quia morbus fallax esse solet, qui interdum inopinato hominem occidit; vel quia in progressu maius contagionis periculum timetur, idque pestis tempore observandum."—*Loc. cit.* (italics added).

[115] ". . . qui secundum humanam aestimationem est in probabili statu moriendi."—*Ibid.*, n. 5.

[116] ". . . extremum remedium hominum infirmorum et morientium quo et in gravissimo mortis periculo iuventur, et ad gloriam introitum, quoad fieri possit, disponuntur."—Disp. XLII, Sec. II, n. 4—*Opera Omnia,* XXII, 852.

one, the sacrament would be invalid.[117] This raises a question also occasioned by the opinion that an illness or a disease which in and of itself is lethal immediately places the recipient in a remote (*in causa*) danger of death sufficient to warrant an anointing if it be necessary not to delay it (Suarez, Laymann). There are diseases that, though once considered incurable or lethal, are no longer so today. According to the opinion, a person contracting such a disease in the past was *"in periculo"; today one contracting the same illness would not be. The disease is still a lethal one, but the treatment and medicines now known render it non-dangerous or relegate it to the class of a "common disease." Is an anointing warranted in either set of circumstances? If not, why not? A parity of condition seems to obtain in both cases. Would the sick man who in 1700 was deemed a fit subject for the sacrament have to be barred as unqualified for the sacrament in 1961?

Following St. Thomas closely, Billuart (1685-1759) looked upon sickness as necessary only because it was an indispensable external sign of spiritual internal sickness. Since to him the sacrament was the *"ultimum remedium immediate disponens ad gloriam"* the recipient had to be dangerously sick, i.e., the illness had to be of such a character as normally to bring on death, and hence the danger of death had to be feared as present. He interpreted the doctrine of the Council of Trent as meaning by *praesertim* that all the dangerously sick, and not only the dangerously sick who were actually dying, were fit recipients of Extreme Unction. How? He does not explain. In support of his doctrine he points to the "perpetual practice of the Church, at least the Western Church, which never gave the sacrament to any sick except the ones *periculose laborantibus*." [118]

117 "Si conferatur infirmo communi morbo, sive non graviter vel periculose laboranti, non est validum."—*Theologia Moralis,* II, n. 208; also Ioannes Clericatus, *De Sacramentis Baptismi, Confirmationis atque Extremae Unctionis Decisiones* (Venetiis, 1703), Decis. LXXIX, n. 10.

118 No proof of this sweeping statement is offered: " . . . Ubi observanda est haec particula "praesertim" qua significatur, etiam periculose aegrotantibus, licet non tam periculose ut videantur in exitu constituti esse

Gotti (1664-1742) looked upon the practice of anointing only those who are in danger of death as "the true and legitimate" practice of the Latin Church.[119] This is far from saying that the only valid subject of the sacrament is one whose death is feared as a danger already present.

Tournely (1658-1729) expressed the rule of anointing this way: "If one is suffering from a slight sickness which cannot evoke a fear that death is a probability he is not to be given the sacrament." [120]

St. Alphonsus in many places speaks about the recipient of Extreme Unction, but it is not always easy (as likewise it is not with Suarez) to know exactly what he demanded for a valid and a licit anointing. There seems no doubt, however, that like Suarez he also believed that a prudent judgment that a danger was present sufficed.

> . . . ad administrandum hoc sacramentum valide et licite, sufficere quod infirmus laboret morbo ita gravi, *ut prudenter putetur esse in periculo proximae mortis.*[121]

In answering the question whether the sacrament when conferred on one not seriously sick is valid, he mentioned the opinion of Coninck and others that it is, but he called the opposite opinion *"communior et sequenda."* The sacrament, he taught, can be given only to the sick who according to human observation seem

---

conferendum . . . ex *perpetua* praxi totius Ecclesiae saltem Occidentalis quae nullibi legitur umquam contulisse hoc sacramentum nisi periculose laborantibus."—*Summa Sancti Thomae* (editio nova, 8 vols., Paris, 1874-1886), VII, Tract. *De Extrema Unctione,* Art. VI, n. 1, 2, 3, 4. Cf. *supra,* pp. 32-34.

[119] "Dico vera et legitima Ecclesiae Latinae praxis est sacramentum Extremae Unctionis illis infirmis, qui periculoso morbo tenentur, de quorum vicina morte timetur, non autem ultimum vitae periodum expectare."—*Theologia Scholastico-Dogmatica* (3 vols., Venetiis, 1763), III, Tract. XI, Quae. IV, dub. I, n. 2.

[120] " . . . infirmis, qui levi aliqua laborant infirmitate, ex qua mors timeri probabiliter non possit, dandam non esse Unctionem Extremam."—*Praelectiones Theologiae* (10 vols. in 13, Venetiis: Pezzana, 1755-1765), IX, Tract. *De Extrema Unctione,* Quae. III, n. 4.

[121] *Theologia Moralis,* Lib. VI, n. 714.

to be approaching death. For this stand he cited the Council of Florence whose *"debet"* (*nisi infirmis, de cuius morte timetur, dari debet*), he submitted, carried with it "not only a precept but a necessity." When the Pontiff designated as the recipients of anointing those sick persons whose death is feared, he thereby excluded all other sick persons. The *"praesertim"* of the Council of Trent he interpreted in the same sense as Billuart.[122]

If there was doubt that the illness was dangerous, then Extreme Unction could not be given. If there was a "prudent fear" or a "true probability" that there might be a danger, the sacrament could be given.[123]

But if it was prudently judged that a danger existed when as a fact it did not exist, was the administration of the sacrament to be deemed valid? If one allowed that a prudent judgment of danger sufficed for validity, then it could hardly be held that an objectively real danger was necessary, and in that case there would be a sacrament whose validity depended on the subjective judgment of the minister.

There are at least three occasions on which the eminent theologian and canonist, Pope Benedict XIV (1740-1758), treated specifically of the recipient of Extreme Unction. On two of these, in the papal Constitution *Etsi pastoralis* of 1742 and in the Encyclical *Ex quo primum,* he wrote as pope; on the third, in *De Synodo Dioecesana* (first edited in 1748), as a private doctor.

In *De Synodo Dioecesana* he wrote:

> . . . (unctionem) solis infirmis esse exhibendam, et quidem tali morbo laborantibus, unde, peritorum iudicio, mors sequutura prudenter timeatur.[124]

122 "[Concilium Tridentinum] docet . . . nisi infirmis qui secundum aestimationem videntur morti appropinquare . . . "debet" [secundum Concilium Florentinum] non tantum importat praeceptum, sed etiam necessitatem. . . . Pontifex cum designavit subiectum huius sacramenti, et designavit tantum infirmum de cuius morte timetur, censetur alios quidem infirmos exclusisse."—St. Alphonsus, *Theologia Moralis,* Lib. VI, n. 713.

123 *Ibid.,* n. 714.

124 Lib. VIII, Cap. V, n. 1.

He did not contend that the sacrament cannot be validly given to other sick persons. He simply set down the rule (of the Latin Church) that *de facto* it is to be administered solely to the sick who are in danger.

The Constitution *Etsi pastoralis* of 1742 was addressed to the Italo-Greeks concerning dogmas and rites to be held and observed by them. In constituted particular law for that rite. In this he wrote:

> Infirmis vero, iuxta verbum Iacobi Apostoli, unctio exhibeatur extrema.[125]

No mention of danger, and no restriction of the use of this sacrament was made for the Italo-Greeks. Such a requirement could not be anything but a legislative precept of the Latin Church. Had Benedict XIV believed that the Council of Trent postulated the necessity of a danger for the valid anointing, he would have added what he wrote in *De Synodo Dioecesana,* but what he omitted here, viz., *"et quidem tali morbo laborantibus, unde peritorum iudicio, mors sequutura prudenter timeatur."*

The papal Encyclical *Ex quo primum* of 1756 was addressed to the Churches of the Greek Rite, relative to a proposed new edition of the Greek *Euchologion* (ritual). In it Benedict treated at length the question of conferring the sacrament on the physically healthy, an abuse that had, it seems, persisted in some sections of the Eastern Church. He stated, quoting a *Monitum* in the *Euchologion:*

> . . . meminisse debent sacerdotes, sacramentum sancti olei, quod Euchelaeon dicitur, a Christo esse institutum, tamquam caelestem medicinam non pro animae tantum, sed etiam pro corporis salute, *solis proinde infirmis administrandum, non autem bene valentibus;* et in eo quidem tempore, in quo sibi constant, et suis compotes sunt; ut ita maiorem sacramenti gratiam recipiant, si cum fide ac devote voluntate accedentes, oleo sancto ungantur.[126]

The question then was taken up whether any of the text of the *Euchologion* should be changed on the grounds that it left the impression of allowing the non-sick to receive the anointing. No

[125] Cap. V, n. 2—*Fontes,* 328.

[126] § 44—*Fontes,* 438.

change was deemed necessary, not even of that passage which allowed the anointing of those who come to the church to receive the sacrament, for this could be understood of those who, while sick, were nevertheless able to come, or at any rate could be brought to church, there to receive the sacrament with greater devotion. The *Monitum* obviated any misunderstanding by reminding priests:

> . . . solis fidelibus graviter aegrotantibus, non autem bene se habentibus, ministretur, neque tamen expectetur tempus illud, quo aeger iam suae mentis compos non est.[127]

According to the *Monitum,* as the pope explained,

> . . . Graecis diserte vetitum fuerit, extremae unctionis sacramentum aliis conferre, praeterquam aegrotis, et quidem gravi morbo laborantibus. [128]

And in another section he mentioned "the standing *prohibition* against administering Extreme Unction outside the necessity of grave illness." [129]

The rule for the Greeks, as expressed in the Encyclical *Ex quo primum,* was that the sacrament be administered to the "seriously sick." The rule in *De Synodo Dioecesana* looked to its administration in favor of "only those sick persons who could prudently be judged to be in danger of death." But the *Monitum,* as also the Council of Trent, directed simply that "the unction is to be used for the sick." These rules seemed to be but working norms that regulated the actual administration of the sacrament. Grave illness could or could not be attended with a danger of death properly so called. An illness can be serious because of the pain it causes, or because of its long duration, or because of the extent to which it debilitates a man. These were

[127] § 46—*Fontes,* n. 438. Benedict pointed out that even in the Latin Church people used to come to church to be anoninted (he cited Martène, *De Antiquis Ritibus,* Lib. 2, Cap. 7, art. 2). Actually the paraphrase of the *monitum* as given in Benedict's words has *"graviter aegrotantibus,"* whereas the *Monitum* has simply *"infirmis."* Neither passage mentions a *"periculum mortis."*

[128] *Ibid.,* § 47—*Fontes,* n. 438.

[129] " . . . stante prohibitione administrandi Sacramentum Extremae Unctionis extra gravi morbi necessitatem."—*Ibid.,* § 48.

norms for determining in practice which sick persons were to be anointed. If a danger of death were an indispensable condition for the administration of the sacrament, then Benedict, who expressed the requisite so clearly in *De Synodo Dioecesana,* would certainly have made it equally clear in the Encyclical *Ex quo primum* and the Constitution *Etsi pastoralis.*

On February 20, 1801, the Sacred Congregation for the Propagation of the Faith decreed that missionaries could anoint persons who were afflicted with a sickness that would, according to common experience, cause death within a year, even though the danger was not yet in any way proximate, under the following condition: when, because of distance or other circumstances, the missioner would not be able to return to the sick person at the time the patient would have reached the normal stage for the reception of the sacrament.[130] Here was sanctioned the teaching of Suarez and of St. Alphonsus and also of other moralists who considered even a very remote (*in causa*) danger sufficient for a lawful administration of Extreme Unction in cases of necessity, although the principle of administration given in the Roman Ritual read, *"ut mortis periculum imminere videatur."* If the administration was lawful, then *a fortiori* it was valid.

On December 11, 1850, the Holy Office confirmed the fact that a prudent judgment of danger proved sufficient for a lawful anointing. The Vicar Apostolic of the Sandwich (Hawaiian) Islands wrote to the Holy Office informing it that "we give Extreme Unction to everyone of the sick whom *we believe* to be in danger, and we follow the Ritual." The Holy Office answered: "You act correctly."[131]

[130] S.C. de Prop. Fide (C. P. pro Sin.), 20 febr. 1801: "Talori i missionari visitando i loro distretti s'incontrano in qualche malato etico o d'altro morbo, che a certa sperienza durerà molti mesi, ma dentro l'anno perisce: si cerca se in tale caso il missionario possa somministrargli il Viatico e l'Estrema Unzione per al ragione che, quando sarebbe veramente nel grado suo di riceverla, allora il missionario non si potrà trovare presente nel luogo per la grande distanza, e per altre circonstanze impeditive? Affirmative." —*Fontes,* n. 4662.

[131] S.C.S. Off. (Vic. Ap. Sandwic.), 11 dec. 1850, n. 17: "Nous donnons l'Extrême Onction à tous les malades *que nous croyons en danger,* et nous suivons le Rituel." "Bene se gerere."—*Fontes,* n. 913.

Before one turns to a consideration of the present law of the Code on the danger of death in the recipient, one may well advert briefly to the teaching of a few eminent theologians, who wrote at the turn of the century or shortly before. Ballerini (1829-1909), writing in 1888, taught that death needed not to be at the door nor was it to be certainly expected to follow from the illness. It was enough to have "a reasonable fear that death was near." This reasonable fear Ballerini equated with a probable judgment of ensuing death (that death would follow). If it was doubtful that the illness really involved a danger, and the doubt was of a purely negative character, then Extreme Unction could not be given. If, on the other hand, the doubt was positive in character, so that there existed the probability of a danger, then it could be administered.[132]

A positive doubt means that there are reasons both for believing that the sickness is dangerous and for believing that it is not. The positive doubt furnishes a basis for the judgment that death will probably follow, and therefore an anointing is permissible. A negative doubt is, for practical purposes, the equivalent of ignorance; there is no reason to believe that the sickness is dangerous and no reason to believe it is not. In this case the sacrament cannot be given because there is no basis for a prudent judgment of danger.

For Lehmkuhl it was necessary that there be a probable danger that life might end shortly. It did not have to be a danger of immediate death, however. It sufficed that a sickness tend to put an end to life shortly, or, if it was a lingering illness (like consumption), that it have reached a stage in which death

[132] ". . . non oportere, ut mors sit in ianuis, imo neque ut certum sit mortem secuturam ex ea infirmitate, sed satis esse, ut de proxima morte infirmi *timeatur,* utique rationabiliter. Rationabilis vero est timor, cum probabile est iudicium de morte secutura. . . . Quid si dubium sit, an infirmitas sit periculosa? Si dubium est negativum, negat cum Castropalao et Laymann, S. Alphonsus, n. 714, dari posse; quia praeceptum est ne aliis quam vita periclitantibus detur. Si vero dubium sit positivum, sive adsit probabilitas periculi, seu prudens timor, tunc potest dari, ut communiter traditur et Eugenius IV docuit."—*Opus Theologicum Morale* (absolvit et edidit Dominicus Palmieri, 7 vols., Prati: Ex Officina Libraria Giachetti, Filii et Soc., 1889-1893), V, 693.

seemed not far off; if old age was the malady, the judgment had to point to a person's death within a few days. As soon as this probable danger existed, the sacrament was to be given. Before it existed, Extreme Unction could not be given.[133] Lehmkuhl seemed to require a probable danger that was somewhat imminent in character.

In his thorough work on Extreme Unction, Joseph Kern (1856-1907) set down the principle that as regards validity the universal norm is this: As long as one is capable of receiving the principal effect of a sacrament, one is capable also of receiving that sacrament validly. Now the principal effect of Extreme Unction is the "comforting of the soul against the depression caused by sickness."[134] A person, then, who is seriously affected with illness is according to this norm capable of receiving the sacrament of the sick. But the universal norm for determining when it is licit, or necessary, to administer the anointing is given in the Roman Ritual: "This Sacrament must be given to those who are *so seriously sick that* the danger of their dying seems to be imminent."[135] What, then, is to be said of the sacrament if one judges an illness to be serious and dangerous while in reality there is in it no danger of death? It is *certain,* says Kern, that the sacrament would be *both validly and licitly* administered.[136]

[133] "Sufficit et requiritur *probabile periculum,* ne brevi vita finiatur; nullatenus requiritur, ut mors iam immineat, aut ut *instantis* mortis periculum adsit. Ergo sufficit morbus gravis seu periculosus, qui vitam brevi finire possit, aut morbi ex natura sua diuturni (ut phthsis) ille status, in quo iuste timeri possit, ne vita brevi finiatur; senectutis talis conditio, ut vires in dies deficere videantur. Quapropter quum primum tale probabile periculum exsistit, multo magis, quando certum est, sacramentum conferri potest, vel potius debet. . . . Si antequam tale periculum probabile existat, extrema unctio dari nequit."—*Theologia Moralis,* II, n. 576.

[134] *De Extrema Unctione,* p. 296.

[135] Pre-Code *Roman Ritual* (all editions), Tit. V, Cap. 1, n. 5.

[136] "Quod spectat *valorem,* norma universalis est: Quodvis sacramentum valide recipiunt, qui sunt capaces effectus eius principalis. Effectus autem principalis Extremae Unctionis est confortatio animae contra depressionem ex morbo causatam. . . . Normam universalem, quando *liceat,* immo oporteat Extremam Unctionem dare, statuit ipsum Rituale Romanum, . . .

Suarez, Coninck, St. Alphonsus and others had all said it, more or less clearly, since the sixteenth century; the Holy Office, sanctioning the practice of anointing absolutely one who was "believed" to be in danger, confirmed it; then Kern spelled it out plainly as his conviction that the existence of a real danger of death is not necessary for the valid reception of Extreme Unction, though it is necessary, by ecclesiastical law, for the licit administration of the sacrament.[137] Not all theologians and canonists were ready to agree, nor are they yet, that a subjectively putative danger is sufficient for the licit, not to say the valid, administration of the sacrament, but it was this opinion that was in fact gaining ground when the Code of Canon Law was formulated in the early part of the twentieth century.

B. *Present Legislation*

1. *Comparison with the pre-Code Law*

The ecclesiastical law governing the administration of Extreme Unction from 1614 to 1918, before the codification of the disciplinary law of the Latin Church, was contained in the Roman Ritual of Paul V.[138] The present law of canon 940, § 1, embodied verbatim in the post-Code editions of the Ritual,[139] is a revision of this former rule. A comparison will show that the new law so modified the old ritual law as to allow for a wider interpretation of *periculum mortis,* an interpretation which, in fact, had been pursued in practice for a long time before the change in the law was realized.

> *Ritual of 1614:* "Debet autem hoc Sacramentum infirmis praeberi, qui cum ad usum rationis pervenerint, tam graviter laborant, ut mortis periculum imminere videatur, et iis qui

---

Si morbus *videatur* gravis et periculosus esse, revera autem nullum adsit discrimen vitae, *certe valide et licite* ministratur sacramentum."—*De Extrema Unctione,* pp. 296-298.

[137] Cf. *infra,* pp. 65-69, 75-76, 83-84.

[138] Tit. V, Cap. I, n. 5. The rule remained the same in the revisions of Benedict XIV in 1752 and of Pius X in 1913.

[139] Tit. VI, Cap. I, n. 8, in both post-Code editions, 1925 and 1952.

prae senio deficiunt, et in diem videntur morituri, etiam sine alia infirmitate."

Canon 940, § 1: "Extrema Unctio praeberi non potest nisi fideli qui, post adeptum usum rationis, ob infirmitatem vel senium in periculo mortis versetur."

The old Ritual called for the danger to be imminent (*ut mortis periculum imminere videatur*); the Code simply requires a danger, and says nothing about whether that danger is to be imminent or remote, certain or probable. How imminent the danger of the old Ritual was expected to be can be judged from what it said of those dying of old age, who were to be anointed when it was foreseen that they would die within the day (*in diem morituri*). The Code makes no such attempt to measure the danger. It merely requires that there be one. The old Ritual described the recipient as one seriously ailing from sickness (*infirmis qui . . . tam graviter laborant*); the Code says nothing of the state or degree of the infirmity, but only that sickness or old age be the cause of the danger (*ob infirmitatem vel senium in periculo mortis versetur*). "*Versetur*" does not point to one "struggling in a danger," it simply implies the presence of a danger in the sick person's condition.

Though dealing with the recipient of Extreme Unction, both laws are directed immediately to the minister of the sacrament. The old Ritual expresses whom he has an obligation to anoint [140] (*Debet . . . praeberi*). The Code, however, tells him whom he is allowed to anoint (*praeberi non potest nisi . . .*).[141]

2. *Definitions of Danger of Death*

The presence of any condition that puts a man's life in jeopardy constitutes for him a danger of death. With reference to Extreme Unction it is always understood that this danger arises internally, from the physiological weakening of the body through sickness or old age.

[140] Not necessarily whom he can anoint.

[141] It positively disallows the anointing of anyone who does not come under the terms of Canon 940, § 1. It sets limits to what subjects can be lawfully anointed.

CERTAIN, PROBABLE AND DOUBTFUL DANGER. When circumstances are such that death is inescapable and unavoidable the danger is called certain. Contracting of what is currently a lethal and incurable disease can bring with it the danger of certain death, a certain danger. A danger of death is probable when in the extant situation there are reasons for believing that death will follow and, at the same time, reasons for believing that the sickness will be overcome. The prospects of life and death need not be equally probable as long as each is truly probable. A ninety percent chance of recovery and a ten percent chance of dying still constitutes a probable, though slight, danger of death, strictly so-called.[142] A probable danger is one with reference to which some positive doubt continues to exist. When in a sickness it is not known whether there is even a probable danger, e.g., a person is taken ill, but it is not known what cause underlies his illness, then there results what is called a doubtful danger. This doubt does not concern itself with whether the patient will live or die, but only with whether there is any probability at all that he may die, i.e., whether there exists any danger at all. Such a doubtful danger always connotes a negative doubt about the danger.

IMMINENT, PROXIMATE AND REMOTE DANGER. An imminent danger of death is present when the person is at the very point of dying; it points to the *articulus mortis,* in which death is expected momentarily. A person in a condition of heart failure, or in a state of asphyxia, or in the extreme stages of a consumptive disease, is in imminent danger of death, a danger in which death could occur momentarily. A proximate danger is one in which death can follow shortly within the immediate future. A remote danger is one in which death can follow, not in the immediate future, but at some later time. Evidently there are degrees of proximate and remote danger.

142 The degree of probability will depend not only on the nature and extent of the illness but also on the age and general constitution of the patient. Pneumonia in one suffering tuberculosis creates a greater danger of probable death (probable danger) than it does in a normally healthy person.

REAL AND ESTIMATED DANGER. A real or objective danger is one that actually exists in the circumstances whether it is known to anyone or not. An estimated or subjectively judged danger is one that may or may not in reality be present. It is a judgment made by the patient, the doctor, the family or the priest, any or all of them, that in the sick man's situation there is a danger to his life. In the nature of things this judgment, though prudently made, remains fallible and can be erroneous, in which case the estimated danger is in fact no danger at all.

3. *What Kind of Danger Is Postulated?*

The Code itself does not define the term danger, *periculum.* It does not attempt to explain what kind of danger is required. From the response of 1801, however, which allowed missionaries to confer Extreme Unction on subjects who had contracted a deadly disease but who would in fact live for months and even a year, it is evident that a proximate danger is not postulated. Wouters (1864-1933) and Regatillo grant that an anointing in such a remote danger as was contemplated in the response is indeed valid, but they further believe that for its lawfulness one must look to further justifying reasons.[143] This view seems questionable in light of the fact that the Code does not distinguish between a danger as necessary for a valid administration and a danger as necessary for a licit administration. As long as one is in danger, in any accepted sense of the term, one can always be both validly and licitly anointed.

The authors in general are in agreement with Cappello, who says:

> Necesse non est, ut periculum sit proximum aut gravissimum aut valde grave. Requiritur et sufficit ut sit moraliter probabile.[144]

[143] Wouters, *Manuale Theologiae Moralis* (2 vols., Vol. II, Brugis: Beyaert, 1932), II, n. 581; Regatillo-Zalba, *Theologiae Moralis Summa* (3 vols., Matriti: Biblioteca de Autores Christianos, 1952-1954), III, n. 649, p. 475.

[144] *De Extrema Unctione,* n. 229; Henry Davis, *Moral and Pastoral Theology* (4 vols., 5. ed., New York: Sheed & Ward, 1946), IV, 7; Kilker, *Extreme Unction,* p. 167; Merkelbach, *Summa Theologiae Moralis* (10. ed.,

The probability of death may not be great when compared with the probability of recovery, but that affects the condition not at all. If any probability of death is present it suffices.[145]

Noldin (1838-1922) distinguished two elements that join to produce a danger. The first is an illness that of its very nature can bring death. The second is the progression of that illness in the recipient to the point where death becomes a probability.[146] It is a bit difficult to see why, if it is known that a sickness can bring death, there is not by that very fact a probability of death as soon as it is certain that the sickness has been contracted. Any waiting for it to progress would only, it seems, be consolidating a probability that is already there. The fact that Suarez allowed for the anointing of persons in time of pestilence as soon as there was some sign of infection,[147] and that the Holy See permitted missionaries to anoint in cases of deadly illness before any notable progression of the illness in the patient, indicates that the probability already existed, at least to the extent required for the administration of the sacrament. Furthermore, there is the problem of knowing precisely what illnesses can inherently (*ex se*) and of their very nature (*natura sua*) lead to death.

---

aucta et emendata, 3 vols., Brugis: Desclée de Brouwer & Cie., 1956), III, n. 704. Fanfani (1876-1955), however, taught that the danger, though not imminent, should be "*satis* proximum et prudenter existimatum."—*Manuale Theorico-Practicum Theologiae Moralis* (4 vols., Romae: Libraria Ferrari, 1949-1951), IV, 608.

145 "Statim atque probabile fit aegrotum ex presenti morbo seu periculo esse moriturum, licet forsan adhuc probabilius sit eum sanatum iri."—Genicot-Salsmans, *Institutiones Theologiae Moralis* (17. ed., quam paravit A. Gortebecke, 2 vols., Bruxelles: L'Edition Universelle, 1951), II, n. 425.

146 "Gravis morbus censetur, qui ex se et natura sua letalem exitum habere potest et ad illum terminum processit, in quo probabiliter iudicari possit mortem allaturus."—Noldin-Schmitt, *Summa Theologiae Moralis* (27. ed., 3 vols., Barcelona: Herder, 1951), III, n. 444. Cf. St. Thomas, *Summa Theologica,* Pars III Supp., Q. XXXII, art. 2: ". . . qui sunt in statu exeuntium, propter hoc quod aegritudo nata est inducere mortem et de periculo timetur." Cf. also Suarez, Disp. XLII, Sect. II, n. 4.—*Opera Omnia,* XXII, 852.

147 Cf. *supra*, p. 39.

Some diseases that were once classified as "killers" are no longer so classified today. The nature of the sicknesses remains the same, and the diseases remain lethal if unchecked, but new remedies have almost completely minimized their danger. A remote danger is produced the moment such a disease is contracted. It is never allowed to become a serious danger in consideration of the extrinsic causes, the remedies, used against it. In the eighteenth century fever in one form or another accounted for eight out of every ten deaths. Fever is still *ex se* and *natura sua* capable of leading to such dread results unless it be expelled, so that today, though the technique of treatment has greatly decreased the *periculum mortis* from fever, it remains *in se* capable of bringing on death.[148]

Potentially every sickness can lead to death if left unchecked or unattended to. Cuttaz rightly observes that in judging a danger one must often necessarily know the constitution of the sick man, his temperament and habits, his physical and moral resistance, for in his particular circumstances an affliction not usually dangerous could be dangerous for him.[149] Pneumonia in an alcoholic is very dangerous as is a strong fever in a cardiac case. It is not quite accurate to say that the illness must of its very nature (*natura sua*) be dangerous; the illness, whether usually lethal or not, must be feared as dangerous in the particular patient. Likewise it does not seem quite reasonable to deny Extreme Unction to one who is known to have contracted a disease considered *in se* lethal until that disease has progressed in the threat of its danger, for as soon as a patient contracts such an illness his life becomes feared for, even though the prospect of death is yet remote. He is in danger, if danger must be the criterion for administration.

Vermeersch (1858-1936) taught that, if a danger exists, Extreme Unction is always conferred validly; if the danger is sufficiently proximate, although there is no "affliction of soul" (the person is really sick and in distress), it is conferred validly and

[148] Cf. Lester King, *The Medical World of the Eighteenth Century* (Chicago: University of Chicago Press, 1958), pp. 123-142.

[149] Cuttaz, *Remède Divin pour les Chrétiens Malades*, p. 73.

licitly; if the danger is remote but there is great affliction, then likewise validly and licitly; if there is doubt about the danger in the affliction which is present, then validly and licitily *sub conditione.*[150] The Code, however, does not advert to the need of any affliction in the sufferer before he can be anointed. It simply points out that there must be a danger arising from sickness. Vermeersch implied that, if the danger was remote and the patient was not in an *"afflictio animi,"* he could not licitly receive the anointing. The Code makes no such restriction.

It is agreed that a probable judgment, or a positive doubt, that death will follow from an illness suffices for a lawful administering of Extreme Unction.[151] Danger in itself is something intangible and imperceptible. Its presence must be deduced from circumstances attending the patient and his illness. But who is to make this deduction, this judgment, about the danger? It is not necessary that it be made by a doctor. It can be the prudent judgment of the sick man himself, of a member of his family, of the priest, or of the physician.[152] The prudent judgment of anyone will suffice, even if others, including the doctor, feel certain there is no danger.[153] This is important. The sacrament can always be conferred absolutely on the prudent judgment of one person that a probable danger exists, even though others may contradict this contention, and even though the priest who administers the sacrament or the physician who attends the patient may not think a probable danger is present.

What is demanded for anointing is a probable danger subjectively conceived to be present, not necessarily the actual and objective existence of a danger.

[150] Vermeersch-Creusen, *Epitome Iuris Canonici,* II, n. 225.

[151] Vermeersch-Creusen, *loc. cit.;* Iorio, *Theologia Moralis* (3. ed., recognita et emendata, 3 vols., Neapoli: M. D'Auria, 1946-1947), III, n. 768; Piscetta-Gennaro, *Elementa Theologiae Moralis,* V, n. 1027, III.

[152] "Non requiritur semper et necessario ut probabile existimetur a medico aut ab infirmo eiusve familia aut communiter. Satis est prudens iudicium unius personae, v.g., parochi seu sacerdotis."—Cappello, *De Extrema Unctione,* n. 229; Genicot-Salsmans, *Institutiones Theologiae Moralis,* II, n. 425.

[153] Iorio, *Theologia Moralis,* III, n. 770, § 2.

> Non requiritur ut sit obiective seu re ipsa probabile; satis est, ut prudenter qua tale existimetur.[154]

> Sufficit prudenter existimatum, quamvis obiectivum non sit. Non requiritur necessario et semper ut tale a medico, familia, etc., existimetur; sat est prudens iudicium unius, ut sacerdotis.[155]

> Nec item necesse est ut sit in se et obiective probabile, sufficit ut sit probabile subiective seu ut tale prudenter aestimetur a parocho aut a sacerdote ministro, licet medicus dicat obiective periculum non haberi.[156]

With this Cance, Ferreres (1861-1936), Abbo-Hannan, Iorio, Romani, Jone, Claeys Boúúaert and Cuttaz agree.[157] Cuttaz points to the phrase used by Saint Thomas and in the Decree to the Armenians, *"de cuius morte timetur,"* and says that, if one prudently fears a danger to be present, that condition is fulfilled, no matter whether one's judgment be erroneous, so that there is

154 Cappello, *De Extrema Unctione,* n. 229.

155 Regatillo-Zalba, *Theologiae Moralis Summa,* III, n. 649, § 3.

156 Conte a Coronata, *De Sacramentis,* I, n. 550, § 4.

157 "Mais il n'est pas requis que ce peril de mort soit certain ou très grave (un danger probable suffit), qu'il soit *objectivement* tel (il suffit qu'on le *regarde prudemment comme tel*), qu'il soit nécessairement regardé comme tel par le médecin ou le malade ou les membres de sa famille (le jugement du curé ou d'un prêtre peut suffire)."—Cance, *Le Code de Droit Canonique,* n. 266, c, note 2; ". . . sufficit ut infirmus laboret morbo ita gravi ut *prudenter existimetur* versari in periculo mortis."—Ferreres, *Theologia Moralis* (13. ed., 7. ed. post Codicem, 2 vols., Barcinone: Eugenius Subirana, 1928), II, n. 845; "Probable danger of death, *subjectively conceived in the mind* of the physician, the minister or the sick person suffices for the valid administration of the sacrament."—Abbo-Hannan, *The Sacred Canons* (2 vols., revised ed., St. Louis: Herder, 1957), II, 62; Iorio, *Theologia Moralis,* III, n. 770; "Requiritur infirmitas eaque gravis et quae infirmum in periculo mortis, licet non prosus proximo, *e prudentibus coniecturis aestimetur constituere.*"—Romani, *Institutiones Iuris Canonici* (2 vols., Romae: Editrice "Iustitia," 1941-1945), II, n. 426; Jone, *Commentarium in Codicem Iuris Canonici,* II, 169; ". . . requiritur probabile iudicium seu dubium positivum de morte secutura ex hac infirmitate."—Ferdinandus Claeys Boúúaert, *Manuale Iuris Canonici* (3 vols., Vol. II, 3. ed., Leodii: Dessain, 1947), II, n. 177, § 3; Cuttax, *Remède Divin pour les Chrétiens Malades,* p. 74.

nonexistent the danger one believes to exist.[158] The sacrament, he adds, must be given to those who according to the estimation of men are threatened with death from sickness.

Essentially, then, it is not a *real* danger at all that is required, but only an *estimated* danger. And if the estimated danger really does not exist here and now in the sick patient, the sacrament is nevertheless conferred validly to him. An inevitable conclusion from this must be that a danger itself is not, and cannot be, a requisite on which the validity of the anointing depends. It must be remembered that what is spoken of here is anointing absolutely, not conditionally. If a danger itself were intrinsically necessary for the validity, the sacrament could never be given absolutely on a subjective probability that a danger is present.

Jone, Cappello, Regatillo, Cuttaz and Kern are explicit in stating that the sacrament when given to one who is thought to be in danger, though no actual danger be present, is both valid and licit.

> Si postea appareat periculum mortis revera non exstitisse, extrema unctio valide et licite administrata fuit, dummodo prudenter gravis et periculosus morbus fuerit existimatus.[159]

> Si morbus videatur gravis et periculosus, revera tamen nullum adsit discrimen vitae? Sacramentum valide et licite administratur.[160]

> Valide et licite confertur . . . in morbo qui videtur gravis et periculosus, etsi obiective non sit vitae periculum.[161]

To deliberately administer the sacrament to a sick person whom no one prudently judges to be in a probable danger would

[158] "Lorsque la vérité (objective) du danger de mort accompagne la certitude (subjective) qu'en a celui qui confère le sacrement celui-ci assurément est valide . . . le sacrement est valide même si cette certitude est erronée et si le danger qu'on croit exister n'est pas rèel."—*Op. cit.*, p. 74.

[159] Jone, *Commentarium in Codicem,* II, 169.

[160] Cappello, *De Extrema Unctione,* n. 237.

[161] Regatillo-Zalba, *Theologiae Moralis Summa,* III, 649, § 7; Kern, *De Extrema Unctione*, p. 298; "Même, si en realité le danger n'existait pas, le Sacrement serait valide."—Cuttaz, *op. cit.*, p. 74.

violate the ruling of canon 940, and therefore be illicit. It would not, however, be invalid provided that the recipient is truly sick.

With this Noldin disagreed completely, saying:

> Si ergo extrema unctio confertur infirmo, qui putatur esse in periculo mortis, reipsa autem non est, invalidum est sacramentum; nam subiectum capax ex institutione Christi est infirmus, qui reipsa in periculo mortis versatur, sicut subiectum capax absolutionis est penitens, qui reipsa est dispositus.[162]

Wouters was in full accord when he wrote that a "merely estimated" danger simply will not do,[163] and he is joined by Doronzo, who feels that this is the "catholic doctrine, to deny which would be temerarious." [164] Kilker (1901-1944) called Noldin's view the more probable one, "for there seems," he said, "to be lacking on the part of the subject an essential condition for a valid reception. In no other sacrament, he continued, does subjective certitude on the part of the minister validate the administration to a man otherwise objectively incapable of reception." [165] He assumes, however, what precisely is to be proved, namely that a danger of death is an *essential* condition, that without it a man is objectively incapable of receiving the sacrament. That "by Christ's institution the *subiectum capax* is a sick person in danger of death truly and actually" [166] is a theological opinion, which indeed lacks unanimity, especially today. All the inspired word of God says about the *subiectum capax* is that he be sick, and the Council of Trent added nothing to further restrict this condition of the man objectively capable of receiving the anointing.[167]

[162] *Summa Theologiae Moralis,* III, n. 444, c.

[163] " . . . sensu obvio periculum vere existens, non autem mere existimatum significant."—*Manuale Theologiae Moralis,* II, n. 582.

[164] "Requiri aliquod periculum mortis, est pariter doctrina catholica cui contradicere *temerarium* esset."—*De Extrema Unctione,* II, 582.

[165] Kilker, *Extreme Unction,* p. 169.

[166] Kilker, *Extreme Unction,* p. 168; Noldin, *Summa Theologiae Moralis,* III, n. 444, c.

[167] The position is a natural conclusion for one who holds that the chief end of the sacrament is "the perfect healing of the soul with a view to its

Yet both Noldin and Kilker taught without hesitation that a probable danger suffices for an absolute anointing. This is a contradiction. If a condition is objectively and really necessary for the validity, then a sacrament could never be given absolutely unless the presence of the condition was morally certain, not merely judged to be probable. A probability involves a positive doubt. A priest would never be justified in conferring absolutely any sacrament on a subject who is but probably capable of receiving it, or with matter that is but probably valid matter. Yet here it is allowed to confer Extreme Unction absolutely on a probably qualified recipient. A probability can be totally wrong in its assumption of a fact, since the fact may lack all existence. On what basis would the exposing of the sacrament to possible (even probable) nullity by way of an ordinary rule of administration be justified?

In 1921, Pope Benedict XV in an allocution to the *Bona Mors* Sodality reminded the members to see that the sick, as the sickness grows, are fortified by the sacrament "when there is a prudent judgment about the danger of death." [168] And, speaking to the same Sodality in 1923, Pope Pius XI said:

> Neque enim, ut sacramentum valide liciteque detur, necesse est ut mors proxime secutura timeatur, *sed satis* est ut *prudens seu probabile adsit de periculo iudicium,* quodsi in ea rerum conditione conferri debet, in hac conferri utique potest. . . . [169]

It is impossible to evade the theological implication here. If Extreme Unction can be given absolutely in the circumstance of a probable danger even only prudently estimated as such, then

---

immediate entrance into glory" (Kilker, *op. cit.,* p. 32) or "ad animam proxime disponendam ac praeparandam, ut sine mora regnum coelorum introire possit (Noldin, *op. cit.,* III, n. 430, a). That it is the chief end, however, is also a theological opinion, never formulated by the Church as dogma.

[168] *Acta Apostolicae Sedis* (*AAS*), *Commentarium Officiale* (Romae: 1909-1928; Civitate Vaticana, 1929-), XIII (1921), 345—" . . . ingravescente morbo, prudens fuit de periculo mortis iudicium."

[169] *AAS,* XV (1923), 105.

the need for a danger exists, not with reference to the validity, but with reference to the element of lawfulness.[170]

Speaking only three and five years respectively after the promulgation of the Code, Benedict XV and Pius XI clearly taught that a probable danger prudently judged to be such warrants the conferring of Extreme Unction. There is no reason to demand more.

According to the present law, sickness is measured not directly by its effect on the body, but by the danger or lack of danger it presents to an individual's life. If an illness causes no great bodily pain and distress to the patient, but nevertheless is one that puts, or is judged to put, his life in danger, he can be anointed. If it cannot here and now be considered to cause any probable danger, he is not to be anointed.[171]

If a doctor or others, e.g., the priest, think the illness not to be serious, but the patient, suffering greatly and thinking himself to be in danger of dying, asks for the sacrament, he is to be anointed.[172] Similarly, if the doctor, or the priest, or any other prudent person believes the patient to be in danger, though he himself does not think so, he can be anointed.

If one is seriously sick with a disease which of its nature is lethal but which does not yet seem subjectively dangerous in him, Cappello, Conte a Coronata and Regatillo agree that Ex-

[170] Kilker gives this explanation to reconcile these papal statements to his view: There is a distinction between valid administration and valid reception. "The permissibility of the administration does not automatically effect the validity of the reception. The lack of an essential [by him so assumed] condition in the subject successfully obstructs such a valid and licit administration. . . . These official pronouncements and private writings speak of the legitimacy of the procedure on the part of the minister, but leave undiscussed the validity of the reception by the subject."—Kilker, *op. cit.*, p. 169. The objection remains unanswered: Why or how can a priest be lawfully permitted to anoint absolutely a subject who is only doubtfully (though by way of a positive doubt or probability) a capable recipient? The obvious intent of the texts is to remind the sodalists that the sick who are in an estimated probable danger are in fact and without doubt capable of receiving the sacrament both validly and licitly.

[171] Kilker, *Extreme Unction,* p. 170.

[172] Cappello, *De Extrema Unctione,* n. 234.

treme Unction can be given.[173] Here it is not really a question of probable danger, for that certainly exists once it is known that the disease is dangerous; it is simply a matter of recognizing the danger.

If the illness carries with it a certain but yet remote danger of death, the sacrament can always be given validly. The question arises, however, of just when to administer the sacrament. This is the case with cancer victims, who may live for months before the disease finally kills them. The writer feels that these people should be anointed as soon as the infirmity begins to restrict them in their normal activity, e.g., confining them to bed. This is when the sickness begins to take its effect in causing that special trial, weakness of body and depression of mind and soul, for which this sacrament is the divine medicine. The *confortatio animae* and the *abstersio reliquiarum peccati* (weakness of will caused by past sin, original and actual) offered by the anointing are intended and needed for the entire time of trial, not only at its end. The fear should not be that this sacrament may be given too soon, but that it might be given too late, thus depriving of much sacramental grace those who in their long trial of suffering could so well have benefited from it, a sacramental grace specifically intended for their situation.[174] If any danger of scandal derive from the giving of the sacrament to a suffering sick person when death is relatively remote, it comes perhaps from not having taught the faithful the tremendous benefits

[173] Cappello, *op. cit.*, n. 239; Conte a Coronata, *De Sacramentis,* I, n. 550, § 4; Regatillo-Zalba, *Theologiae Moralis Summa,* III, n. 649, § 7, c; cf. also Suarez, Disp. XLII, Sect. II, n. 5: "Quoties morbus ex se fuerit periculosus et gravis, existimo sacramentum esse validum, etiamsi ad statum morbi vel non satis vel etiam nihil attendatur."—*Opera Omnia,* XXII, 852.

[174] "[The anointing] should bring to the sick one, for the entire period of his trial, a spiritual comfort, and secondarily a corporal one. It is only eventually and by way of consequence that this sacrament should procure the grace of a good death by continuing its supernatural work to this decisive moment and by giving also to the dying all necessary encouragement."—F. Meurant, "L'Extreme-Onction, Est-elle le sacrament de la dernière maladie?" *La Vie Spirituelle,* XCII (1955), 245. (Writer's translation.)

accruing from the sacrament *during the time of sickness,* except perhaps to inform them that sometimes it may bring about a complete physical recovery; most of the time, however, they hear what it can do for them in their dying moments.[175]

The fact that a danger can be removed, with more or less certainty, by means of medical treatment or surgery does not *ipso facto* change the present condition of the patient. If he is considered sick enough to be anointed, he can and should be, even though he may consent to undergo an operation that will with moral certainty accomplish his recovery.[176] An operation would affect the question of the anointing in no way whatsoever. If a person is considered so ill that a serious operation is deemed necessary (e.g., as with patients suffering greatly from intestinal ulcers and tumors), it seems that the person should already have been anointed before the time of operation is at hand. Whether the operation itself be considered safe or dangerous is not the point at issue,[177] since it is something extrinsic to the patient's present condition. It is fallacious and detrimental to believe that until an actual crisis of life or death looms up the anointing should be deferred, such as the anointing of a seriously sick cancer patient because he may be taking radium or X-ray treatments and is not yet in immediate danger, or the anointing of a man with a severe bleeding ulcer, while treatments are being given, until the time when an operation is judged expedient. Certainly many such patients were and are in a "prudently judged probable danger" long before they are actually anointed. Such people unfortunately go through the agony and trial of

[175] Cf. The Council of Trent on effects of Extreme Unction, *supra,* pp. 49 ff.

[176] Kern held that if the patient agreed to the operation he eliminated himself from being a fit recipient, but there is no sound reason for this. If one is here and now a fit subject, there is no barrier in the way of a valid reception. Cf. Kern, *op. cit.,* p. 299; Cappello, *op. cit.,* n. 242; Regatillo-Zalba, *op. cit.,* III, n. 649, § 7, e; Kilker, *op. cit.,* p. 179.

[177] Kern apparently felt that it was, since he allowed a dangerously sick man consenting to a dangerous operation to be anointed, whereas he disallowed it if the operation was sure to produce a certain recovery. Cf. *op. cit., loc. cit.*

their illness without the mighty fortification and consolation of the sacrament of the sick, which all too often is given them only toward the end of their illness.[178]

Lanza (1905-1950) seems wrong, as also those who follow him, when he wrote that, although one becomes eligible to receive Extreme Unction once a danger of death is judged probable, one should be given the sacrament not immediately but only when death has become imminent with moral certitude.[179] One should again recall the words of Pius XI: "To give this sacrament validly and licitly it is enough that there be a prudent or probable judgment about the danger." There is no justification for keeping the sacrament from the faithful once they fulfill this minimum condition of being in danger.[180]

When one cannot be sure that even a probable danger is present in a sick person's condition, but suspects that there may be, then one is in doubt. As was seen, a probability of danger itself involves a doubt, but indeed a positive doubt. In this type of doubt Extreme Unction is conferred absolutely. When canon 941 states "Quando dubitatur num infirmus . . . in periculo mortis reipsa versetur . . . hoc sacramentum ministretur sub conditione," its concern relates not to a positive doubt but simply to a nega-

[178] The unconscious thinking behind such a deferral may be expressed in McReavy's words: "It will be evident that the further the administration of the sacrament is removed from the moment of death, the less effectually, owing to the subsequent accumulation of inevitable daily faults, can it produce this proper effect of preparing the way for prompt entry into glory."—"Extreme Unction—How Near to Death?" *The Clergy Review*, XL (1955), 491. Cf. The Council of Trent, where none of this theological opinion receives mention among the given effects of the sacrament. *Supra*, p. 10.

[179] A. Lanza–P. Palazzini, *Principi di Teologia Morale* (3 vols., Roma: Editrice Studium, 1952-1956), III, 308.

[180] Classical authors and some modern ones too discuss the question about giving Extreme Unction to women in childbirth. Childbirth itself is not an illness. On that account, despite the ordinary pains of parturition, Extreme Unction is not warranted. If the woman is ill or becomes ill so as in the light of a prudent judgment to be constituted in danger, then she could be anointed. For more on this cf. Kilker, *op. cit.*, pp. 173-177; Conte a Coronata, *De Sacramentis*, I, n. 550, § 7.

tive doubt. What this amounts to is a doubt about the existence of even a probability of danger.[181] The question here is not whether there is a sufficient measure of danger (if there is any probable danger then an absolute anointing is licit), but whether there is any measure of danger at all. In such a doubt Extreme Unction can be given, but conditionally.

This becomes important in an illness the nature of which is not known but which is apparently making the patient quite sick. Suspicion that a danger may be probable clearly justifies a conditional anointing. A sickness that greatly affects the body, e.g., with high fever, and whose nature is not precisely known is reasonably to be considered as at least doubtfully dangerous. Only when a disease is known in its source and its cause can it be counteracted effectively. The discovery of the nature of the disease and the subsequent discovery of efficient remedies is exactly what has turned once dangerous illnesses into now generally nonfatal illnesses. The very distress of the patient furnishes the suspicion that a danger may be present in the still mysterious sickness, and thus a conditional anointing is licitly administered.

Again this is important with reference to the cases which involve old people. Their condition may not induce a solidly estimated probability that a danger is present, but it may give rise to a founded suspicion thereof. If so, then there exists a doubt, and a conditional absolution is in order. There must, however, be a founded suspicion before there can ensue a reason for anointing conditionally. This suspicion can arise in consequence of the individual and specific circumstances surrounding the sick person. If a priest fears to go away from a sick person without anointing him, and yet cannot reach a solid judgment that a

[181] "Extrema Unctio conferri potest quoties prudenter *existimatur* infirmum versari in periculo mortis etiam dubio tantum seu probabili. *Existimare* autem est moralem *certitudinem* habere, et heic quidem, de *existentia* talis periculi. *Dubitare* vero idem est ac suspicionem habere. Unde discrimen; in *existimatione* de existentia periculi etiam dubii seu probabilis, conferri potest extrema unctio, et quidem *absolute,* ut dicitur . . . in *dubio* vero seu quando dubitatur an revera existat tale periculum eadem conferri potest, sed *sub conditione.*"—Iorio, *Theologia Moralis,* III, n. 768, § 2.

danger really exists, then he should anoint the sick person conditionally, without scruple.[182]

Canon 940 requires that the admissibility of the sick to the reception of Extreme Unction be measured by whether they can be considered to be in danger of death. This means whether there is in their situation, as arising from sickness or old age, a prudently estimated probability that their infirmity is likely to bring on death. If so, the sick person can be anointed absolutely.

Canon 941 makes provision for the case in which even the probability itself cannot be established with certainty. Accordingly, if there be reason to suspect a danger, then Extreme Unction is to be administered conditionally.

4. *Is This Danger Essential for the Sacrament?*

That for centuries it has been the danger of death that has served as a norm by means of which one determined whether or not a sick person should be anointed is a fact. That any such condition, however, is a requirement *de necessitate sacramenti* for the valid reception of Extreme Unction has never been set forth by the Church as Catholic doctrine. Aside from the fact that Saint James never mentioned it, that the practice of the Church for at least the first ten centuries seemed to contradict it, that the Council of Trent, in dealing specifically with the recipient, refused to declare it (and this at a time when not only a danger but an actual *labor in extremis* was deemed most desirable for the administration of the sacrament), that there have always been theologians who denied it (even among those who wanted the administration of the sacrament limited to those who were in danger), and that the matter is still controverted, there is yet another consideration that makes it seem very unlikely that the danger of death is an essentially necessary requisite for a valid anointing.

Over the years the notion of what danger is required has been stretched in a manner in which no objective requisite for validity

[182] Cf. Woywod-Smith, *A Practical Commentary on the Code of Canon Law* (revised and enlarged edition of combined Volumes I and II, New York: Joseph F. Wagner, 1957), 547.

could ever have been stretched. Today the common opinion of theologians and canonists, an opinion verbally expressed also by both Pope Benedict XV and Pope Pius XI, teaches that for the valid and licit administration of Extreme Unction it is sufficient that there be a prudent or probable judgment that there is a danger.[183] This amounts to saying that a judgment in good faith which regards a danger to be present is sufficient to warrant an absolute administration, and therefore sufficient for the valid reception of Extreme Unction. If, however, the condition were *de necessitate sacramenti* (or even *de precepto ecclesiae*) for validity, such a subjective judgment, no matter how probable and prudent in its background of good faith, could never be enough for the valid administration or reception of the sacrament, if in reality that danger did not exist.

Besides, it is agreed that the judgment of danger need not be made by any exclusively specified person. It can be the judgment of the patient himself, of the doctor, of the family, or of the priest. Some may judge that there is a danger, some that there is not. Yet the "probable and prudent" judgment of any of them suffices for a lawful and valid anointing, not conditionally but absolutely. To allow an anointing in these circumstances is to display no fear or anxiety that the actual presence or absence of danger will have any effect on the validity of the sacrament, or even that the sacrament may be exposed to nullity. It is difficult to see how the setting of this condition could involve anything more than a disciplinary law which controls the administration of Extreme Unction, like the ecclesiastical law which limits a Catholic to receiving Communion (except Viaticum) once a day, though he is capable of receiving it often during the day, or the law limiting priests to offering the Mass once a day, a law which in fact allows exceptions on All Soul's Day, on the day of Christmas, and on days when bination or trination be-

[183] Pius XI, litt. ap. *Explorata res est,* 2 febr. 1923: "Neque enim, ut sacramentum valide liciteque detur, necesse est ut mors proxime secutura timeatur, sed satis est ut prudens seu probabile adsit de periculo iudicium, quodsi in ea rerum condicione conferri debet, in hac conferri utique potest. . . ."—*AAS,* XV (1923), 105.

comes allowable, or the old law that once required satisfaction to be made before absolution was to be given.

Writing, however, in 1926 Kilker said:

> It is certain now that a person in order to be a *valid* subject for Extreme Unction must 1) be afflicted with a serious disease which is putting him *in danger of death*. . . . The present canon of the Code confirms this. The subject is one *"qui ob infirmitatem in periculo mortis versetur."* Hence, the subject must be sick, *and in danger of death* from the sickness. *Neither without the other is sufficient.*[184]

And writing in 1953, Doronzo cites canon 940, § 1, in proof of his conclusion that "ad valorem sacramenti requiritur aliquod verum, seu actuale et obiectivum, mortis periculum." [185] Many authors take for granted that canon 940, § 1, is one that spells out the conditions necessary for validity in the recipient.[186] A close look, then, must be taken at this canon to see if, in fact, it intends danger of death to be a requirement for validity, rather than simply for lawfulness.

When the law intends to demand something or to declare something that is necessary for validity it seeks to make that fact unmistakably clear, by stating it either expressly or in obviously equivalent terms. Unless it does, the law is not to be understood as being an invalidating or incapacitating law.[187] Any demands which a law makes for validity are to be considered as imposing a burden and accordingly must be susceptible of proof beyond all reasonable doubt.[188]

[184] *Extreme Unction*, p. 164. (Emphasis added.)

[185] *De Extrema Unctione*, II, 641-643.

[186] Germain Lesage, "Sources textuaires des canons relatifs à l'extrême-onction," *Revue de l'Universitè d'Ottawa*, XXIX (1959), 71; Blat, *Commentarium Textus Codicis Iuris Canonici*, III, n. 284, p. 343; Abbo-Hannan, *The Sacred Canons*, II, 61; Vermeersch-Creusen, *Epitome Iuris Canonici*, II, n. 225, "subiectum capax."

[187] "Irritantes aut inhabilitantes eae tantum leges habendae sunt, quibus aut actum esse nullum aut inhabilem esse personam expresse vel aequivalenter statuitur."—Canon 11.

[188] "Leges etiam irritantes et inhabilitantes, in dubio iuris non urgent. . . ."—Canon 15.

Canon 940, § 1, reads:

> Extrema Unctio praeberi non potest nisi fideli, qui post adeptum usum rationis ob infirmitatem vel senium in periculo mortis versetur.

At first glance the words *"praeberi non potest nisi"* might indicate that anyone not coming under the terms of the canon is incapable of receiving the sacrament. The former law of the *Ritual,* which the Code revised, had stated: *"Debet* autem hoc sacramentum infirmis praeberi qui . . . tam graviter laborant ut mortis periculum imminere videatur." The directives, old and new, are alike in the use of the word *praeberi* which indicates that, though it adverts to the recipient of the anointing, the law primarily speaks to the minister of the sacrament. The old *Ritual* told the priest to what subjects he was bound to make the sacrament of Extreme Unction available (*debet praeberi*), namely to the gravely sick who were in imminent danger of death. It did not strictly deal with what sick people were essentially qualified to receive it, and therefore the sacrament was in fact given to other sick people who did not fall within the category designated by the *Ritual,* i.e., to such who were in imminent danger.[189]

The new law in canon 939, sets down the obligation in justice of a pastor to administer the sacrament, and the obligation in charity for any priest to do so in a case of necessity. Then, in canon 940, § 1, it sets down to whom he can give (*praeberi*) Extreme Unction.[190] The question is, does the canon mean that he can give it validly only to the ones there specified, or, are those whom by this canon he is allowed to anoint the only and exclusively capacitated recipients of the sacrament? The canon says to him, you cannot give the sacrament except to these, but

189 The Ritual told the priest whom he had an obligation to anoint, but the zealous priest, desirous to make the sacrament available to others who were sick, looked to the authors, both canonists and theologians, to find out whom he *could* anoint.

190 The construction has, "Extreme Unction cannot be given . . . ," but since only a priest gives the sacrament the canon is obviously addressed to him.

does it necessarily say that none but these are capable of receiving it validly? A canon similar in structure to 940, § 1, legislates that one who is not keeping a natural fast for the prescribed time *cannot* be admitted to Holy Communion except in urgent danger of death and for the prevention of irreverence to the Eucharist.[191] There is no doubt that the priest "cannot" admit such a one to Communion, and that it would be gravely sinful to deliberately do so. But there is likewise no doubt that, if he did, the person would receive the Sacrament of Holy Communion validly.

Canon 940, § 1, does not read *"praeberi valide non potest,"* but simply *"non potest,"* which phrase of itself constitutes no proof that an action to the contrary automatically becomes infected with invalidity.[192] Such words as *potest* and *non potest* or *nequit* do not expressly involve or equivalently point to invalidating laws. If they did the Code would not find it necessary to modify them by adding the word *valide* as it does in many canons.[193]

The absence of *valide* or of any other word or phrase definitely pointing to canon 940, § 1, as incorporating exclusively conditions for validity cannot be considered accidental when one studies with what care and accuracy all the other canons treating of the valid minister and recipient of the sacraments are drawn up. Canon 745 states: *"Subiectum* CAPAX *baptismi est* OMNIS ET SOLUS *homo viator, nondum baptizatus."* It is absolutely clear who the valid subject of baptism is. The subsequent canons use the word *licite* when treating of who can be baptized licitly.

[191] Canon 858, § 1.—"Qui . . . ieiunium naturale non servaverit, *nequit* ad sanctissimam Eucharistiam admitti, nisi. . . ."

[192] "Lex irritationem et inhabilitatem statuit expresse, quando conceptis verbis declarat actum esse nullum aut personam esse inhabilem, sive positive sive negative; aequivalenter, quando adhibet terminologiam quae idem importat quin id disertis verbis exprimat. Exempla expresse declarationis sunt; error actum irritum reddit, ipso iure nulla, inhabiles sunt, invalide admittuntur, ad validitatem requiritur, ea tantum valida sunt quae. Formulae aequivalentes sunt, v.g. effectum non sortitur, nullum habet (parit) iuridicum effectum, nihil est actum."—Udalricus Beste, *Introductio in Codicem* (editio quarta, Neapoli: M. D'Auria, 1956), p. 69.

[193] Cf. canons 147; 154; 157; 170; 758; 964, § 2; 1147; 1316, § 2; 1450.

Canon 786 states: *"Aquis baptismi non ablutus* VALIDE *confirmari nequit,"* and then adds: *"Ut quis licite et fructuose confirmetur. . . ."* Would not the use of *valide* be redundant if *confirmari nequit* necessarily included the notion of validity along with that of lawfulness? Yet canon 940, § 1, simply reads, *praeberi non potest.*

Canon 853: *"Quilibet baptizatus qui iure non prohibetur, admitti potest et debet ad sacram communionem."* It is clear that anyone who has been baptized is *capable* of receiving the Eucharist sacramentally. The following canons determine which of these essentially capacitated recipients are prohibited by law from receiving Communion. Thus a sharp and clear distinction is made between who can validly and who can licitly receive this sacrament.[194]

Canon 902 makes it perfectly clear that anyone who has sinned even venially after baptism can receive valid absolution, while canon 901 tells what sinners are obliged to use this sacrament.

Canon 968 states: *"Sacram ordinationem* VALIDE *recipit* SOLUS *vir baptizatus,"* but then adds: *"Licite autem ad normam sacrorum canonum. . . ."*

Further examples occur in canon 737: *"Baptismus . . .* VALIDE NON CONFERATUR NISI *per ablutionem aquae verae et naturalis cum praescripta verborum forma"*; in canon 758: *"Licet baptismus conferri* VALIDE *possit . . ."*; in canon 851: *"Minister huius sacramenti* [*poenitentiae*] *est* SOLUS *sacerdos"*; in canon 872: *"Ad* VALIDAM *peccatorum absolutionem requiritur in ministro potestas iurisdictionis . . ."*; in canon 879: *"Ad confessiones* VALIDE *audiendas . . ."*; in canon 881: *"Omnes utriusque cleri sacerdotes . . . possunt . . .* VALIDE *et licite absolvere"*; in canon 882: *"In periculo mortis omnes sacerdotes . . .* VALIDE *et licite absolvunt quoslibet poenitentes a quibusvis peccatis aut*

[194] Baptized children, even though only infants, could before attaining the use of reason receive the sacrament of Holy Communion validly, but canon 854 prohibits the administration to them. Excommunicates, too, could receive the sacrament of Holy Communion validly but they cannot receive it licitly, according to canon 855.

censuris."[195] Even when listing the qualifications for the valid recipient of indulgences the Code uses the word *capax* of him,[196] leaving no doubt that what follows is required for the valid gaining of the indulgences. And canon 1094 declares outright that the observance of the canonical form is a requirement for the validity of a Catholic's marriage: "*Ea tantum matrimonia* VALIDA *sunt quae. . . .*"

Likewise when it deals with the minister of Extreme Unction the Code is absolutely clear about the element of validity: "*Hoc sacramentum* VALIDE *administrat* OMNIS *et* SOLUS *sacerdos.*"[197]

If the lawgiver wanted to decree that only a subjcet who has qualified under the various conditions stated in canon 940, § 1, is capable of being the recipient of a *valid* anointing, he knew indeed how to give expression to that with positive and unmistakable clearness. With reference to other comparable situations, it is not gratuitous to expect that the canon could have been formulated, for instance, to read: "*Extrema Unctio praeberi valide non potest nisi . . . ,*" or, "*Extremam Unctionem valide adhibere potest omnis et solus qui . . . ,*" or, "*subiectum capax Extremae Unctionis est omnis et solus fidelis qui post adeptum usum rationis ob infirmitatem vel senium in periculo mortis versetur.*" Instead, the wording of the canon seems content with setting down the ecclesiastical law as it binds the priest: "*Extrema Unctio praeberi non potest nisi. . . .*" Neither the words in the canon itself expressly or equivalently state, nor does a comparative study of similar canons suggest that the danger of death is a requisite for validity in the recipient.

The use of the word "*fideli*" in canon 940, § 1, likewise nullifies the contention that *all* requirements there stated look to validity. In the Code *fidelis* is most often, if not exclusively,

[195] Similarly canons 883 and 884.

[196] "Ut quis *capax* sit sibi lucrandi indulgentias, debet esse baptizatus, non excommunicatus, in statu gratiae saltem in fine operum praescriptorum, subditus concedentis."—Canon 925.

[197] Canon 938. To designate precisely who can validly administer Extreme Unction, the law does not content itself with stating simply: "*Hoc sacramentum administrat sacerdos.*"

used in designation of one who is not only baptized but also an actual member of the Church, a Catholic. The contrast between a *fidelis* and a non-Catholic is perfectly exemplified in canon 1258, § 1: *"Haud licitum est* FIDELIBUS *quovis modo active assistere seu partem habere in sacris* ACATHOLICORUM." Another equally obvious example occurs in canon 1152: *"Exorcismi a legitimis ministris fieri possunt non solum in* FIDELES *et catechumenos, sed* ETIAM IN ACATHOLICOS *vel excommunicatos."* Canon 467 obliges a pastor to administer the sacraments to the faithful (*fidelibus*), and since canon 731, § 2, explicitly forbids the administration of the sacraments to non-Catholics, even to those who are in good faith and ask for them, it seems evident that the word *fideles* points to Catholics. In consequence of the prohibition contained in canon 731, § 2, there is no doubt that only Catholics are bound to confess and receive Communion once a year according to canons 859 and 906, both of which employ the phrase: *"Omnis utriusque sexus* FIDELIS." In canon 863 the "*fideles*" are encouraged to receive Communion frequently, and in canon 892, § 1, pastors are seriously bound in justice to hear the confessions of the "faithful" committed to them (FIDELIUM *sibi commissorum*). The meaning is clear. The bodies of the faithful (*fidelium*) are to be buried in blessed ground, and the funeral rites in their full sequence, as found in the liturgical books, are to be performed for them.[198]

Vermeersch, noting that non-Catholics are not formally excluded, left room for the possible gaining of indulgences on the part of such as were in good faith. The reason apparently why they are not considered excluded is that in canon 925 the *subjectum capax* is delineated simply as one who is *"baptizatus, non excommunicatus, in statu gratiae."* Had the word *fidelis* been employed in place of *baptizatus*, the same conclusion could not have been reached.[199]

A final example of the Code's use of "*fidelis*" may be cited as

[198] Canons 1205 and 1215 both make mention of the *cadavera fidelium*.

[199] Cf. Vermeersch-Creusen, *Epitome Iuris Canonici*, II, n. 214 (footnote to paragraph 1).

it occurs in canon 1325, § 1, which deals with the obligation of the *fideles Christi* to profess their faith.[200]

In expressing the essential and indispensable need for baptism in order to be a recipient of the other sacraments, the Code uses the word *baptizatus,* except when it deals with the recipient of Extreme Unction. For Confirmation one must be *"ablutus aquis baptismi"*;[201] for the reception of the Eucharist *"quilibet baptizatus qui iure non prohibetur"*[202] qualifies; for Penance the sins to be remitted are such as have been committed *"post baptismum"*;[203] for Orders, *"solus vir* BAPTIZATUS*"*[204] can look to a valid reception; for Matrimony, *"Matrimonium* BAPTIZATORUM *validum dicitur . . .* BAPTIZATORUM *matrimomium regitur iure non solum divino sed etiam canonico. . . ."*[205] Yet for the recipient of Extreme Unction the word *fidelis* is employed. The Code here asks for more than the essential baptism of water; it asks also for *fides catholica.*[206] The element of baptism contained in the word *fidelis* is certainly an indispensable prerequisite for the valid reception of Extreme Unction. The element of *fides catholica*—actual membership in the Church—which is also contained in the word *fidelis* is not, however, a necessary prerequisite for the *valid* reception of the sacrament. Only one of the

[200] Cf. also canons 1154; 1169, § 1; 1188; 1245; 2003.

[201] Canon 786.

[202] Canon 853.

[203] Canons 901 and 902.

[204] Canon 968, § 1.

[205] Canons 1015, § 1, and 1016.

[206] "Extreme Unction can be given only to a Catholic . . . ," Woywod's translation of canon 940, § 1—*A Practical Commentary on the Code of Canon Law,* p. 545; " . . . *fideli,* id est, baptizato habenti fidem."—Blat, *Commentarium Textus Codicis Iuris Canonici,* III, n. 284; cf. also Kilker, *Extreme Unction,* pp. 123-126; " . . . nowhere in the Code can *"fidelis"* be construed to include those outside the fold of faith."—p. 126; "Dans le Code, ce terme désigne souvent non seulement les baptisés, mais uniquement les membres de la véritable Eglise."—Charles DeClercq, in *Traité de Droit Canonique,* publié sous la direction de Raoul Naz, Vol. II, *Des Sacrements* (Paris: Letouzey et Ané Editeurs, 1947), p. 304.

two conditions postulated by the use of the word *fidelis* in canon 940, § 1, is a requisite in the recipient for *valid* reception. The other is a requisite solely for the *lawful* administration of the sacrament. When the canon prohibits the administration of the sacrament to all except the *fideles* it excludes not only the unbaptized who are essentially incapable of receiving Extreme Unction or any other sacrament, but also baptized non-Catholics who are *essentially* capable of receiving the sacrament *validly*, all other conditions being fulfilled. It cannot be said therefore that this canon deals *solely* with those conditions that are necessary for a *valid* reception. The law does not read, *"praeberi non potest nisi baptizato,"* but rather, *"nisi fideli."* One need not be a *fidelis* in order to receive Extreme Unction *validly*. Nevertheless one who is not a *fidelis* is excluded from the class of lawful recipients by canon 940, § 1.

If one should argue that perhaps *fidelis* could here have been intended to equal the simple notion of *baptizatus* (an assumption that would bear the burden of proof), it would still be difficult to explain the use of the word for this sacrament alone, when in all similar canons on the sacraments the term *baptizatus* is employed to express the essential and fundamental prerequisite of baptism. The Code would not use a word that implies more than baptism, especially in these circumstances, unless it meant more. To say that it does not mean more is to imply that the Code abstracts from the use of a clear word to replace it with one that is misleading and which obfuscates the intended simple notion of baptism.

All that can be said about the element of danger from canon 940, § 1, is that it is a requirement for the licit administration of Extreme Unction. The canon cannot rightly be interpreted to state expressly or equivalently that it is necessary for validity. This is not surprising, for it would be startling indeed for a Code of disciplinary law to define something never defined by the Church. Neither St. James, nor the Council of Trent set the danger of death as a requirement for the valid reception of Extreme Unction. Nor is it the unanimous teaching of theologians. Canon 940, § 1, gives no proof of being a dogmatic canon.

The wording of canon 941, however, seems to provide a strong objection to holding that the danger of death is postulated simply for the lawful administration of the sacrament. The canon provides that, when there is doubt whether the patient is in a real danger of death, he is to be anointed conditionally.

> Quando dubitatur num infirmus . . . in periculo mortis reipsa versetur . . . hoc sacramentum ministretur sub conditione.

A general theological principle states that sacraments are given *sub conditione* only when some requirement for validity is in doubt, so that their administration would thereby be exposed to possible nullity. Accordingly, since the anointing is to be conditional when there is doubt about any danger being present, the danger must be postulated as a condition for validity.

The doubt to which canon 941 adverts is a doubt which relates to the *de facto* presence or absence of a danger of death. The important word is *reipsa.* The doubt turns not about the degree of probability in the danger, but solely about the fact whether a danger is really (*reipsa*) present. If a priest, for instance, judges that there is some danger in the condition of the sick person, though he is not sure how much of a danger, he is not in doubt from the viewpoint of canon 941. The question is not one of a grave or slight measure of probability. It is when the priest is not sure whether there is even a probable danger that he is in doubt from the viewpoint of canon 941. It is not a question of saying, "I am really not sure that the person's likelihood of dying from this sickness is very great," for the supposition here is that there is a likelihood, though perhaps not a grave one, and in the presence of this likelihood one prudently judges a danger to be present. Anointing would be unhesitatingly absolute. When the question is, "I am not sure that what he has is dangerous," then there is a doubt about the real presence of a danger and anointing is to be conditional.[207]

[207] Danagher, however, advises: "If there is a real doubt as to the very existence of danger of death, the anointing should be postponed if possible." But if it were not convenient to return quickly should a danger surely arise, he then allows a conditional anointing according to canon 941.—"Extreme Unction in Doubtful Danger of Death," *The Homiletic and Pastoral Review,* LVII (1957), 656. But since the canon deals precisely with the doubt of the very existence of any danger, and directs that the

There was no provision in the earlier law for a conditional anointing in a doubtful danger, nor was there one in the *1913 Schema* of the Code.[208] Before the Code was finally completed, however, this provision was added to canon 941. Prior to the Code any doubtful danger generally had as its consequence a deferring of the anointing, though it were only conditional. St. Alphonsus had said: *"In dubio an infirmitas sit periculosa mortis . . . non posse Extremam Unctionem ministrari."* [209] Lehmkuhl, while agreeing with others that any danger, even though only probable, proved sufficient for the administration of the sacrament cautiously added: *"Sed antequam tale periculum probabile existat, extrema unctio dari nequit."* [210] And Kern, admitting that one who is suffering from an illness known to bring on death, but who is not yet in danger, can be validly anointed, nevertheless thought it better to put off the anointing until the danger became patent: *". . . censeo, melius expectari tempus, quo periculum iam sit apertum."* [211]

In stating that the sacrament should be administered conditionally when there is doubt about the presence of any danger, the Code actually extended the use of Extreme Unction beyond the limits previously allowed by the authors, at least with reference to its lawful administration. But why is the administration to be conditional, unless it be for the reason that a danger is indispensable for validity?

---

sacrament be administered conditionally in that case (the text reads, not *administrari potest,* but *ministretur*), there is no reason why the administration should be put off. No reason, like inconvenience in returning later, is demanded for this conditional anointing and none is needed.

[208] "Quando dubitetur num infirmus usum rationis attigerit vel num mortuus sit, hoc sacramentum ministretur sub conditione."—Canon 217, Gasparri, *Schema Codicis Iuris Canonici* sub Secreto Pontificio Sanctissimi Domini Nostri Pii PP. X, cum notis Petri Card. Gasparri (4 vols. in 2, Romae: Typis Polyglottis Vaticanis, 1912-1914). This with the addition of *"num infirmus in periculo mortis reipsa versetur"* became canon 941 of the Code.

[209] *Theologia Moralis,* Lib. VI, n. 714.

[210] *Theologia Moralis,* II, n. 576.

[211] *De Extrema Unctione,* pp. 298-299.

The writer believes that it is for the same reason that conditional absolution is allowably given to the unconscious who are not capable of performing the acts of the penitent. This is permitted on the very slight but still probable opinion that these acts of the penitent are not necessary for validity. The Church has never definitely settled the question, though almost no theologian now is inclined to favor the tenuously probable opinion which is the basis for such a conditional absolution. Similarly, the Church has never defined that any danger of death is necessary for the validity of the sacrament of Extreme Unction, nor has it ever been the unanimous opinion of the theologians that the presence of a danger is *de necessitate sacramenti.* Cappello writes:

> Qua in re, ut accurate tota doctrina catholica exponatur, distinguere oportet inter *morbum* simpliciter et *morbum gravem* et *periculosum.* . . . Quod subiectum capax extremae unctionis sit solus *infirmus* ac propterea quod *morbus* sit de necessitate sacramenti, certum est. . . . An ulterius, etiam *peculiaris gradus infirmitatis* seu morbus *gravis* sive *periculosus* sit de necessitate sacramenti, dissentiunt theologi. Plerique affirmant, propter easdem rationes.[212]

Suarez thought that *"probabilius"* such a danger was essential for the sacrament.[213] Billuart regarded this doctrine as certain.[214] But Coninck, Kern and others believed that such a danger was not a necessary prerequisite. What had not been decided by the Church at the Council of Trent, or at any time since, was surely not to receive its dogmatic decision in the compilation of the Church's disciplinary laws in 1918. Desirous to extend the use of Extreme Unction as far as possible while re-

[212] Cappello, *De Extrema Unctione,* n. 230. One of the reasons for this affirmation derives *"ex fine huius sacramenti,"* which the Scholastics had taught was "ut ultimum remedium . . . immediate disponens ad gloriam . . . unde sacramentum exeuntium." This too, however, has never been defined, and the development of the theology of Extreme Unction has by no means ended on this point.

[213] Disp. XLII, Sect. II, n. 5.—*Opera Omnia,* XXII, 852.

[214] *Summa Sancti Thomae,* VIII, Tract. *De Extrema Unctione,* Art. VI, n. 4.

taining, though modifying, the now traditional norm of giving it to those who are somehow in danger, the Church had to take into account both theological probabilities. Either a danger is postulated for the element of validity or it is not. Therefore, when there remains a doubt about the presence of a danger the Church ordered a conditional anointing. Thus, if in fact the presence of a danger is postulated for validity, then in the act of administration the sacrament is not exposed to nullity; if it is not, as the other school holds, then no otherwise capacitated recipient of the sacrament will be deprived of its benefits. The occasion for the conditional anointing is the doubt *"num infirmus . . . in periculo mortis reipsa versetur."* [215] The condition itself is: "If the presence of a danger of death is postulated for the validity of this sacrament," just as in conditional absolution to the unconscious the condition is: "If the acts of the penitent are not necessary for validity." [216]

By the unmodified use of the word *periculum,* canon 940 allowed for the widest interpretation of what is meant by the danger of death. By the prescription of canon 941, which allows a conditional anointing when even the existence of any danger to the sick person is doubtful, the Church made the sacrament available to many to whom it was not at all offered before. The condition of danger in canon 940 is one that restricts a Catholic who is sick and otherwise qualified in his right to receive a sacrament, and all such restrictions should always be interpreted as favoring the free exercise of rights.[217]

From the considerations presented above the writer believes that the danger of death is not a postulated prerequisite affecting the valid administration of Extreme Unction to the sick, but a condition on which hinges the administrative norm for the lawful conferring of the sacrament, a norm which the Church could

[215] Canon 941.

[216] All such conditions, of course, are in the intention to administer as the Church wishes, and need not be even mentally formulated in this specific manner.

[217] "Leges quae poenam statuunt aut *liberum iurium exercitium coarctant* . . . strictae subsunt interpretationi."—Canon 19.

change for some other norm such as the one stated in the words of the Council of Trent: "This sacrament is to be given to the sick, especially to those who are so dangerously sick as to be in danger of death." Meanwhile the minister of the sacraments is obliged to confer them not only validly but also licitly. By canon 940 he is allowed to administer Extreme Unction absolutely only to those sick persons who are judged to be in at least a probable danger of death, but by canon 941, he is also allowed to administer the sacrament conditionally to those sick persons who are judged to be in a doubtful danger, i.e., doubtfully in danger. The two canons conjointly provide a wide scope of action in the ministrations, which the Church contemplates for the sick.

Article III. New Danger in the Same Illness

The state of sickness which entitles a person to receive Extreme Unction as a sacramental remedy can exist, disappear and reassert itself many times during the course of the same person's life. It is evident, therefore, that the sacrament can be received again by the same recipient as often as upon his recovery a new illness besets him. There seems to be, furthermore, no *intrinsic* reason for denying that Extreme Unction could also be received more than once during the same illness. There is, in fact, evidence that such a repetition was actually practiced in the Church for many centuries.

A. *The History of the Requirement*

1. *Before the Council of Trent*

In the oldest Rituals for administering Extreme Unction, the rubrics called for a repetition of the entire rite for seven consecutive days if necessary.[218] Pope Benedict XIV (1740-1758) referred to this practice in his *De Synodo Dioecesana,* citing a Code of the eleventh century which prescribed the seven anointings, and attested that this procedure was the ancient custom of

[218] Martène, *De Antiquis Ecclesiae Ritibus* (3 vols., Venetiis, 1783), I, Cap. VII, art. I, n. 5; art. IV, Ordo V; cf. also Kern, *De Extrema Unctione,* pp. 338-345.

the Church.[219] Ruch (1873-1945) considered it undeniable that Extreme Unction was once repeated in the same illness.[220]

In time, however, legislation limiting the repetition of Extreme Unction began to appear. In the twelfth century Ivo, Bishop of Chartres (1090-1117), concurred with others in the opinion that, like Baptism, Extreme Unction could be received only once in a lifetime.[221] The Code of St. Martin of Tours provided that a person could be anointed only one time during the year, and Bishop Durantis (1237-1296) added that this held true no matter how often the subject became ill during that year.[222] Others limited the anointing to once every three years. In such regulations, the norm for repetition was strictly one of time.

The Scholastic theologians, believing that Extreme Unction was instituted primarily in view of the danger of death brought on by sickness, rather than in view of sickness itself, developed the principle that the sacrament could be repeated only when a new and distinct danger arose, whether it arose in the same illness or from a new illness. The sacrament, they said, given for one particular danger, has its effect only for the duration of that danger. Once that danger has ceased, the effect of the sacrament is lost. If a new danger arises, even in the same illness, the patient, who is no longer benefiting from the previous anointing, can be anointed again.

It must be remembered that danger for St. Thomas and the Scholastics meant a proximate or imminent danger. Recovery

[219] Lib. VIII, c. VII, n. 4. The fact that the rubric, *si necessitas fuerit*, appears in these rituals which prescribe an anointing for seven days is another indication that each rite was a separate administration of the sacrament, and not merely part of one cumulative rite that resulted in one administration of the sacrament.

[220] "Il semble indeniable qu'à certaines époques et à certains endroits, l'extrême-onction ait été réitérée durant la même maladie."—Ruch, "Extrême-Onction du Ier au IXe siècle," *Dictionnaire de Theologie Catholique* (15 vols. in 30, Paris: Letouzey et Ané, 1903-), V, 1980.

[221] Sainte-Beuve, *Tractatus de Sacramentis Confirmationis et Unctionis Extremae,* Disp. II, art. III, p. 430.

[222] Martène, *op. cit.,* I, Cap. VII, art. I, n. 3; art. I, n. 6.

from danger meant recovery from a proximate or an imminent danger; a new danger meant a new imminent danger.[223]

Of repeating the anointing during a long illness St. Thomas taught:

> Quaedam vero sunt aegritudines diuturnae, ut hectica, hydropisis, et huiusmodi; et in talibus non debet fieri unctio, nisi quando videntur perducere ad periculum mortis; et si homo illum *articulum evadat,* eadem infirmitate durante, et iterum *ad similem statum* per illam aegritudinem reducatur, iterum potest inungi, quia iam quasi est alius infirmitatis status, quamvis non sit alia infirmitas simpliciter.[224]

The picture was this. A sick man should not be anointed until his illness had reached a stage that seemed to forbode his imminent death. St. Thomas called this crisis the *articulus.* If the patient survived that *articulus,* but during the same illness was reduced again to a *similar state,* that is, to another imminent danger of death, he could be anointed again. The remote, but very real, danger the sick man remained in after surviving a crisis of imminent death—especially if he was suffering from a disease that was consumptive and surely led to death—was not considered. What sufficed for anointing and for reanointing in the same illness were the distinct crises, wherein death was feared to be imminent, i.e., separate and distinct imminent dangers.

William of Paris († *circa* 1314) repeated this common Scholastic teaching:

> Similiter est notandum, quod hoc sacramentum non solum respicit infirmitatem, sed infirmitatis statum; ideoque pro qualibet infirmitate dari potest; sed non in quolibet statu infirmitatis; sed *solum in extrema necessitate in articulo mortis, in quo speratur homo mori.* Ideo pro infirmitatibus diuturnis non datur, sicut est paralysis, lepra, et huiusmodi;

223 Cf. *supra,* pp. 25-26.

224 *Summa Theologica,* Pars III Supp., Q. XXXIII, art. 2. In the same article he had said previously: ". . . hoc sacramentum non respicit tantum infirmitatem, sed etiam infirmitatis statum; quia non debet dari nisi infirmis, qui secundum humanam aestimationem videntur morti appropinquare."

> nec etiam pro quibusdam infirmitatibus non diuturnis, sicut febris continua et huiusmodi, *nisi periculum mortis immineat.* Nota etiam si quis inunctus fuerit, infirmitate durante *in eodem statu* (in extrema necessitate in articulo mortis in quo speratur homo mori) non iterum debet inungi quia est eadem infirmitas . . . si periculum mortis evadat (ut supra), et durante adhuc infirmitate, et iterum per eandem infirmitatem *ad simile periculum* reducatur, potest iterum inungi, quia iam est quasi alius infirmitatis status.[225]

It was not enough that the sickness be an incurable and a deadly one. It must have brought about an actual crisis during which death was expected to ensue. As often as such a crisis arose after a previous one had receded, there was verified that new "*status infirmitatis,*" for which there could be a new anointing.

2. *The Council of Trent*

> Declaratur etiam, esse hanc unctionem infirmis adhibendam, illis vero praesertim, qui tam periculose decumbunt, ut in exitu vitae constituti videantur, unde et sacramentum exeuntium nuncupatur. Quod si infirmi post susceptam hanc unctionem convaluerint, iterum huius sacramenti subsidio adiuvari poterunt, cum in aliud simile vitae discrimen inciderint.[226]

The Council indirectly settled the question whether a recipient could receive Extreme Unction more than once in his lifetime or once a year, and also whether he could receive it more than once in the same illness. It taught that he can, and it set down the circumstances in which a repeated anointing in the same illness was permissible.[227] The Council accepted and approved the norm established by the Scholastics, that one could be anointed again in the same illness as often as there was present a new and

[225] *Dialogus de septem sacramentis,* c. 23, quoted in Doronzo, *De Extrema Unctione,* II, 329.

[226] Sess. XIV, c. 3, *de extrema unctione*—Schroeder, *Canons and Decrees of the Council of Trent,* 376.

[227] This does not necessarily mean that the sacrament could not be validly repeated in other circumstances if the Church, in its discipline regarding the sacraments saw fit to allow it. Cf. Kern, *De Extrema Unctione,* p. 360.

distinct danger. The expression used in the declaration of the Council of Trent was not *periculum mortis,* but *discrimen vitae.* Actually the word *discrimen,* which means a real crisis or struggle, more accurately described the situation in which the Scholastics taught that the sacrament should be given, and in which it could be repeated, than does the word *periculum. Discrimen vitae* gives the picture of life here and now hanging in the balance, or currently in jeopardy. *Periculum* does not necessarily imply such a situation, since a danger can be imminent or remote. There can be a *periculum mortis* in an illness without a *discrimen vitae.* A person who is in the first stages of cancer is put in the *periculum mortis* thereby, but not yet in the *discrimen vitae.* Only in the last stages, when he is actually fighting for his life, is he in the *discrimen vitae,* in a struggle for life. As has been seen, this notion of the *discrimen vitae* is what the Scholastics had in mind when they treated of the *periculum mortis.*

The Council taught that only in another similar *discrimen vitae* (*aliud simile*), was the anointing to be repeated, and this indicated what the Council implied with the word *convaluerint.* One cannot speak of another, similar struggle for life unless there has been a previous one that has already been overcome. *Convaluerint,* then, must mean that the sick person who was anointed in a *discrimen vitae,* or in a *periculum* but before the actual *discrimen,* must have successfully survived that first *discrimen,* and without fully recovering from the illness or without necessarily having extricated himself from all *periculum mortis,* then found himself once more in a real struggle with death, a new *discrimen vitae.*[228]

The Council stated that a person could be reanointed when he fell into another *similar* crisis (*aliud* SIMILE *vitae discrimen*). The crisis described by the Council, however, was not merely

[228] The Council did not use the phrase *periculum mortis* at all in its declaration about the recipient. When singling out those sick persons who should especially be fortified with the sacramental strength of Extreme Unction, it described them as *"illi qui tam periculose decumbent, ut in exitu vitae constituti videantur,"* and not as *"illi qui in periculo mortis sunt."*

that of a man who was dangerously ill, *in periculo* (*illi qui tam periculose decumbunt*), but of a man who was so dangerously ill as to appear to be actually close to death, *in vitae discrimine* (*ut in exitu vitae constituti videantur*).

The ones "*tam periculose decumbentes ut in exitu vitae constituti videantur*"—that is, those who are in the *discrimen vitae* —should especially be given Extreme Unction. If a sick person was subjected to such a *discrimen vitae* more than one time in an illness he could be anointed again, in each separate and distinct instance. The Council did not specify that any certain time had to elapse between anointings. It postulated only the need for a new danger (*discrimen*) and, *a fortiori*, the cessation of the old.

3. *The Law of the Roman Ritual of 1614*

Particular rituals and synods after the Council of Trent generally began to direct a second anointing in the same sickness after a partial recovery and a subsequent relapse into a new danger. The Manual of Rheims stated:

> Denique potest hoc sacramentum iterari, et quidem in eadem infirmitate, quandoquidem quis est *in articulo* mortis, modo casus sit diversus, ut, qui in hydropisi, aut longa febri, postquam evasit *periculum*, rursus post aliquot menses *de vita periclitatur*.[229]

Here there appears a new element not in the declaration of the Council of Trent, namely, the provision that some months pass between the first *articulo mortis* and the second (new) struggle with death (de vita periclitatur).

St. Charles Borromeo decreed for his Church at Milan:

> Quod si unctione suscepta convaluerit, quoties postea *vitae discrimen* inciderit, toties hoc sacramentum ei adhibebitur. Item in morbis quibusdam diuturnis, puta in hydropisi, si ob mortem *impendentem* quis unctus fuerit et evaserit, deinde ex eodem morbo in *alium similem casum* et periculum mortis inciderit, rursus etiam ungi debebit.[230]

[229] Quoted in Kilker, *Extreme Unction*, p. 190; also in Doronzo, *De Extrema Unctione*, II, 330, where other manuals and rituals are quoted.

[230] *Acta Ecclesiae Mediolanensis*, Pars IV, "Instructiones Variae," Tit. "De Sacramento Extremae Unctionis," p. 543.

Here too, as in the Council of Trent, recovery meant recovery from imminent, impending death, and a new danger meant a recurrence of a similar crisis of impending death (*discrimen vitae*).

In 1614, legislation for the whole Latin Church on this matter was set forth in the *Roman Ritual* of Pope Paul V. It prescribed:

> In eadem infirmitate hoc sacramentum iterari non debet nisi diuturna sit, ut cum infirmus convaluerit, iterum in periculum mortis incidit.[231]

The word "*convaluerint*," which the Council of Trent had used, the *Ritual* likewise used, but the phrase "*in aliud simile vitae discrimen inciderint*" of the Council was changed to "*iterum in periculum mortis incidit.*" Since a new danger in the same illness was commonly understood to mean a new danger of proximate or impending death, the new phrase *periculum mortis* in this context actually expressed the same idea as the Tridentine phrase *discrimen vitae*. Thus Baruffaldo (1675-1755) commented that to satisfy the demands of the word *convaluerit*, the sick person must have been delivered from a proximate danger, and the new danger he described as a "*diversa dispositio ad moriendum.*" [232]

The rubric, however, added a new qualification to the sickness in which one needed to be (not in which one could be) [233] in order to be reanointed in the event of a new danger. It specified that the illness in question had to be one of notable duration "*nisi diuturna sit.*" A certain period of time was expected to elapse, it seems, between the anointings. Baruffaldo thought a few weeks constituted a long enough interval.[234] The passage of

231 *Rituale Romanum* (1614 ed.), Tit. V, Cap. V, n. 14.

232 "Medicorum iudicio, idem infirmus prius esse debet extra probabile, *seu propinquum* mortis periculum, et de novo in morbum periculosum incidisse, mutata corporis valetudine; et hoc potest fieri quamvis intervallum non longum temporis, sed paucarum habdomadarum intercesserit, dummodo prudenter censeatur diversus status, diversum periculum, et *diversa dispositio ad moriendum*."—*Ad Rituale Romanum Commentaria* (editio tertia Veneta, Venetiis: Typographia Balleoniana, 1792), Tit. XXVII, n. 14.

233 *The Ritual* read "*iterari non* DEBET *nisi.*"

234 *Loc. cit.*

some time was considered necessary before a present danger could really subside and a recovery from it take place. Thus there was employed the construction, "*diuturna sit ut cum infirmus convaluerit, iterum in periculum mortis incidit.*" The sickness had to be of a sufficiently long duration to allow for these changes in the patient's condition to be realized.

Elbel (1690-1756), citing Barbosa (1590-1649) and Gobat (1600-1679), agreed with them that, if a week had passed since the first serious danger of an illness, then the particular crisis could safely be judged to have passed, and should the patient's life again be threatened after the seven days then he could be anointed again. That Elbel understood the rule for reanointing to allow a reanointing in every separate danger of proximate or imminent death is evidenced when he said that the old danger need not have vanished altogether from the illness.[235]

Laymann (1574-1635) too had believed that a new danger meant a new proximate or imminent danger:

> . . . postquam semel inunctus fuerat, melius habere *coepit* ut medicorum iudiciis extra probabile seu *propinquum* mortis periculum constiturus esset, mutata corporis constitutione recidit. . . . Ergo dum *idem status,* quamvis diuturno tempore, durat, non est repetendum sacramentum; secus si uno periculo remoto *diversus moriendi status* incidat.[236]

If the sick man's condition did not change but remained critical, then no matter how long it lasted there should be no further anointing.

In long illnesses, such as consumption for instance, the sick person after being anointed might live on for some length of time making only a partial recovery. In a relapse was he to be

[235] "Necesse tamen minime est . . . ut infirmus plene recuperet sanitatem et denuo incidat in simile periculum, sed satis est iam de novo instare periculum; quinimmo, tametsi antiquum periculum, non tamen ita urgens, cum antiqua aegritudine perseveret . . . accedente novo periculo, possunt denuo inungi absque scrupulo."—Elbel, *Theologia Moralis* (novis curis edidit F. Irenaeus Bierbaum, 9 vols. in 3, Paderbornae, 1891-1892), III, n. 219. Elbel actually spoke here of the new danger arising from a cause other than the one which even for the present kept the patient in a remote danger.

[236] *Theologia Moralis,* II, Lib. V, tract. VIII, cap. IV, n. 5.

anointed again? Could the present danger be considered a new danger? Many theologians, along with St. Alphonsus, adopted the working rule that, if the patient had survived the first danger for a period of thirty days, and then there arose a doubt whether the danger in which he was laboring was the same danger or a new one, he could be anointed again.[237] This rule was not at all intended to be a substitute for the "recovery–new danger" rule of the *Ritual,* but it was offered simply as an aid for determining whether the "recovery–new danger" conditions as required by law were actually fulfilled in doubtful cases. If it was certain that the conditions were verified before the lapse of a month, then the patient could certainly be anointed again. If it was certain that the conditions were not verified even after that lapse of time, then the patient could not be anointed again. *If there was doubt* whether these conditions were verified, then the presumption was to favor their fulfillment, and therefore a re-anointing.[238]

In his *De Synodo Dioecesana,* Benedict XIV taught:

> Durante autem eadem infirmitate, [si] post susceptam extremam unctionem morbus ita remittat, ut aegrotus mortis periculum evasisse videatur, sed, antequam convalescat iterum *in vitae discrimen relabatur,* etiam iuxta presentem disciplinam, poterit, absque scrupulo denuo Sacra Unctione muniri.[239]

That the danger postulated for a repetition of Extreme Unction in the same illness was a proximate or imminent danger, according to Pope Benedict, is suggested by his reverting to the use of the phrase employed by the Council of Trent, *vitae discrimen,* when he adverted to the new condition. In the presence of this new crisis it was enough to have a probability that the previous danger had receded (*evasisse videatur*), and this probability

[237] *Theologia Moralis,* Lib. VI, n. 715.

[238] The doubt could arise, however, only if there was some amelioration of the patient's condition during that lapse of time. It was not doubted that a person in a coma for several months or a year, and without any change of condition, was in the same danger even after all that lapse of time. Cf. St. Alphonsus, *loc. cit.*

[239] Lib. VIII, cap. VIII, n. 4.

rested on the fact that there had been an improvement in the sick person's condition after the first anointing (*morbus ita remittat*). With such a probability at hand, Benedict encouraged a priest to again anoint a patient in the new *discrimen vitae,* and to do this apart from all scruple whether the law has been adequately complied with.

Lehmkuhl (1834-1918) likewise furnished testimony of the pre-Code teaching that the new danger in question was to be identified with a proximate or imminent danger of death, a crisis, and that an adequate recovery from the previous danger meant a probable recovery from a previous proximate or imminent danger, which for the present could nevertheless still exist as a remote danger. The passing of the earlier danger did not mean a total and a complete extinction of all the previous danger whatsoever. Mindful perhaps of the words of the *Ritual, "nisi diuturna sit,"* Lehmkuhl added that a suitable period of time, such as a month, must intervene between anointings.[240]

B. *Present Legislation*

> In eadem infirmitate hoc sacramentum iterari non potest, nisi infirmus post susceptam unctionem convaluerit et in aliud vitae discrimen inciderit.[241]

In determining in what state of illness or old age a recipient must be before he can be given Extreme Unction, canon 940, § 1, uses the general and expansive phrase, *periculum mortis.* In determining, however, what new exigency must be present before Extreme Unction can be repeated in the same illness after a previous administration, the same canon, departing from the wording of the Ritual which had read, *iterum in periculo mortis,*

[240] "Iterare potest resp. debet extrema unctio . . . in morbo diuturno, si periculum mortis evanuit et *post notabile tempus* denuo periculum *propinquum probabiliter* cessaverit et iterum inducatur, modo intervallum satis diuturnum, ut unius mensis, intercesserit.—Ita in phthisi, hydropisi aliisque morbis tenendum est, ex quibus *saepius* mortis periculum *imminere* probabiliter videri potest, imo etiam re ipsa adesse, postea tamen satis iterum remotum exsistere."—*Theologia Moralis,* II, n. 577, § 4.

[241] Canon 940, § 2; repeated verbatim in *Rituale Romanum* (1925, post Code ed.), Tit. VI, Cap. I, n. 8.

reverts to the use of the more specific phrase, *aliud vitae discrimen inciderit,* which the Council of Trent had employed. The change seems to offer a clarification of precisely what is required for a reanointing, for the two expressions, *periculum mortis* and *discrimen vitae,* are not synonymous. Every *discrimen* is a *periculum,* but not every *periculum* is necessarily a *discrimen.* A *discrimen* is a danger that has reached a crisis of life or death, a danger that is proximate or imminent.

If this be so, then it is the meaning of canon 940 that a person suffering from sickness or old age can be anointed as soon as it is prudently feared that the effects of his sickness or old age could lead to his death, that is, as soon as it is prudently judged that there is in his condition a danger of death, not necessarily a proximate danger or one that immediately puts his life in jeopardy. This suffices to justify an initial administration of Extreme Unction.[242] Once anointed, however, the patient cannot receive the sacrament again unless he falls into *"aliud vitae discrimen."* The *"aliud"* implies that there was a previous *discrimen.* If there was not, the present *discrimen* does not fulfill the requirement of the canon for a reanointing. Thus a person anointed in a remote danger, say a cancer victim in the middle stages of the disease, who later reaches a crisis in the illness, when his life is put in immediate danger, could not be anointed again at this time, for this is the first and not another *discrimen vitae.* If he survives that crisis, on the other hand, and later falls again into such a struggle for his life, there is a new crisis, an *"aliud vitae discrimen,"* and a second anointing would be in order.

"Convaluerit," then, means a recovery from the crisis of impending death, and not a recovery to the extent that all danger whatsoever in the condition has ceased.[243] If then a patient who has been anointed in a proximate danger of death survives that particular danger, even though the lessened danger in his illness

242 Cf. *supra,* pp. 57-67.

243 "Il faut et il suffit qu'une distinction entre les deux *crises dangereures* soit incontestable. . . ."—Cuttaz, *Remède Divin pour les Chrétiens Malades,* p. 76; Lehmkuhl, *Theologia Moralis,* II, n. 577, § 4; Laymann, *Theologia Moralis,* II, lib. V, tract. VIII, cap. IV, n. 5.

continues in a more remote degree, but later takes a turn for the worse whereby his life once again hangs in the balance, he can be given Extreme Unction once more.[244]

The rule regulating the repetition of Extreme Unction in the same illness is, therefore, that it cannot be repeated again in the same *proximate* danger of death, in one and the same crisis, no matter how long that crisis lasts. Strictly it can be given again in the same danger when that danger once proximate and now remote becomes proximate once more. This is the case in many illnesses, such as cancer, leukemia, tuberculosis, and certain conditions of old age, which when once they have reached a point of danger always remain dangerous to a greater or lesser degree. If one would demand that a patient convalesce to a point in which the danger which warranted his earlier anointing has disappeared before he be anointed again, then there could hardly ever be a reanointing in these illnesses, no matter how long the victim continued to suffer from them.

Many, however, deny that Extreme Unction can be validly received in the one same sickness and danger, but none of the reasons alleged for this position are peremptory or decisive, and the opinion, though rather common, cannot be called certain.[245] The chief argument for this stand is that Extreme Unction is given specifically for the danger of death, and that its effects endure as long as the danger for which it was given.[246] This reasoning has

[244] "Communi usu recepta et approbata sententia . . . permittit huius sacramenti iterationem quotiescumque fidelis in novum incidit morbum, immo et in eadem infirmitate, si morbus post unctionem susceptam ita remittat ut infirmus periculum *proximum* mortis evasisse videatur, et deinde iterum in *vitae discrimen relabatur*."—De Augustinis, *De re sacramentaria,* II, p. 408, quoted in Cappello, *De Extrema Unctione,* n. 288; Laymann, *loc. cit.;* " . . . *post susceptam unctionem* de qua est inscriptio *convaluerit* respective ab infirmitate vel evaso mortis *proximae* periculo propter quod recte ac proprie subiungitur."—Blat, *Commentarium Textus Codicis Iuris Canonici,* III, n. 284, p. 344.

[245] Cappello, *De Extrema Unctione,* n. 308.

[246] " . . . quia efficacia huius sacramenti tamdiu durat, quamdiu remanet idem mortis periculum, pro quo fuit collatum."—Prümmer, *Manuale Theologiae Moralis* (12. ed. recognovit a Engelberto M. Munch, Friburgi Brisgoviae: Herder, 1955), III, n. 582; Noldin, *Summa Theologiae Moralis,* III, n. 448; "Non potest in eadem infirmitate et eodem mortis periculo

its basis in the Scholastic doctrine that the sacrament is a sacrament of the dying and is given in view of death, a doctrine not taught by the Council of Trent.[247]

Granted that its efficacy does last as long as the danger,[248] this statement offers no proof that the sacrament cannot therefore be repeated validly in the same illness and the same danger. It is true, as Billot (1846-1931) wrote, that Extreme Unction "commends the sick man to God," giving him the right to special sacramental graces of alleviation for the time of his trial. But to add, as Billot did, that these effects can neither be increased nor multiplied is something else again. This proposition needs to be proved and not merely assumed.[249]

What precise theological truth prevents a sick man from being "commended to God" again in a sacramental way during his illness, especially if it is a long one? What prevents an increase of sacramental grace in this instance? In directing that priests always administer Extreme Unction again when in doubt about whether the danger is a new one, Benedict XIV gave as his reasons that in so doing a priest acts more in conformity with the practice of the ancient Church and that "by the reanointing a new spiritual uplifting and assistance comes to the sick man."[250]

Following an argument of St. Thomas, Billot, Doronzo and Blat, among others, state that a sacrament which has produced its principal effect should not be repeated. To do so would be to irreverently question the efficacy or the sufficiency of the sacrament, and this would result in grave disrespect (sacrilege says Blat)[251] to the sacrament.[252] Now no one denies that Penance

---

(iterari). Quia eius efficacia tamdiu durat, quamdiu periculum."—Regatillo-Zalba, *Theologiae Moralis Summa,* III, n. 650, § 2.

247 Cf. The Council of Trent, Sess. XIV, "On Extreme Unction."

248 Would it not be more accurate to say that it lasts as long as the *sickness* lasts? Cf. Suarez, Disp. XLII, sect. IV, n. 6—*Opera Omnia,* XXII, 853.

249 Cf. Cappello, *op. cit.,* n. 308; Madden, "Repetition of Extreme Unction," *The Australasian Catholic Record,* XXIX (1952), 147.

250 *De Synodo Dioecesana,* Lib. VIII, cap. VIII, n. 4.

251 *Commentarium in Textus Codicis Iuris Canonici,* III, n. 284, p. 344.

252 St. Thomas, Pars III Supp., Q. XXXIII, art. 1; Doronzo, *De Extrema Unctione,* II, 353-355; Billot, quoted in Cappello, *op. cit.,* n. 308.

is efficacious in forgiving sins. Yet cannot a man who has confessed his sins and received valid absolution go again to confession a day or a week or even an hour later, confess the very same sins and validly receive the sacrament of Penance again? Would such a submission of the same sins for valid absolution be an affront to the sacrament, a questioning of its efficacy or sufficiency for the forgiveness of sin in the first confession? Cannot a dying man receive Viaticum on Monday and then again on Tuesday and Wednesday if he hangs on to life during these subsequent days? Would the repetition of Viaticum, which repetition is urged by the law itself,[253] be a disrespect to the sacrament or imply any doubt about the efficacy of the Viaticums already received? Once Holy Communion was received little more than once or twice a year.[254] Today the law itself urges pastors to encourage the faithful to daily Communion.[255] Is this to question the infinite effects inherent in one fruitful reception of the Eucharist? Is the sacrament of the Holy Eucharist to be thought less efficacious now than when it was received infrequently?

The principle stressed by these authors fits in well with those sacraments which produce a constitutive change in the Christian, namely Baptism, Confirmation and Orders,[256] but it seems inapplicable to those other sacraments whose purpose is to nourish, heal and strengthen the Christian life of grace. There seems no more theological necessity for saying there can be only one anointing for each sickness or danger than there is to permit only one administration of Penance for each sin.[257]

[253] Canon 864, § 3.

[254] The Code of St. Martin of Tours decreed: "Non nisi mense semel aliquis communicet aeger."—Martène, *op. cit.*, I, Cap. VII, art. 1.

[255] Canon 863. The faithful are encouraged to communicate again on the same day by way of Viaticum if death becomes imminent for them after their earlier reception of Holy Communion on the same day.—Canon 864, § 2.

[256] And with Matrimony insofar as this sacrament is the contract itself which perdures till death.

[257] Some argue that a repetition in the same danger is null, otherwise the Church would not forbid it.—Regatillo-Zalba, *op. cit.*, III, n. 650, § 7. The Church ordinarily does not allow a priest to offer Mass more than once a

Vermeersch believed that, although the repetition of Extreme Unction in the same danger is gravely prohibited and illicit, such a repeated administration would be valid. This was likewise explicitly held by Kern before the Code.[258] Iorio thinks that *more probably* such a repetition is valid.[259] Cance apparently agrees with this view, for he treats of repetition under the question of lawfulness, but he admits that the opposite opinion is more common (not more probable).[260] Conte a Coronata states that the opinion which acknowledges validity for the repeated administration does not lack probability.[261]

Regatillo feels that such a repetition is *multo probabilius* invalid,[262] as does also Lanza.[263] Prümmer and Doronzo explicitly hold that it is invalid.[264]

Others content themselves with saying that a repeated administration is seriously forbidden, though it might perhaps be valid.[265]

The writer believes that the canon law seriously forbids repe-

---

day. Is it, therefore, proved that, if he offered Mass repeatedly, the Mass is invalid? Besides, as Benedict XIV attested, it was once allowed by the Church to reanoint in the same circumstances of an illness. Ab esse ad posse valet illatio.

Often the reviviscence of Extreme Unction is explained by the fact that it is never repeated in the same danger (cf. Leeming, *Principles of Sacramental Theology* [Westminster, Md.: Newman, 1956], p. 275). But then it is said that the sacrament is not repeated because of the capacity for reviviscence inherent in it. Reviviscence is offered as a proof that it cannot be repeated, and the fact that it cannot be repeated is given as a proof of reviviscence, the while neither claim is established with certainty or sustained with intrinsic proofs.

258 Vermeersch-Creusen, *Epitome Iuris Canonici,* II, n. 229; Kern, *op. cit.,* p. 338.

259 *Theologia Moralis,* III, n. 771.

260 *Le Code de Droit Canonique,* II, n. 267, p. 406.

261 *De Sacramentis,* I, n. 553.

262 Regatillo-Zalba, *op. cit.,* III, n. 650, § 7.

263 Lanza-Palazzini, *Principi di Teologia Morale,* III, n. 164.

264 Prümmer, *op. cit.,* III, n. 582; Doronzo, *De Extrema Unctione,* II, p. 305.

265 Claeys Boúúaert-Simenon, *Manuale Juris Canonici,* II, n. 178; Noldin, *op. cit.,* III, n. 448.

tition in the same *proximate* or *imminent* danger, but that such a repetition would not be invalid.

The fact that the great majority of authors hold the validity of such a repetition to be probable shows that the *"iterari non potest, nisi"* of canon 940, § 2, does not clearly express a prohibition affecting both the validity as well as the lawfulness of the act of conferring the sacrament.[266]

Even the authors who contend that a new danger is postulated for validity with reference to a repeated administration of the sacrament hasten to quote the admonition of Benedict XIV, and in urging a reanointing when one is in doubt about the reality of a new danger, they do not generally mention that such an anointing should be conditional.[267]

Benedict XIV taught that if a patient *seems* to have escaped a danger, but before fully recovering has fallen back into a crisis, "even according to the present discipline he can *without scruple* be fortified once more with Extreme Unction." [268] Then, dealing precisely with the question of doubt, he continued:

> . . . si dubitent, an revera morbi status sit mutatus, seu num idem, vel diversum sit vitae periculum, in quo aegrotus versatur, expedire ait [Van-Espen], ut ad Sacramenti iterationem propondeant, . . .[269]

The whole tenor of Benedict's statement, when he commented on a law which was the same as that of the Code today, shows that he looked on it as a disciplinary norm for the lawful administration of Extreme Unction—*iuxta praesentem disciplinam*, he says —not as a norm affecting the element of validity. Provided a priest conscientiously attempts to carry out its prescriptions, he need have no fear in reanointing when he is in doubt about the fulfillment of the postulated conditions, for he acts lawfully and commendably in doing so.

[266] The structure of § 2 of canon 940 is identical with that of § 1, *"praeberi non potest nisi."* Cf. *supra*, pp. 71-73, for a study of the wording.

[267] Wouters does.—*Manuale Theologiae Moralis*, II, n. 586; Noldin suggests the use of the condition *"si nondum es unctus."*—*Op. cit.*, III, n. 446.

[268] *De Synodo Dioecesana,* Lib. VIII, cap. VIII, n. 4.

[269] *Loc. cit.*

Benedict XIV and the authors did not consider as mandatory a reanointing in a doubtfully new crisis, and neither does the present Code.[270] But in any such doubt it seems commendable to anoint again.

In the law of the Code there is deleted the phrase *"si diuturna sit"* of the old *Ritual*, and there is omitted all mention of any time period that should elapse between anointings. Time is not a factor directly affecting the administration or the non-administration of another anointing. The only measure of the law is the recession of the former proximate danger and the appearance of a new proximate danger or crisis. Accordingly an asthma victim who can be in a severe danger one day and out of it the same day could be anointed again the following day if another such crisis should develop. On the other hand, an auto-accident victim who remains in a critical condition for months without any improvement could not be anointed again as long as that same crisis persists without interruption.[271]

Connell writes that "if at least three months have elapsed since the anointing, the sacrament may be repeated, *even though there has been no apparent improvement.*" [272] And Davis (1866-1952) wrote:

> It is the practice of prudent parish priests to administer the Sacrament once a month to a sick person who having first received it in danger of death gives *no evident signs of getting much better.* It is reasonably thought that such a one

[270] Parres feels that when there is doubt whether the former danger has actually passed and that a new danger is present, the reanointing should be conditional.—"Repetition of Extreme Unction in the Same Illness," *The Homiletic and Pastoral Review,* LVIII (1958), 1166. The writer feels that it should not be conditional. ". . . ne nimium scrupulose in hoc se gerant, sed, si dubitent, . . . ad Sacramenti iterationem propondeant, eo quod haec iteratio conformior sit veteri Ecclesiae consuetudini, et per eam novum spirituale subsidium et levamen infirmo obveniat."—Benedict XIV, *De Synodo Dioecesana,* Lib. VIII, cap. VIII, n. 4.

[271] "Unde adverte quod in morbo diuturno, si infirmus post unctionem *certe* manserit in *eodem* periculo mortis, non poterit rursus ungi."—St. Alphonsus, *Theologia Moralis,* Lib. VI, n. 715. (Italics added.)

[272] "The Hospital Chaplain and the Administration of Extreme Unction," *The American Ecclesiastical Review,* CXIX (1948), 100-101. (Italics added.)

must have got well of his first danger and is now in a fresh danger of death.[273]

Madden says that "a person who is still alive after some weeks (a month or more) of dangerous illness probably has recovered at least for a while in the meantime, that the same danger is no longer present." [274]

Such rules as have here been presented cannot be reconciled with the Code. No time measure can supplant the *convaluerit–aliud discrimen* norm established by the law to allow for re-anointing. To speak of anointing again "even though there has been no apparent improvement," "no evident signs of getting much better," so long simply as a certain period of time has elapsed is to substitute a rule of thumb for the prudent judgment one must exercise to determine whether in fact the requirements of canon 940, § 2, and the *Ritual* have been at least probably fulfilled in a particular case.[275]

If a patient after being anointed in a remote danger falls into an imminent danger a month later he cannot be anointed again, for this imminent danger would evince indeed a *discrimen,* but not an *aliud discrimen.* If he was anointed in a proximate danger and his condition does not improve so as to give probability that he has escaped that particular crisis of the illness, he cannot be anointed a month, three months, or six months later, as long as he continues in that same condition. If he was anointed in a proximate danger which is overcome in a matter of days, and

[273] *Moral and Pastoral Theology,* IV, 8.

[274] "Repetition of Extreme Unction," *The Australasian Catholic Record,* XXIX (1952), 150. He does not feel, however, that anointing every month should be made a practice. He does not explain, however, why he would not every month administer Extreme Unction to a recipient whom he deems probably eligible to receive it again. Piscetta-Gennaro (*Elementa Theologiae Moralis,* V, n. 1030) and Genicot-Salsmans (*Institutiones Theologiae Moralis,* II, n. 428) maintain that, if one who has been anointed lives on for a year and the danger remains *physically one and the same* during that time, one could be anointed again, for according to the common estimation of men the danger in his present condition would be considered *morally* distinct from the former danger.

[275] Cf. Lynch, "Notes on Moral Theology," *Theological Studies,* XX (1959), 262.

then, within the same week, he becomes critically ill again, he can be anointed immediately. Recovery from one crisis, and this usually means an obvious physical improvement in the patient's condition, and relapse into another are essential elements. A relatively notable lapse of time is not essential.

No certitude about the reality of these changes is necessary; there is needed only a sound probability that they have occurred, a probability deduced from the patient's condition.[276]

Authors have set up employable presumptions for the cases in which there is doubt about whether the crisis is really a new one. If after the first anointing the patient's condition has noticeably improved for a month, say Genicot, Conte a Coronata and Noldin,[277] or for even a week, according to Regatillo, Cappello and Prümmer,[278] the presumption is that the danger is a new one. If the improvement has run for only a few days, the former danger is considered as continuing. These presumptions must always of course yield to contrary proof. The writer feels that the use of such presumptions often complicates matters rather than simplifies them. Let the conditions postulated by the law be adjudicated in each case, regardless of the greater or lesser lapse of time, and if there remains any doubt as to their fulfillment, any doubt as to whether the present crisis is a new crisis, let the patient be anointed again, as Pope Benedict urged.

According to the present discipline, there is no justification for anointing old people every month as a matter of routine. There must be a new crisis.[279]

[276] " . . . aliud discrimen . . . quando eadem persona in eadem detineatur infirmitate, et *melius se habuerat ita ut saltem probabiliter* extra mortis periculum constituta *iudicaretur,* deinde vero talis mutatio obvenit qua iterum eius vita in discrimen poneretur."—Raus, *Institutiones Canonicae* (altera editio, Paris: Typis Emmanualis Vitte, 1931), n. 264.

[277] Genicot-Salsmans, *Institutiones Theologiae Moralis,* II, n. 427, III, b; Conte a Coronata, *De Sacramentis,* I, n. 553; Noldin, *Summa Theologiae Moralis,* III, n. 448, § 3.

[278] Regatillo-Zalba, *Theologiae Moralis Summa,* III, n. 650, § 4; Cappello, *De Extrema Unctione,* n. 286, § 2; Prümmer, *Manuale Theologiae Moralis,* III, n. 582.

[279] Can a patient who while in danger suffers another illness that brings with it another danger be anointed again in view of this new danger?

Admittedly the norms existing today for the administration of Extreme Unction with regard to the condition of danger of death leave much to the prudent judgment of the ministering priest. He should have no fear of making these judgments as best he can, always anointing when he is satisfied in his own mind that the requirements are fulfilled so far as he can determine, always anointing conditionally when he has doubt whether any danger at all is present, always reanointing when in doubt about the reality of a new crisis in the same illness. If in the development of the theology of Extreme Unction it is determined that no danger at all is required for the valid reception of this sacrament (as this writer from his study has been led to believe) but only a real bodily debility, and the Church deems it profitable thus to determine its discipline, a change in the present discipline could someday ensue. In consequence thereof serious sickness, as judged by its visible effect on the person, could warrant an anointing, and a definitely specified lapse of time (every week, or two weeks, or every month) could mark the instant at which a reanointing within the same serious sickness would become permissible.[280]

Elbel-Bierbaum (*Theologia Moralis,* III, n. 219), Kilker (*Extreme Unction,* p. 202), and Conte a Coronata (*op. cit.,* I, n. 553, p. 609) say that he can. Noldin (*op. cit.,* III, n. 448, § 3), Cappello (*op. cit.,* n. 285), Regatillo-Zalba (*op. cit.,* III, n. 650, § 5), and Doronzo (*op. cit.,* II, 362) say that he cannot. The writer agrees with the latter group. Danger is a single condition caused by one or several agents. The sacrament is given with regard to the physical condition of the body, and not in view of the causes of that condition. If the new illness brings a proximate danger while the current danger is remote, however, then the conditions for reanointing are verified, unless the former danger has never yet reached a critical stage.

280 If ever sickness is judged by its effects on the person rather than by the danger of death it can bring, then perhaps those people who suffer psychosomatic illnesses that truly make them sick and not themselves—that make it therefore so much more difficult for them to live full spiritual lives in their condition—may become (as they once seem to have been, cf. Palmer, *Sources of Christian Theology,* II, 398) the recipients of this "Sacred Unction of the Sick."

CHAPTER III

THE MENTAL REQUISITES IN THE RECIPIENT

Article I. The Attainment of the Use of Reason

There were times in the past when particular legislation required the recipient of Extreme Unction to be of a fixed age, an age beyond that which brings the use of reason. The Code of St. Martin of Tours and Bishop Durantis (1237-1296) too prescribed that the recipient must be at least eighteen years old. A Synod of Paris of the twelfth century admonished pastors to give the sacrament especially to those who had reached their fourteenth year, though it also allowed all who had reached the age of discretion to receive it.[1] In 1748 Benedict XIV quoted and condemned the practice of synods and particular rituals that had called for the deferring of the sacrament until the fourteenth year or until the subject had received Holy Communion. The practice, though not universal, had been general enough up to the sixteenth century. Others, like Cardinal de Rohan (1674-1749) in the Ritual of Strasbourg, prescribed that it was not to be denied to children who had reached their seventh year, nor to those less than seven years old who had already come to know right from wrong.[2]

The Roman Ritual of 1614, in listing those to whom Extreme Unction was not to be given stated simply, *"pueris rationis usum non habentibus."* [3]

To receive this sacrament, said Suarez, it was enough that one be capable of committing actual sin, capable of being tempted and of resisting temptation, capable of devotion and trust in

[1] Martène, *De Antiquis Ecclesiae Ritibus,* I, cap. VII, art. I, n. 3.

[2] "Non denegetur etiam pueris si septimum attigerint annum, nec iis in quibus malitia supplet aetatem, etiamsi septenarii non sunt."—Quoted in *De Synodo Dioecesana,* Lib. VIII, cap. VI, n. 2.

[3] Tit. V, Cap. V, n. 9; The Council of Avignon (1594) had decreed: ". . . ita istis ne ministret; nempe pueris rationis usu carentibus ad iudicium parochi. . . ."—Hardouin, X, 1848; *Acta Ecclesiae Mediolanensis,* Pars I, p. 140.

God.[4] Laymann taught that whoever had reached the age of reason, thereby becoming capable of sinning, so that he was a fit recipient for the sacrament of Penance, was also capable of receiving Extreme Unction. He cited Scotus (1266-1308) and Vivaldus (1544-1605), who held that children who had not reached that age and disposition in which they could receive Viaticum could not be anointed. Remarking that many places still followed this rule, Laymann called the practice *"minus rationabilis,"* for there was no necessary connection between the two sacraments. One capable of receiving Extreme Unction was not to be deprived of it simply because he might be prevented from receiving Viaticum.[5]

St. Alphonsus taught that children with the capacity for wrongdoing (*doli capaces*) could receive Extreme Unction even though they had not yet received Communion. And if there was doubt whether they had actually reached the use of reason, the sacrament could be given to them conditionally.[6]

Benedict XIV put it very emphatically: "*As soon as* children are judged capable of knowing right from wrong and of being answerable for their acts they can be anointed should they fall seriously ill." [7]

[4] "Ut persona absolute sit capax illius (sacramenti) sufficit quod fuerit capax peccati actualis, devotionis, tentationis et resistentiae et fiduciae in Deum. . . ."—Disp. XLII, Sect. I, n. 5—*Opera Omnia,* XXII, 850.

[5] Laymann, *Theologia Moralis,* II, Lib. V, Tract. VIII, c. IV, n. 2. If the custom was tolerated by the bishop, said Laymann, the pastors were excused if they did not administer Extreme Unction to children under fourteen or fifteen years of age, except in cases of necessity when it was evident that a child who had reached the use of reason would otherwise die without receiving any sacrament.

[6] *Theologia Moralis,* Lib. VI, nn. 719, 720.

[7] "Sed statim ac pueri rationis compotes iudicantur doli et culpae capaces, si in gravem incidant morbum poterunt infirmorum oleo muniri . . . quandocumque censentur capaces Sacramenti Poenitentiae sunt pariter idonei reputandi ad Extremam Unctionem quae est illius complementum, quamvis nondum tanta polleant iudicii maturitate, ut videantur apti ad rite participandam Eucharistiam."—*De Synodo Dioecesana,* Lib. VIII, cap. VI, nn. 2, 3.

A Synod of Pistoria and Prato, held in 1892, insisted that previous Communion was not necessary, but that the capacity to commit *mortal* sin sufficed.[8]

The present Code reads: "fideli, qui post adeptum usum rationis. . . ."[9] Since, according to canon 88, § 3, all children who have reached their seventh birthday anniversary are presumed by law to have attained the use of reason, they are always to be anointed when they are seriously sick. This is a *presumptio iuris simpliciter* and admits of contrary proof, but until it is proved beyond doubt that a child of seven does not yet have the use of reason the presumption stands in his favor and he is to be anointed.[10] While a child under seven is not presumed to have the use of reason, he may in some cases actually have attained it before that time. If so, he fulfills the requirement signalized in the phrase *"post adeptum usum rationis,"* and is to be anointed. The attainment of the use of reason is not measured by the capability of committing mortal sin—were that true, then the age at which the use of reason is to be presumed should stand higher than at seven years—but by the first signs of being able to distinguish between right and wrong.

Whenever there is any doubt that a child has in fact reached the use of reason, canon 941 provides that Extreme Unction be conferred on him conditionally.[11]

That the Church feels it most important that young children be not deprived of Extreme Unction is witnessed by the legislation of many recent synods, including that of Rome in 1960 under Pope John XXIII which decreed:

> Extrema Unctio administretur etiam in casibus dubiis, scilicet sub conditione, et etiam pueris qui rationis usu polleant, quamvis nondum ad sacram Synaxim admissis.[12]

[8] *Synodus Pistoriensis et Pratensis,* Cap. VII, n. 6.

[9] Canon 940, § 1.

[10] Cf. canons 1825, 1826, *De praesumptionibus.*

[11] "Quando dubitatur num infirmus usum rationis attigerit . . . hoc sacramentum ministretur sub conditione."

[12] *Prima Romana Synodus,* n. 461; also cf. *Synodus Dioecesana I Ravenna-*

It is not necessary that the child be seven years old or have received first Communion or even have gone to confession or have ever sinned, as long as he is probably thought to have attained the use of reason.[13] Not to administer Extreme Unction to children who have reached the use of reason was described by the Decree *Quam singulari* of 1910 as "a detestable abuse." [14]

Those, on the other hand, who have never attained even the temporary use of reason, no matter what their age, are ineligible (*incapax*) to receive Extreme Unction. Such are the perpetually insane and infants.[15] Care must be taken not to deprive the so-called feeble-minded or mentally retarded of this sacrament too quickly. Many of these, though they will not have attained the perfect use of reason compatible with their age group will, nevertheless, have reached the imperfect use of reason of a six- or seven-year-old child. If so, they are fit recipients for Extreme Unction. In any doubt they are to be favored with a conditional anointing.[16]

A person who has once had the use of reason, even for the shortest period of time, and subsequently lost it permanently by becoming insane, or temporarily by becoming unconscious, delirious or momentarily deranged, still fulfils the condition inherent in the phrase *post adeptum usum rationis,* and can in

---

tensis et Cerviensis (1955), canon 300; *Patriarchalis Ecclesiae Venetiarum Synodus XXXI* (1957), canon 324.

13 "Pueris, qui vel septimum aetatis annum expleverint vel ante septennium usum rationis iam adepti sint, extrema unctio conferatur absolute, etiamsi forte nondum sacrementum poenitentiae susceperint."—*Synodus Dioecesana Aprutina et Hatriensis,* canon 208; Lehmkuhl, *Theologia Moralis,* II, n. 576, § 2.

14 S. C. de Sacramentis, 8 aug. 1910: "Detestabilis abusus est non ministrandi extremam unctionem pueris post usum rationis."—*Fontes,* n. 2103; *AAS,* II (1910), 583.

15 Mothon, *Institutions Canoniques* (3 vols., Vol. II, Bruges: Société Saint-Augustin, Desclée de Brouwer, 1924), II, art. 2025; Cappello, *De Extrema Unctione,* n. 219.

16 Canon 941; *Prima Romana Synodus* (1960), n. 461.

those states be anointed.[17] The actual use of reason at the time of reception is not necessary. It is only necessary to have once had it. The importance of conferring Extreme Unction on the insane is magnified when one remembers the words, "And if he be in sins, they shall be forgiven him." [18] These people are no longer capable of using the sacrament of Penance. Yet, if they went insane in the state of mortal sin and before making an act of perfect contrition, Extreme Unction is the only certain means available to extricate them from sin and its consequence of eternal damnation. For them, the *ex opere operato* effect of this sacrament seems the only hope of salvation.[19]

The Ritual of 1614 stated specifically that those who had lost their speech or become insane, delirious, or unconscious could be given the sacrament. It added, however, that, if in his delirium or insanity the recipient was thought likely to act in a manner disrespectful to the sacrament he should not be anointed unless all such danger was completely obviated.[20] Commenting on this rubric, Baruffaldo (1675-1755) cited Barbosa (1590-1649) and

[17] "Igitur deneganda non est: 1) amentibus et delirantibus, qui unquam antea rationis usum habuerint. . . ."—Lehmkuhl, *Theologia Moralis,* II, n. 576, § 2.

[18] St. James, V:14.

[19] Again Extreme Unction shows itself the true complement of Penance in forgiving the sins of those to whom the ordinary way, Penance, is no longer available. If danger of death were not required for the reception of Extreme Unction, these "insane" who are really "sick" would stand to benefit immeasurably by the speedy reception of the sacrament in their particular "sickness." Now, if they are perhaps in mortal sin, their only hope seems to lie in their dying of some physical bodily illness and being fortunate enough to have the ministration of a priest at that time. Is it saying too much to suppose that they too perhaps were included in the "Is anyone among you sick?" of St. James?

[20] "Infirmis autem . . . etiamsi deinde loquelam amiserint, vel amentes effecti sint, vel delirent aut non sentiant, nihilominus praebeatur (hoc sacramentum).

Sed si infirmus, dum phrenesi aut amentia, verisimiliter posset quidquam facere contra reverentiam Sacramenti, non ungatur, nisi periculum tollatur omnino."—Tit. V, Cap. V, nn. 6, 7.

other theologians who suggested that this danger could best be averted if the recipient were tied down. This procedure, he said, was sometimes necessary when the man would otherwise die without receiving any of the sacraments.[21]

St. Thomas had demanded more. He believed that personal devotion was necessary in the reception of Extreme Unction just as it was necessary in the receiving of the Eucharist. The recipient had to know and recognize the sacrament he was receiving. It was not to be given, therefore, to the delirious or the insane, unless they had lucid intervals in which they knew what they were receiving. Only in those moments could it be conferred on them.[22] It followed that St. Thomas did not allow Extreme Unction to be administered to the unconscious. St. Bonaventure, Scotus and Gerson agreed that the recipient should possess the actual use of reason when he received Extreme Unction.[23]

That this opinion was no longer generally accepted in the sixteenth century is evidenced by the rubric in the Ritual of 1614. Suarez (1548-1617) had summed up the true doctrine. It is fitting and proper that one should receive Extreme Unction with attention and devotion if at all possible, but this is not essential to the validity of the sacrament.

[21] *Ad Rituale Romanum Commentaria,* Tit. XXVII, n. 7; also, "praecavenda . . . irreverentia . . . etsi forte aegrotus propter furorem ligari debeat."—Lehmkuhl, *Theologia Moralis,* II, n. 576, § 2.

[22] "Respondeo dicendum, quod ad effectum huius sacramenti percipiendum plurimum valet devotio suscipientis . . . et ideo illis, qui non possunt recognoscere, et cum devotione suscipere hoc sacramentum, dari non debet, et praecipue furiosis et amentibus, qui possunt irreverentiam sacramento per aliquam immunditiam facere; nisi haberent lucida intervalla, in quibus sacramentum cognoscerent; et sic conferri in statu illo posset."—*Summa Theologica,* Pars III, Supp., Q. XXXII, art. 3.

[23] ". . . dari debere solis infirmis ratione utentibus."—St. Bonaventure, *Opera Omnia,* IV, Dist. XXIII, quae. II; Duns Scotus, *Summa Theologica,* VI, *Tract. de Extrema Unctione,* Q. XXXII, art. 3: ". . . requiritur actualis devotio in suscipiente; item non dari furiosis et similibus, nisi per intervalla resipiscant, seu utantur ratione. . . ."—Gerson, *Summa Theologica et Canonica,* Liv. IV, *De Extrema Unctione,* p. 280.

> . . . non est necesse, ut qui illud recipit, *tunc* sit compos aut habeat usum rationis, *satis* enim est, quod aliquando *habuerit* et peccare actualiter *potuerit.*[24]

Once a person has attained the mental capacity to commit so much as a venial sin he is, as far as this requisite is concerned, ever after a fit subject for Extreme Unction, no matter what his mental condition later reflects.[25]

The rubric of the old ritual which forbade the administration to the delirious or the insane when there was danger of irreverence to the sacrament was dropped completely in the post-Code edition of the ritual; no such disciplinary law is incorporated in the Code itself. This seems most wise, since in reality a person in such a condition is incapable of any disrespect to the sacrament. His acts are not human acts morally imputable to him. He would be no more disrespectful in his ravings than is a baby crying loudly and tugging at the priest's stole during his baptism. And should it be difficult to anoint such a recipient, the short form could always be applied easily and lawfully.

Given the fact that the former prohibition has been revoked through its deletion from the Ritual after the Code, and the fact that one deals here with the restriction of a Christian's right to receive a sacrament, there seems no basis today for holding, as Merkelbach (1871-1942) did, that those who are raving and delirious cannot be anointed except in lucid intervals, or only in times of the most urgent crisis, if there is no danger of irreverence to the sacrament.[26] The anointing of any sick person, when otherwise he is judged to be a fit recipient, should not be post-

[24] Disp. XLII, Sect. I, n. 5—*Opera Omnia,* XXII, 850. (Italics added.)

[25] "Nec requiritur aegrotum perfecte pervenisse ad usum rationis; sufficit talis usus rationis quo potuit veniale committere peccatum."—Jone, *Commentarium in Codicem,* II, 169; Bucceroni, *Institutiones Theologiae Moralis* (4 vols., 6. ed., Romae: Ex Typographia Pontificia in Instituto Pii IX, 1914-1915), III, n. 871.

[26] "Item furiosis et phreneticis; ipsis tamen sacramentum non est conferendum nisi in lucidis intervallis, at necessitate *omnino urgente,* ministrari poterit etiam *in crisi,* dummodo non sit periculum irreverentiae pro sacramento."—*Summa Theologiae Moralis,* III, n. 705.

poned solely because he has lost the use of his reason and is perhaps raving. The salutary effects of this sacrament for the sick are too helpful to suffer any delay.

In canon 943 there is confirmation of what, from the preceding considerations, is already clear, namely, that the recipient of Extreme Unction need not be conscious, though that state is certainly the ideal and desirable one for its reception. The canon speaks of anointing absolutely the sick who have the required intention, *"etiamsi deinde sensus vel usum rationis amiserint."* [27]

SCHOLION. ANOINTING AFTER APPARENT DEATH

"The Sacraments are destined, by divine institution, for men in this world for the duration of their earthly life. . . . One who is not a man, or not yet a man, or no longer a man, cannot receive the Sacraments." [28] Whether a sick man is still alive, and therefore still a *homo viator* capable of receiving sacraments, or whether he is dead and no longer a man, is something not easily verifiable in many cases. Yet, as long as the slightest waning degree of human life remains in his body he is a fit subject for the reception of Extreme Unction. Anxious that no one be deprived of any possible sacramental help, and realizing that for an unconscious dying man Extreme Unction may be the only certain means of salvation,[29] the Church directs that, when a priest

[27] "Subiectum Extremae Unctionis est homo baptizatus, qui ad usum pervenerit rationis . . . licet sensibus destitutus. . . ."—Bucceroni, *Institutiones Theologiae Moralis,* III, n. 871; "Danda est extrema unctio iis omnibus . . . etiamsi . . . sensibus desituantur."—Genicot-Salsmans, *Institutiones Theologiae Moralis,* II, n. 427.

[28] Pope Pius XII, Allocution to Anesthetists, Nov. 24, 1957—*Acta Apostolicae Sedis,* XLIX, 1027; translation in T. Lincoln Bouscaren, *The Canon Law Digest* (4 vols. and supplement, Milwaukee: Bruce, 1934-1960), IV, 300.

[29] "Poterunt tunc administrari sub conditione sacramentalis absolutio et praecipue extrema unctio, quae certiorem habere potest in casu effectum."—Bucceroni, *Institutiones Theologiae Moralis,* III, n. 754. Such a person, if in mortal sin and incapable of eliciting an act of perfect contrition, can regain the state of grace only through the *ex opere operato* effect of a sacrament, provided always he has at least attrition for his sin (cf. M. J.

doubts whether one who seems to have died is really dead, he anoint that person conditionally.[30] St. Charles Borromeo (1538-1584) enunciated the same principle over four hundred years ago, as did also Suarez (1548-1617), Laymann (1574-1635), LaCroix (1652-1714), and St. Alphonsus (1696-1787) after him.[31]

Given the definition of death as the separation of body and soul,[32] the doubt mentioned in canon 941 (*num mortuus sit*) turns on the fact of this separation. A doubt about death is a doubt that the soul has actually left the body. The departure of the soul from the body cannot be seen, but it is manifested by the *final and complete* cessation of human life in the body. Once, through a sudden indisposition or from the effects of a gradual

---

Scheeben, *The Mysteries of Christianity* [translation by Cyril Vollert, St. Louis: Herder, 1954], p. 577). Conditional absolution would be of doubtful efficacy, since the recipient is incapable of performing those external acts which theologians commonly hold to be necessary for the valid reception of Penance (cf. Ad. Tanquerey, *Synopsis Theologiae Moralis et Pastoralis* [3 vols., Vol. I, editio decima quarta quam quarto post Codicem recognovit F. Cimetier, Parisiis: Desclée et Socii, 1955], pp. 49-52). Without any manifestation of guilt, sorrow or satisfaction on the recipient's part, however, Extreme Unction would restore him to God's friendship immediately for, "If he be in sins, they shall be forgiven him" (St. James, V:15). When necessary this sacrament directly effects the remission of sin. It affords a Christian who is sick and unable to use the ordinary means (Penance) another sacramental means of forgiveness. There is reason for calling it, as The Council of Trent did, the *"complementum poenitentiae."*

30 "Quando dubitetur num infirmus . . . mortuus sit, hoc sacramentum ministretur sub conditione."—Canon 941; *Rituale Romanum,* Tit. VI, Cap. I, n. 9.

31 "Si vero aliqua morbi vis de repente illum oppressit ut dubitetur, vivus ne sit, an mortuus, ea conditione in unguendo utatur; si es vivus."—*Acta Ecclesiae Mediolanensis,* Pars II, p. 223; "In dubio vero de vita, detur sub conditione."—Suarez, *Opera Omnia,* XXII, Disp. XLII, Sec. II, n. 1; Laymann, *Theologia Moralis,* II, Tract. VIII, Cap. 4, n. 5; LaCroix, *Theologia Moralis,* II, Tract. V, Cap. I, n. 208; St. Alphonsus, *Theologia Moralis,* Lib. VI, n. 712.

32 Francesco Roberti, *Dizionario di Teologia Morale* (Roma: Editrice Studium, 1954), p. 858; Cappello, *De Extrema Unctione,* n. 243: "Mors realis habetur cum homo reapse moritur, seu cum anima a corpore separatur." Cf. Pope Pius XII, Allocution—Bouscaren, *Digest,* IV, 301.

deterioration, the body is no longer capable of sustaining the basic and essential vital functions, the separation of the two constituent parts of the creature man takes place.

The essential vital functions are the activities of the nervous, respiratory and circulatory systems. So interdependent are these, that the failure of one brings on the inevitable destruction of the others. When they have come to a definitive and final end—beyond any hope of resuscitation—the body is really dead.[33] That human life ceases and that, therefore, the soul separates from the body at this time seems to be the contention of Pope Pius XII (1939-1958), who wrote:

> (But) considerations of a general nature permit the belief that human life continues as long as vital functions—as distinct from simple organic life—are manifested spontaneously, or even with the aid of artificial processes.[34]

This is in reply to the question whether death has already taken place when a serious skull injury has brought a complete paralysis of the central respiratory nerves, "whose *immediately fatal* consequences have been effectively retarded by artificial respiration," or whether it takes place "only with the *final* stopping of the circulation" in spite of prolonged artificial respiration. In another place he stated: "The possible danger that a man might be buried alive can be neglected, since the removal of the breathing apparatus must produce, after a few minutes, the stopping of circulation and so death." [35]

The distinction between human life and the life of individual (minor) organs, made twice in the Allocution, is important, for the continued existence of the latter does not have to be attrib-

[33] Cf. John J. Lynch, "Autopsy—How Soon After Death," *The Linacre Quarterly,* XXVII (1960), 98.

[34] Pope Pius XII, Allocution, Nov. 24, 1957—Bouscaren, *Digest,* IV, 303.

[35] *Ibid.*, p. 301. The general topic of the Allocution is the state of those whose principal vital functions are preserved solely by mechanical apparatus. This is reanimation as opposed to resuscitation, which is the revival of the functions to the point where they momentarily or permanently continue spontaneously. Cf. Eugene Tesson, "Réanimation et Casuistique," *Etudes,* CCXCVI (1958), 96-98.

uted to a persistence of the former.[36] Molecular and cellular activity continues for a time after death as is evidenced by the continued growth of hair, and nails, by the fact that organic transplantation is sometimes possible if accomplished immediately after death, by the fact that the supply of chemical matter necessary for metabolism is not immediately exhausted upon the failure of the vital functions that supply it to the entire body. This activity, however, is no longer geared and co-ordinated to the maintenance and preservation of the body; it cannot restore the life of the organism as a whole, and without that life is itself doomed to quick destruction. Such life is not to be considered a continuation, in lesser degree, of human life. "If, in the opinion of the doctors," said Pius XII, "this definitive stoppage indicated the certain separation of soul and body—even if some particular organisms continue to function—Extreme Unction would certainly be invalid, since the recipient would no longer be a man." [37]

To know that the cessation of essential vital activity marks the advent of real death is one thing, to determine with certitude that these functions have actually and finally stopped is quite another. These functions, chiefly respiration and circulation, could end abruptly by the violent destruction of the organs through which they operate, and such an event would be readily observable. Such, however, is not ordinarily the case. The process of dying is not usually the phenomenon of an instant but one that is gradual and progressive. The vital functions do not cease all at once but diminish in force until they can no longer survive. They can become so feeble and weak that the victim may evidence signs of having died while human life persists latently within him. The observable fact that one has drawn

[36] Against those who attributed cellular life to the action of the human soul, E. Hugon (1866-1929) wrote: "Ratio est, aiunt, quia anima non exit de corpore, quamdiu tot vivant in illo cellulae; quaenam autem veram vitam, etiam post mortem apparentem, expromere pergunt. . . . Nec sufficit opponere quasdam cellulae adhüc vitae munia retinere; sed probandum esset illas vivere per animam humanam, quod quidem nulla facta censere sinunt."—In Doronzo, *De Extrema Unctione*, II, 460.

[37] Allocution, Nov. 24, 1957—Bouscaren, *Digest*, IV, 302.

his last breath and that his heart no longer beats and that his pulse cannot be felt does not necessarily indicate that the processes of respiration and circulation have been entirely extinguished as yet.

There are several conditions that give a body the semblance of being dead while actually it is not—at least not yet. The most common of these is partial asphyxia induced by drowning, electrocution, strangulation, suffocation, and some types of poisoning. All respiratory and circulatory activity seems to have halted and, in some types of asphyxia, the body may even have become stiff. The conditions are extremely serious and, if they last, surely lead to real death. The body, if recoverable, will not revive spontaneously but only with the aid of timely, adequate and prolonged artificial respiration. Victims of asphyxia have been resuscitated, which means that, despite some external appearances to the contrary, vital activity had not ceased entirely.[38]

Such neuro-psychotic states as catalepsy, trance and lethargy also resemble the state of death. In catalepsy consciousness is usually lost, body temperature diminished, and respiration and circulation are seemingly discontinued. The muscles may be generally rigid, but the limbs are easily movable. The state of catalepsy is rarely encountered, but, when found, is easily distinguished from real death, at least by trained physicians.[39] In

[38] Cf. "Death," *The Encyclopedia Americana* (30 vols., 1957 ed., Chicago: Americana Corporation, 1957), VIII, 540; Austin O'Malley, *The Ethics of Medical Homicide and Mutilation* (New York: Devin-Adair, 1922), pp. 85-86, where examples are cited. "To resuscitate a person apparently dead, the maintenance of the blood circulation is the chief end. If, however, the blood is not oxygenized, the circulation will not go on automatically."—O'Malley, *op. cit.*, p. 84. There is no recovery without the essential functions.

[39] Giuseppe De Ninno, "Morte," *Enciclopedia Cattolica* (12 vols., Città del Vaticano: Ente per L'Enciclopedia Cattolica e per il Libro Cattolico, 1948-1954), VIII, 1433; "Respiration and heart action while reduced are apparent."—"Death," *Encyclopedia Americana*, VIII, 539. In speaking of cases of apparent death as cited by older writers, in which cases the pulse was reported missing up to 14 days before death, O'Malley (1858-1932) stated: "These all were apparently cataleptic cases, where the circulation was very feeble and the radial pulse was not palpable."—*Ethics of Medical Homicide and Mutilation*, p. 86.

a true trance state there is more similarity to death. The face is pale, the limbs often rigid, reflexes may be lost, the pupils may be dilated and immobile, but here too there are signs that distinguish the condition from death, such as the persistence of electrical excitability, normal ophthalmoscopic appearance of the fundus of the eye, and the absence of decomposition.[40]

Is there any one sign that by itself can offer certitude of real death? Having made a study of the question in the early part of this century The Medical Academy of Paris concluded that there exists no sign that can give certitude about death in every case except manifest putrefaction of the body, and that all other signs, taken individually, must be considered doubtful.[41] Brouardel, with whom D'Angelo (1885-1930) concurred, further held that not even a complexity of these signs taken cumulatively can suffice to give certitude about real death if putrefaction has not begun.[42] From such an affirmation De Ninno dissents. It is true, he says, that if you ask for one unique and unequivocable proof of death there is only one, namely, the putrefaction of the body. But it is just as true that from the organs and functions of the body there can always be derived some proofs which taken together in their cumulative force are capable of giving certitude that real death has occurred.[43] The matter is a serious one to adjudicate, nonetheless, and De Ninno adds that full certitude

[40] "Death," *Encyclopedia Americana,* VIII, 539-540.

[41] Cf. Sosio D'Angelo, *La Morte Reale ed Apparente* (2. ed. corretta ed ampliata, Torino: Lega Italiana Cattolica Editrice, 1928), p. 41.

[42] Cf. D'Angelo, *op. cit.*, p. 43. Some who hold this make this distinction: the complexity of signs in the absence of putrefaction cannot afford certitude of real death, but it could indicate with certitude that a return to life is impossible.—*Ibid.*, p. 42.

[43] "Per quanto reguarda, da ultimo, la questione della constatazione de morte, è vero che non esiste un segno *unico* e in*equivocabile* del suo avvenimento, a eccezione della putrefazione del corpo; ma è pur vero che può sempre rilevarsi, dai vari organi e dalle varie funzioni, un *complesso* di segni capaci, nel loro insieme, di dare la certezza della morte reale."—"Morte," *Enciclopedia Cattolica,* VIII, 1432. In col. 1433 De Ninno gives a brief exposition of the various signs that join to form this cumulative proof of death.

can be derived from these signs only when the examination is conducted by one competent in medicine.[44]

The fact that human life can and often does remain for a time in a body that shows the common signs of death gives rise to the doctrine of apparent death as contrasted with real death. Simply defined, apparent death is that state in which one is still alive, his soul not yet separated from his body, although he exhibits no signs of life or cannot exhibit them exteriorly.[45] Maroto (1875-1937) described it as the state of those who, according to the thinking of the ordinary man, seem to have died; who no longer use their senses; who lack external signs of life and perhaps even the principal vital functions, but who nonetheless still retain within themselves latent life and have not yet yielded up their souls.[46] "From the moment that external signs signifying the advent of death appear in consequence of the suspension of the major functions essential to the preservation of life (respiration and circulation) to the moment in which life in an individual is totally extinguished through real and definitive death," says Doctor Laborde, "there exists a period of latent life which will vary in length depending on the cause of death."[47] Writing in 1928 D'Angelo felt that from current studies and the most accurate experience it could be said that, despite the signs of death, life continues for minutes, hours and sometimes even days.[48]

It is surely undeniable that a period of latent life may often

[44] Remarking on the fantastic figures and accounts often given of premature burials, De Ninno suggests that the cause of these terrible events was not the fact that death could not be objectively determined by competent men, but wrongful presumptions of death based on summary observation rather than thorough examination—this especially in times of war, plagues and epidemics, when haste and fear of contagion resulted in little care and attention for the apparently dead and consequently quick burials.—"Art. cit.," col. 1433.

[45] Cappello, *De Extrema Unctione,* n. 243.

[46] Philippus Maroto, "Dubia circa canones Extremae Unctionis applicandos casibus mortis apparentis," *Apollinaris,* I (1928), 177.

[47] D'Angelo, *La Morte Reale ed Apparente,* p. 39.

[48] D'Angelo, *op. cit.,* pp. 39-40.

exist after the appearance of death, but can such a period be said to follow in every case of death? In 1914 Professor Bitonti held as an incontrovertible thesis and universal doctrine that *no one* dies in that moment which is commonly believed to be the last of his life, but actually dies only sometime later.[49] Kilker writes that "all authorities are inclined to agree . . . that the patient *usually* is not dead immediately upon the cessation of circulation and respiration."[50] McFadden says simply, "Medical science agrees that there is an indeterminable period of latent life after the patient has apparently died."[51] O'Malley maintained that even in cases of decapitation it is probable that the victim does not die at once.[52] Ferreres (1861-1936), who made a special study of the entire doctrine of apparent death, concluded: "*Probably* every man goes on living for some space of time after the instant in which he is considered to be dead, the length of this latent life depending upon the nature of the causes bringing death."[53]

The generalization that life survives latently in *every* case of death seems too wide a conclusion. Doronzo calls it exaggerated and adds: "Id nullo satis probabili argumento ostenditur."[54] In the absence of *certain* signs of death, however, the probability, slight though it may be, that life does continue latently is enough to constitute the doubt, *num mortuus sit*.

[49] Cf. D'Angelo, *op. cit.*, p. 38.

[50] *Extreme Unction,* p. 211. (Emphasis added.)

[51] Charles J. McFadden, *Medical Ethics* (3. ed., Philadelphia: F. A. Davis Co., 1953), p. 421.

[52] *Ethics of Medical Homicide and Mutilation,* p. 63.

[53] *Compendium Theologiae Moralis,* II, n. 850: "Probabiliter omnes homines, post instans in quo iam mortui censentur, adhuc perstant in vita per aliquod temporis spatium, longius vel brevius iuxta naturam causarum mortem afferentium."

[54] *De Extrema Unctione,* II, 461. The arguments of Lépicier (1863-1936) against the opinion *"quae tenet, semper et in omnibus casibus distingui debere mortem apparentem a morte reale,"* and which he termed *"periculosa"* and *"ad minus tamquam suspecta,"* are quoted briefly by Doronzo on pages 458-460.

> Doctrina de morte reali et apparente profecto attendenda est, ubi agitur de extrema unctione ministranda necne; nam sacramenta sunt instituta propter homines ideoque, cum extrema unctio hominem a morte aeterna salvare possit, ipsi in gravissima necessitate constituto succurrendum est, meliori quo fieri possit modo, etiam cum levi aut levissima probabilitate.[55]

Life is a fundamental right received from the Creator and the loss of it must be demonstrated with certainty,[56] especially when loss of this right puts one outside the scope of the sacraments which may be necessary for his salvation.

The pastoral importance of considering the doctrine of apparent death in the administration of Extreme Unction is evidenced by specific legislation about the matter in many recent particular synods. The Synod of Bergamo, held in 1952, states:

> Cum iuxta peritorum sententiam communem, mors realis aliquamdiu post apparentem saepe sequatur, ideo tum absolutio tum extrema unctio ministrari possunt, sub conditione quidem etiam aliquo temporis intervallo, postquam mortem secutam esse vulgo censetur; nempe eo longiore intervallo, quo celerior mors acciderit.[57]

The synod accepts it as the common doctrine of experts that real death often, not necessarily always, follows apparent death, and therefore sees it permissible to anoint conditionally for some time after death is commonly thought to have occurred. It makes no attempt to measure the length of this period of probable latent life except to say that it may be longer following a swift and sudden death than it is when it comes after a slow death.

The Synod of Ravenna of 1955 directs a priest when he is called to one who to all appearance died within the previous three hours to administer Extreme Unction conditionally unless

[55] Cappello, *De Extrema Unctione,* n. 245; also Iorio, *Theologia Moralis,* III, n. 777, § 2; Pope Pius XII, Allocution, Nov. 24, 1957—Bouscaren, *Digest,* IV, 300.

[56] Pope Pius XII, Allocution, Nov. 24, 1957—Bouscaren, *Digest,* IV, 301.

[57] *Synodus Dioecesana Bergamensis XXXVI (1952),* C. 287, § 2; the identical paragraph is found also in *Synodus Dioecesana Aprutina et Hatriensis (1956),* C. 208, § 2.

there is danger of causing contempt for the sacrament or unless a doctor declares that the person is dead.[58] In its wording the synod implies two things that are worth noting. By calling for a conditional anointing within three hours after apparent death it implies that up to this time the probability of latent life exists. By adding the condition "unless a doctor declares the patient dead," it implies that certitude of death can be had through examination made by a competent doctor, and that once death is thus certified no reasonable ground for doubt remains.

The Synod of Reggio Emilia, held in 1956, admonishes priests to keep before their eyes what the convictions of medical men are concerning apparent death and latent life, and, priests who have come upon someone who has just died should anoint him conditionally as long as not more than three hours have elapsed since he seemed to expire in a case of sudden death, and not more than half an hour if he succumbed to a long illness.[59]

In the Synod of Novara of 1955 there is found perhaps the widest possible application of the doctrine of apparent death.

> Cum incipiens corporis dissolutio, ut nunc arbitrantur, unum sit signum mortis certae, impense hortamur ut Extrema Unctio sub unica unctione, remoto scandalo et sub conditione, "si vivis," iis omnibus conferatur qui sine ea vita functi sint sine temporis praescriptione.[60]

What the synod says in substance is that until a body begins to decompose there is not offered any certain proof that it is really dead, and consequently, regardless of how long ago death seemed to come, the body can be anointed conditionally until that dissolution begins. Till the beginning of decomposition there is probability of life in some degree. The source of this doctrine might well be Ferreres who wrote:

58 "Quod si vocetur in casu quo quis paulo (quod probati Auctores concedunt ad tres horas) morte correptus videatur, tum absolutionem, tum Extremam Unctionem sub conditione administret, dummodo non adsit contemptus sacramentorum vel iudicium medici qui mortem testetur."—*Synodus Dioecesana I Ravennatensis et Cerviensis (1955)*, C. 311, § 2.

59 *Synodus Dioecesana Regiensis (1956)*, C. 326.

60 *Synodus Dioecesana Novariensis XIX (1955)*, Art. 203.

> Igitur in *praxi* semper (vel fere) poterit sacerdos absolvere et extrema unctione munire adultum qui *vulgo* recenter mortuus absque ultimis Sacramentis credatur, nisi mors per generalem cadaveris corruptionem fuerit certo comprobata.[61]

Kilker, who claims that a priest is "amply justified in anointing a man supposedly dead from a sudden and unexpected cause up to the time when advanced decomposition has set in," adds that this period may last "for many hours and even through several days "depending upon the rapidity with which putrefaction occurs." [62] Repeating that putrefaction is the only certain sign of death, Healy too concluded that "any time before general putrefaction sets in Extreme Unction may be given." [63]

In this line of reasoning there is assumed a fact which by no means is admitted by everyone today. To hold that in the absence of bodily decomposition there can be no certitude of real death is not only to say that putrefaction is the only (single) proof of death, but also to deny the possibility that any number of other proofs can produce that certitude independently of dissolution. But De Ninno insists:

> It can be affirmed that a proof of death which gives full certitude is always possible when obtained by a competent person (doctor) employing a complexity of signs obtainable from the different functions of the organism.[64]

The recent Roman Synod asks priests to keep in mind the doctrine of apparent death and to confer conditional Extreme Unction after apparent death, especially if it has come on suddenly, only, however, "within a short period of time." [65]

[61] Ferreres, *Compendium Theologiae Moralis,* II, n. 855.

[62] *Extreme Unction,* p. 219. Climate, cause of death and physical condition of the body will all affect the time at which decomposition begins.

[63] Edwin F. Healy, *Medical Ethics* (Chicago: Loyola University Press, 1956), p. 382.

[64] "Si può quindi affermare che una constatazione di morte che dia piena sicurezza è sempre possibile, purche fatta da persona abile e utilizzando un complesso di segni rilevabili dalle differenti funzioni dell'organismo."—De Ninno, "Morte," *Enciclopedia Cattolica,* VIII, 1433.

[65] "Sacerdotes, doctrinam de morte apparenti meditantes, Extremam Unctionem post apparentem, repentinam praesertim, mortem, intra breve

Scientific biological knowledge and factual human experience permit two universally acceptable conclusions about apparent death: 1) that human life can persist in the body even when it has ceased to exhibit external signs of life, and 2) that the duration of this latent life, though not determinable to the exact minute or moment, is longer or shorter depending upon the cause of death and the physical condition of the body at time of apparent death. The vital forces of a healthy body struck by sudden, accidental death will have more resistance than those of a body that has succumbed to the lethal effects of a lingering illness which has slowly been causing physical deterioration.

Given these facts plus the lack of positive proofs of death in any particular case, there is basis for a doubt, slight though it might be at times, that real death has come. Lacking *positive* proof of death, the minister of Extreme Unction is faced with an insoluble doubt, in which case he should judge "in favor of the presumption of human life, because there is here a question of a fundamental right received from the Creator, the loss of which must be demonstrated *with certainty.*"[66] In case of extreme necessity the Church has recourse to extreme measures in order to communicate to a man grace and sacramental aid,[67] so that when there exists the least probability, as long as it is a probability, that one apparently dead is still a fit recipient of the sacrament, he is licitly anointed conditionally. Only *positive* proof that he is no longer a man can exclude him from the class of at least doubtful recipients.[68]

---

tamen tempus, ministrent, praemissa absolutione sub conditione."—*Prima Romana Synodus MDCCCCLX,* n. 462.

[66] Pope Pius XII, Allocution, Nov. 24, 1957—Bouscaren, *Digest,* IV, 301. (Emphasis added.)

[67] *Ibid.,* p. 300.

[68] "Nam quamdiu spes probabilis adest vitam adhuc permanere neque certum est mortem vere intrasse, tamdiu possunt et debent saltem conditionate conferri sacramenta quibus talis forte indigeat; haec autem sunt Poenitentia ex Extrema Unctio."—Aloysius Sabetti, *Compendium Theologiae Moralis* (33. ed., 7. ed post Codicem, concinnata A. Timotheo Barrett, Neo Eboraci: Pustet, 1931), p. 806; ". . . ad licite administrandum sacramentum praecipue in casibus necessitatis, sufficit etiam minima solida

Taking the information available from medical science, in which sphere it lies to pronounce on the fact of real death,[69] the authors attempt to determine in a general manner how long after apparent death there remains enough probability of latent life to give rise to the doubt, *num mortuus sit.* It is the common opinion that after death from a long illness this probability lasts for about half an hour. Iorio says that a conditional administration is admissible within half an hour from the moment of the last breath, and up to an hour if death comes prematurely before the illness has run its course.[70] Aertnys (1828-1915)–Damen (1881-1953) likewise allow an administration within a half hour,[71] as do Jone, Regatillo-Zalba, Genicot (1856-1900)–Salsmans (1873-1944), Arregui (1867-1942), and Vermeersch (1858-1936), among others.[72] Cappello grants half an hour from the estimated time of death, but extends the time to one hour "or even two" if death is attributed partly to the illness and partly to another unexpected cause.[73] Ferreres at all times granted half an hour as a minimum, but he specified that his starting point is not the moment when, by the common estimation of men, death seems to have come, but from the time at which a doctor, employing the

probabilitas. . . ."—Doronzo, *De Extrema Unctione,* II, 461; cf. also D'Angelo, *La Morte Reale ed Apparente,* pp. 53-61.

[69] Cf. Pope Pius XII, Allocution, Nov. 24, 1957: "As for establishing the fact in particular cases, the answer cannot be deduced from any religious or moral principle; and under this aspect it is outside the competence of the Church."—Bouscaren, *Digest,* IV, 303; also p. 302.

[70] *Theologia Moralis,* III, n. 779.

[71] J. Aertnys–C. A. Damen, *Theologia Moralis* (15. ed., 7. ed. post Codicem, 2 vols., Taurini: Marietti, 1947), II, n. 338: "Practice ergo illis qui ex diuturna infirmitate censentur mortui *post semi-horam* . . . non facile sunt sacramenta ministranda."

[72] Jone, *Commentarium in Codicem Iuris Canonici,* II, 170; Regatillo-Zalba, *Theologiae Moralis Summa,* III, n. 484, § 14; Genicot-Salsmans, *Institutiones Theologiae Moralis,* II, n. 426; Antonius M. Arregui, *Summarium Theologiae Moralis* (20. ed., 17. ed. latina, Bilbao: Editorial El Mensajero del Corazón de Jesús, 1952), n. 666; Vermeersch-Creusen, *Epitome Iuris Canonici,* II, n. 225.

[73] *De Extrema Unctione,* n. 246, § 3.

most accurate tests and observations, can no longer perceive any vestiges of life.[74]

Merkelbach, on the other hand, saw no probability of latent life in ordinary cases of death following upon long and consumptive illnesses, and therefore allowed no conditional conferring of the sacraments. If, however, during such an illness there arose complications which accelerated the expected time of death he permitted a conditional anointing within half an hour.[75] Healy and McFadden extend the time to one hour after a long and protracted illness.[76] O'Malley did not hesitate to state that the probability of the soul's not yet having left the body is so strong for a whole hour after apparent death that he considered a priest neglectful if he would not minister conditional Extreme Unction.[77] Connell believes Extreme Unction *should* be given up to half an hour, but *may* be given up to an hour after apparent death from illness.[78]

Admitting the grave difficulty for a layman (but not generally for a trained medical man) to distinguish apparent death from real death, De Ninno regards it to be licit to administer conditional Extreme Unction within a half hour from the time the victim has drawn his last breath and his heart has stopped beating.[79]

If death has resulted from some sudden and unexpected cause,

[74] *Compendium Theologiae Moralis,* II, n. 855. As has been seen, Ferreres justified a conditional anointing up to the time decomposition of the body has begun.—*Supra,* p. 197.

[75] *Summa Theologiae Moralis* (10. ed. aucta et emendata, 3 vols., Brugis: Desclée de Brouwer, 1956), III, n. 654: "In casu mortis *ordinariae* ex diuturno et paulatim consumptivo morbo, non possunt absolvi, quia vitam manere non est probabile. In casu mortis *intermediae,* ex morbo diuturno sed cum influxu repentino novo, quae 'complicatio' audit et expectatam mortem valde accelerat, videntur posse absolvi per lapsum circiter semihorae post apparentem obitum."

[76] Healy, *Medical Ethics,* p. 382; McFadden, *Medical Ethics,* p. 421.

[77] *Ethics of Medical Homicide and Mutilation,* p. 88.

[78] "The Hospital Chaplain and the Administration of Extreme Unction," *The American Ecclesiastical Review,* CXIX (1948), 97.

[79] "Morte," *Enciclopedia Cattolica,* VIII, 1434.

the period of time after apparent death in which latent life is probable is agreed to be considerably longer. Authors allow anywhere from one to four hours in such cases, and some add "as long as the signs of death are not clear." De Ninno grants two hours, as does Cappello;[80] Wouters and Regatillo-Zalba, two or more, especially in cases of asphyxia;[81] Arregui, Noldin, Maroto, Bucceroni, Aertnys-Damen, two or more;[82] Vermeersch, Jone and Merkelbach, three hours. Merkelbach added that after three hours the probability of latent life is gone. Accordingly, though the possibility of a continued latent life could not be denied in an extraordinary case, still no anointing should be conferred after that time.[83] Romani holds a full hour as an allowable time for a conditionel anointing, but he likewise regards an anointing as licit as long as the signs of death are not clear.[84] Connell and Healy allow four hours. Connell writes: "For a period of about four hours after all signs of life have ceased (unless the body has been greatly macerated or dismembered) the sacraments may be administered."[85] Healy, pointing to deaths which result from sudden accidents such as drowning, lightning, fire, wounding, hemorrhage, apoplexy, or asphyxiation, remarked: "This norm merely indicates the amount of time after apparent death before putrefaction usually begins."[86]

[80] De Ninno, *loc. cit.;* Cappello, *De Extrema Unctione,* n. 246.

[81] Wouters, *Manuale Theologiae Moralis,* I, n. 477; Regatillo-Zalba, *op. cit.,* III, n. 484, § 14.

[82] Arregui, *Summarium Theologiae Moralis,* n. 666; Noldin-Schmitt, *Summa Theologiae Moralis,* III, n. 246; Maroto, "Dubia circa canones Extremae Unctionis applicandas casibus mortis apparentis," *Apollinaris,* I (1928), 177; Bucceroni, *Institutiones Theologiae Moralis,* III, n. 754; Aertnys-Damen, *Theologia Moralis,* II, n. 338.

[83] Merkelbach, *Summa Theologiae Moralis,* III, n. 654; Jone, *Commentarium in Codicem,* II, 170; Vermeersch-Creusen, *Epitome Iuris Canonici,* II, n. 225: ". . . a momento quo, *vulgari iudicio,* mors secuta est, immo intra duas tresve horas."

[84] *Institutiones Iuris Canonici,* II, n. 436.

[85] Connell, "Case for the Apparently Dead," *American Ecclesiastical Review,* CXXXVII (1957), 346.

[86] Healy, *Medical Ethics,* p. 382.

It has been seen that some consider it licit to anoint until the beginning of bodily decomposition, regardless of time.[87]

From the views and opinions cited thus far it is clear that, lacking positive moral certitude of real death, a priest can find justification, at least from extrinsic if not always intrinsic probabilities, for administering conditional Extreme Unction after apparent death according to canon 941. But, are there times when he can have such certitude, so that he may not anoint, even conditionally? All agree that bodily putrefaction definitely rules out any possibility of continued human life. True *rigor mortis,* which can be identified, at least by a competent doctor (if not also by a layman at times), gives moral certitude of real death.[88] The patent condition of a body so violently mutilated or macerated as to preclude any possibility of the latent operation of vital human functions would likewise yield moral certitude.[89] If the head is so completely crushed that the brain is obviously destroyed; or the chest so torn or punctured that the heart is manifestly ruptured beyond the possibility of functioning; or the body decapitated, there seems no doubt that the essential vital functions have ceased beyond any hope of resuscitation, since the very organs through which they operate are hopelessly destroyed. Even though a particular organ may continue to function in that body for a time, the essential vital functions are irreparably lost.[90] Such a body is no longer disposed to bear human life, and any presumption that the human soul still remains in it appears

87 McCarthy calls this procedure "sound and logical." Cf. "Anointing after Apparent Death," *The Irish Ecclesiastical Record,* 5th Series, LVIII (1941), 371. He quotes Drum as saying, "so long as we have any doubt about the presence of total decomposition it is probable that we should administer conditionally."

88 Cf. McFadden, *Medical Ethics,* p. 421.

89 "Excipitur, si mors fuerit *violenta,* v.g. ex compressione vel abruptione membrorum principalium, quia tunc mors est evidens."—Merkelbach, *Summa Theologiae Moralis,* III, n. 654; Connell, "Case for the Apparently Dead," *American Ecclesiastical Review,* CXXXVII (1957), 346.

90 "En effet si les blessures du cerveau sont importantes, la survie est presque certainement impossible." Cf. Eugène Tesson, "Réanimation et Casuistique," *Etudes,* CCXCVI (1958), 96. This holds true *a fortiori* if the brain itself is wholly destroyed.

gratuitous.[91] In these cases death has struck quickly, like the thief in the night. If, on the other hand, bodily damage is severe, but the destruction of the vital organs is not obvious, there is not certitude of real death. The human body is capable of tremendous endurance, as has often been proved by the long survival or even permanent survival of people after suffering serious multiple injuries externally and internally, or being burned extensively and severely.

It also seems true that employing all the present-day techniques available to determine death,[92] a competent doctor can give a priest moral certitude in a particular case.[93] It is the priest, however, who must have the certitude so that if he should have reason to question the fact that real death has resulted despite the certification of death by a doctor, he would be justified in anointing conditionally.[94] In such a case it is especially

[91] If the possibility of the soul's presence in a body devoid of the basic functions of human life were acknowledged, who is to say that the soul may not remain until the body has wholly disintegrated?

[92] Cf. *supra*, pp. 113, 114.

[93] Merkelbach supported this view when in prefacing his remarks on anointing after apparent death he wrote: "In praxi, deficiente certo mortis signo, si non possit hic et nunc haberi iudicium medici: . . ."—*Summa Theologiae Moralis*, III, 654. De Ninno certainly shares this view. Cf. "Morte," *Enciclopedia Cattolica*, VIII, 1433. Pope Pius XII (Allocution, Nov. 24, 1957) seemed to regard such certitude as within the reach of doctors when he said: "If, in the opinion of the doctors, this definitive stoppage indicated the certain separation of soul and body—even if some particular organisms continue to function—Extreme Unction would be certainly invalid, since the recipient would no longer be a man."—Bouscaren, *Digest*, IV, 302.

[94] If he looks for at least extrinsic probability to do so he will easily find it among the authors: ". . . tuto minister sequi potest plurium doctorum regulam iuxta quam, nisi adsit evidens (iuxta omnes) signum mortis, ut generalis corporis putrefactio, sacramenta Poenitentiae et Extremae Unctionis conferri possunt in omni casu usque ad dimidiam circiter horam a morte apparente (seu a momento quo, *etiam ex iudicio medici*, mors ex apparentibus signis contigerit) et in casu repentinae vel violentae mortis usque ad unam vel duas circiter horas."—Doronzo, *De Extrema Unctione*, II, 462; "Celle-ci (la mort) peut n'être qu'apparente; en cas de maladie, la vie risque encore de se prolonger une demi-heure *après la constatation médical* de la mort; si cette constatation n'est pas faite, et elle ne le sera

important to take measures to avoid the possible scandal ensuing to bystanders who see a priest anointing someone already pronounced dead, and to the doctor himself should he be a non-Catholic. A doctor is, after all, a professional man who deals with life and death; he does not make hasty and premature judgments about a matter so serious as the declaration of death. Unless a priest anointing in such circumstances makes it clear that he is acting on the medical doctrine of apparent death, and that the sacrament is given only on condition that the soul has not yet left the body, he will give the obvious impression that he is conferring the sacrament on a corpse. This can only bring contempt for the sacrament. The authors all agree that a conditional anointing based on the doctrine of apparent death is allowed always provided there is no danger of scandal or contempt for the sacrament.[95] They suggest that when possible it be conferred surreptitiously, which often enough is possible, since the short form is used.[96]

The fact that the Ritual calls for the specific pronunciation of

---

que très rarement, on peut encore administrer le sacrement plusieurs heures après le décès supposé."—DeClercq, *Traité de Droit Canonique,* II, p. 206, n. 236; Ferreres, *Compendium Theologiae Moralis,* II, n. 855; Vermeersch-Creusen, *Epitome Iuris Canonici,* II, n. 225: ". . . saltem per semi-horam ex quo peritus medicus omni inspectione facta, personam defunctam esse declaravit."

[95] Cf. Doronzo, *De Extrema Unctione,* II, 463; Synod of Novara, *supra,* p. 117; also J. C. Didier, "Faut-il donner facilement l'Extrême-Onction sous condition, ou vaut-il mieux s'abstenir?" *L'Ami du Clergé,* 7th Series, XVI (1959), 249-50.

[96] McCarthy, "Anointing after Apparent Death," *Irish Ecclesiastical Record,* 5th Series, LVIII (1941), 371; Doronzo, *op. cit.,* II, 463: "Admonet autem doctores, in tali conditionata administratione utriusque sacramenti, et signanter Extremae Unctionis, removendum esse, quantum fieri potest, periculum contemptus sacramenti oriens ex adstantium scandalo seu admiratione, ita nempe ut Extrema Unctio non solum conferatur in unica unctione, omissis omnibus aliis caeremoniis et orationibus, set etiam veluti furtive, seu tali modo quo adstantium attentio eludatur (puta ungendo celeriter frontem infirmi aut etiam ungendo solam manum, si unctio frontis nequeat fieri sine certa ac gravi adstantium admiratione, cum, ut dictum est . . . valde probabiliter valida sit unctio in qualibet corporis parte); quod si attentio eludi non possit, congrua admonitio et explicatio facti praedictum contemptus periculum praecavere poterit."

"si vivis" when anointing in doubt of death [97] shows how solicitous the Church is that there be no misunderstanding in the matter. Since most bystanders could not hear or understand the "si vivis," the priest should enlighten them on what is being done. His failure to do this, especially when such an administration is performed publicly in times of a great accident or disaster, could, and perhaps has, put the Great Sacrament of the Sick in a bad light, as a magical rite to unbelievers, and as something to be associated with the dead or the dying in the minds of believers, perhaps even as a "catchall" available and efficacious always.

Often a priest will arrive on the spot of the apparently dead person and see in him the usual signs of death; he may not know the cause of death or how long the victim has been as he is now; a doctor may not yet have come, or may yet be examining or attempting to resuscitate the victim. The priest, knowing the doctrine of apparent death, wonders *"num mortuus sit"*; he must act quickly, however, for if that fateful moment of separation, soul from body, has not already passed, it may be the very next. He cannot wait for examinations to be concluded, nor can he spend time considering the circumstances at length. If upon arriving at the scene he cannot tell himself, "I am sure this man is really dead" (getting this certitude from his own observations or from others who can supply it), he is in doubt and therefore *"hoc sacramentum ministretur sub conditione."* But there are times when he can be sure. As a zealous minister of the sacraments he will dispense Extreme Unction generously where he can, realizing at the same time that there are those—painfully true as it is—for whom he can do nothing.

Article II. The Intention to Receive the Sacrament

Theologians teach that to receive a sacrament validly an adult possessing the use of reason must have an intention of receiving it.[98] This intention need not be actual or even virtual. An inten-

[97] "Quod si dubitet an vivat adhuc, Unctionem prosequatur sub conditione pronuntiando formam dicens; si vivis, per istam. . . ."—*Rituale Romanum,* Tit. VI, Cap. I, n. 13.

[98] Prümmer, *Manuale Theologiae Moralis,* III, n. 87. With others Prümmer holds that no intention is necessary for the valid reception of the Eucharist.

tion once made and never afterward revoked, though never again adverted to even at the time the sacrament is received, suffices. This is a habitual intention. Furthermore, the habitual intention required for the reception of Extreme Unction need not have been explicitly formulated, for it can be implicitly contained in some other intention. Thus, Cappello, citing De Lugo (1583-1660), teaches that a person who wishes to live and die a Catholic necessarily wishes also, at least implicitly, to be helped to accomplish this by means of the sacraments which are given precisely for this purpose.[99] Genicot-Salsmans hold that this habitual implicit intention is embraced in the general intention, once made and never retracted, of utilizing all the means useful or necessary for salvation.[100] Regatillo adds that such an intention exists in one who is contrite or attrite,[101] and this is logical, for one who is sorry for sins desires implicitly at least their forgiveness and the help necessary to avoid them in the future.

Kilker and Conte a Coronata write that a man who has at any time manifested, either explicitly or implicitly, a desire to live according to the dictates of his conscience, and to do all necessary for salvation, though giving no thought to Extreme Unction, has an intention sufficient to receive this sacrament. And this, they say, would be true even if the man, knowing little or nothing at all about the sacrament, should out of ignorance decline to receive it when it is offered to him.[102]

An intention is something internal that can be known to others only through some express or equivalent external manifestation.

99 Cappello, *De Extrema Unctione*, n. 259; Prümmer, *loc. cit.*

100 Genicot-Salsmans, *Institutiones Theologiae Moralis*, II, n. 27.

101 Regatillo-Zalba, *Theologiae Moralis Summa*, III, n. 28: "Quam voluntatem (recipiendi sacramenta) Ecclesia praesumit de omnibus, qui signa poenitentiae suo tempore dederunt."—De Lugo, quoted in Cappello, *loc. cit.*

102 Kilker, *Extreme Unction*, pp. 251-252; Conte a Coronata, *De Sacramentis*, I, n. 551. Since this habitual implicit intention truly resides in the general intention actually present it cannot accurately be called an interpretative intention. An interpretative intention (actually not an intention) is one that presumably would have been elicited had something been known, or had certain conditions been present. It cannot be considered to exist implicitly in any act of the will.

When a person is conscious it is not difficult to ascertain whether this minimum required intention exists in a recipient. It should be remembered, however, that a refusal to receive a sacrament at a given time does not thereby necessarily destroy the habitual implicit intention to receive it. One who defers ordination for a time does not thereby intend to withdraw his intention of receiving Orders. So a patient, who for some faultless reason declines to receive Extreme Unction here and now [103] does not in doing that retract his intention of being anointed sometime.[104]

Determining whether one who is now deprived of the use of reason by unconsciousness or insanity has the requisite intention to receive Extreme Unction may not always be an easy task. Canon 943 tells how the presence of an adequate intention in the unconscious or the insane can be established.

> Infirmis autem qui, cum suae mentis compotes essent, illud saltem implicite petierunt aut verisimiliter petiissent, etiamsi deinde sensus vel usum rationis amiserint, nihilominus absolute praebeatur.

Kilker correctly observes that this canon does not deal strictly with the intention itself, but with its external manifestation in the form of a petition or request to receive the sacrament. If it is established that there was or would have been such a petition on the part of the recipient, the priest is assured that an intention to receive the sacrament does exist.[105]

Only when a man is conscious and rational can he express outwardly, even though it be only implicitly, the state of his mind

[103] He may think that this sacrament is only for those who are actually dying, and may feel that he is not at this point in his sickness.

[104] "Si suscipiens ex errore duas contrarias intentiones habet, alteram qua actu respuit, alteram qua habitu desiderat sacramentum, valide suscipit, si intentio illud suscipiendi praevalet."—Noldin, *Summa Theologiae Moralis,* III, n. 41, § 5, d.

[105] *Extreme Unction,* p. 252. In older rituals for anointing the sick, it was required that the recipient formally ask for the sacrament before he could be anointed. This was done, not so much to assure the presence of an intention, it seems, as to literally comply with the words of St. James, "Let him call in the priests." Cf. Bord, *L'Extrême-Onction, d'après l'Epitre de Saint Jacques Examinée dans la Tradition,* p. 57.

and soul. Once he is irrational or unconscious, all that can be known of his interior dispositions of mind and soul with any moral certitude must be deduced simply from his conduct before he actually lost the use of his reason or his senses. The internal state of the insane and the unconscious must be judged not on what changes of heart and mind might possibly take place within them while they are unconscious (for these, if any, can be known only to God Himself), but on the facts that emanated from their rational and conscious life. Canon 943 adverts to this in its opening statement: *"Infirmis, autem qui, cum suae mentis compotes essent. . . ."* [106]

Illud saltem implicite petierunt. The recipient need not have asked that the sacrament of Extreme Unction be administered to him. Any request that implicitly includes this petition suffices. A sick person asking to have a priest summoned for him asks implicitly for the sacrament of the sick.[107]

Aut verisimiliter petiissent. In the absence of any external manifestation of intention which implicitly includes the petition to receive the sacrament, an interpretative petition is enough. This is not identifiable with an interpretative intention. It means that had the patient known of or adverted to the sacramental assistance available to him in his condition, he would surely have asked to receive Extreme Unction. This interpretative petition, of course, could only be presumed if the conduct of his life indicated its plausibility. Such an interpretative petition, and therefore the supposed habitual implicit intention, is presumed in every Catholic unless the contrary is clearly proved.[108] Unless there is certain proof that a Catholic has positively withdrawn or retracted his habitual implicit intention to receive the sacra-

[106] The law of the 1614 Ritual read: *"Infirmis autem, qui dum sano mente et integris sensibus essent. . . ."*—Tit. V, Cap. V, n. 6.

[107] Blat, *Commentarium in Textus Codicis Iuris Canonici,* III, n. 287; Cappello, *De Extrema Unctione,* n. 261.

[108] ". . . de quolibet Fideli, de quo contrarium non constat, praesumendum est, fuisse hoc Sacramentum (Extremam Unctionem) petiturum, si potuisset."—Benedictus XIV, *De Synodo Dioecesana,* Lib. VIII, Cap. VI, n. 5; "(si) antequam insanierit, expresse aut tacite petierit illud, aut, si meminisset, petiturus fuisset."—*Ibid.,* n. 4.

ment, it is presumed that he would ask for it if he were able.[109]

What of the Catholic who steadfastly refuses the sacrament to the very time that he becomes unconscious? If the refusal was made while he was delirious or insane, it was not truly a human act, and does not revoke any intention to receive.[110] If it was made while the sick man was conscious and well aware of and intent upon what he was doing, there must be a distinction. A patient may refuse Extreme Unction because he does not believe himself sick enough to be anointed, or in order to avoid letting his family know how seriously ill he is.[111] Such refusals do not imply any positive retractation of the general intention to receive the sacrament. If any such reasons for refusal are known or suspected, he can certainly be anointed when unconscious. If, on the other hand, no such reasons exist and his refusal is purely a contemptful scorn for the sacrament, an attitude of "I don't need it" or "I don't want it," there is no doubt that he revokes any intention he may have had to receive this sacrament. While he was conscious—and only at this time can a priest judge it—he neither implicitly nor interpretatively asked for the sacrament. Quite to the contrary, he explicitly denied any desire and intention to receive it.[112]

109 "Aegris ratione iam privatis, recte datur Unctio, non tantum si ante petierit, sed etiam si fuerint Catholici, neque constet esse in mortali, nam hoc ipso censentur interpretative voluisse et petiisse, quod alii Christiani, etiamsi de ea numquam audierint . . . tum non possint eam (Unctionem) petere, merito praesumitur omnes eam velle, nisi de contraria voluntate constet."—LaCroix, *Theologia Moralis,* II, *Tract. de Sacramentis in Genere,* Cap. III, dubium I, nn. 163, 172.

110 LaCroix, *ibid.,* n. 174: " . . . quando erat compos rationis, voluit, aut probabiliter praesumitur voluisse illud, quamvis postea in amentia vel phreneti expresse dicat se nolle, quia haec revocatio non est actus humanus vel liber, ergo prior volitio humana permanet habitualiter."

111 Circumstances that are indeed possible if Extreme Unction is looked upon as the harbinger of death.

112 Innocentius III, ep. *Maiores Ecclesiae Causas,* a. 1201: "Ille vero, qui nunquam consentit, sed penitus contradicit, nec rem nec characterem suscipit sacramenti, quia plus est expresse contradicere, quam minime consentire. . . . Dormientes autem et amentes, si prius quam amentiam

Davis and other authors think it is wrong to refuse Extreme Unction to one "who has positively repudiated the ministry of a priest up to the moment of unconsciousness." [113] Joseph Genicot, citing E. Genicot and Davis, writes that an intention is not wanting in unconscious Catholics, not even if they had rejected the Faith and had refused to be converted at the moment of death.[114] Commenting on E. Genicot's view, Mahoney (1888-1954) taught that the Catholic who had refused the sacrament up to the time of becoming unconscious (he spoke of a lapsed Catholic) could be anointed conditionally, because "we can indulgently allow for an adequate intention owing to the resurgence of convictions formerly held." [115]

The reasons offered to justify this practice are principally two, namely that the refusal was perhaps not genuine, and that, through God's goodness, an interior change in intention may have been effected between the time of becoming unconscious and the time the priest anoints conditionally,[116] and who, said Davis, can judge the state of soul of one who is apparently unconscious? [117]

Davis was right if he spoke about an unconscious man of whose state of soul nothing was known before he became unconscious. For in this case one is bound to presume that the man does have a desire for salvation, and therefore for its means until the contrary is certainly proved.[118] But this is not the situation with a man "who has positively repudiated the ministry of a

---

incurrerent aut dormirent, *in contradictione persisterent; quia in eis intelligitur contradictionis propositum perdurare. . . .*"—Denz., n. 411.

[113] Davis, *Moral and Pastoral Theology*, IV, 9. Cappello calls this view probable.—*De Extrema Unctione*, n. 264, § 3.

[114] J. Genicot, "Casus," *The Clergy Monthly*, XIX (1955), 227; E. Genicot, *Institutiones Theologiae Moralis*, II, n. 427: "Probabiliter tamen conferri potest . . . immo iis qui usque ad sensuum destitutionem *sacramenta respuerunt*."

[115] Mahoney, *The Clergy Review*, XXXV (1951), 105.

[116] Cf. Kelly, *Theological Studies*, XIII (1952), 97.

[117] *Loc. cit.*

[118] Benedictus XIV, *De Synodo Dioecesana*, Lib. VIII, Cap. VI, n. 5; Suarez, Disp. XLII, Sect. I, n. 6—*Opera Omnia*, 850.

priest up to the moment of unconsciousness." If anything is known of a man's state before he becomes unconscious, then there can be a prudent judgment about his state after be becomes unconscious. If he had a habitual implicit intention while conscious, we can have moral certainty that he retained that disposition after becoming unconscious. It is precisely on this logical judgment that canon 943 rests.[119]

One can be morally certain that the patient's state will remain in unconsciousness what he manifested it to be while he was conscious. Therefore the canon enjoins an absolute anointing, not a conditional one. Granted, anything is *possible,* and he actually could have fallen a victim to despair and retracted the intention at some time before the sacrament was administered, but to act on any such extreme possibility is wholly unreasonable and is not, indeed, prudent human exercise of judgment expected in a minister of the sacraments. Moral certitude always leaves "possibilities" of error, but moral certainty is the only certitude on which one can reasonably act. Otherwise there would never be a time when sacraments could rightfully be administered apart from a condition. It is "possible" that some candidates for Confirmation may not have been validly baptized, but would a bishop act reasonably if he always administered Confirmation *sub conditione* on that possibility?

If a man has "positively repudiated" the reception of Extreme Unction while he was conscious, if he has "rejected his faith and refused to be converted" up to the time he loses consciousness, he has made it expressly clear that he has no intention to receive the sacrament. If this refusal persists to the time he loses consciousness despite the actual grace God certainly gives him to be converted while he can, and despite the promptings of the priest and others that he set things straight, then there can be moral certitude that his state remains the same after he becomes unconscious. There is no *reason* to suppose a change.[120]

[119] ". . . cum suae mentis compotes essent . . . deinde sensus vel usum rationis amiserint, *nihilominus absolute* praebeatur."

[120] "Quia semel malus semper malus, quare, *si certum* sit hominem fuisse in statu peccato mortali, nisi postea iudicium aliquid mutatae voluntatis

If God should, by a singular grace, enlighten an unconscious man so as to effect in him a total change of the disposition he persevered in while conscious, this would be an extraordinary working of Divine Providence, a working we have no right to suppose or expect.[121] A man must work out his salvation while he has the light, for when darkness comes, at the end of his conscious life, he cannot work.

"If a person expressly refuses them (the sacraments)" said Pope Pius XII, "they cannot be administered against his will. God forces no one to accept sacramental grace." [122]

Suarez wrote that it would be a grave sin to administer Extreme Unction to a man who neither expressly nor implicitly even interpretatively asked for it, even if only through some sign of attrition or by leading a good life.[123]

A man who *in his right mind and without any justifiable reason* refuses the sacrament to the time he becomes unconscious must be taken to mean what he says, and what he says clearly evidences a lack of any interior intention to receive it. To give him Extreme Unction, or to attempt to do so, would be to force him against his will. It seems unreasonable to wait until that man has become unconscious and can no longer refuse, and then on the extreme possibility that he did not really mean what he said, or that he had a last-second change of heart, or special Divine inspiration while unconscious, to anoint him even conditionally. In one who so positively refuses the sacrament to the end, there cannot be presumed even a habitual intention.[124]

---

praebeat, potius existimatur in statu antiquo permansisse."—Laymann, *Theologia Moralis,* II, Lib. V, Tract. VIII, cap. IV, n. 3.

121 God's salvific will, having afforded many opportunities for him to repent and to be converted, should not now, if such opportunities were refused constantly and with full intent, be expected to perform a miracle of grace on his behalf. "If they do not hearken to Moses and the Prophets, they will not believe even if someone rises from the dead."—Luke XVI:31.

122 Allocution of Nov. 24, 1957.—Bouscaren, *Digest,* IV, 300.

123 Disp. XLII, Sect. I, n. 8.—*Opera Omnia,* XXII, 850.

124 Fanfani, *Manuale Theorico-Practicum Theologiae Moralis,* IV, 609. God treats man as the rational, free creature He created him, and so must God's priest. He will extend himself surely to do all he can for a man's

The law of the 1614 Ritual, from which canon 943 is taken, read: "seu verisimiliter petiissent, *seu dederint signa contritionis.*" These last four words do not appear in the present law, most likely because they are really contained in the words *verisimiliter petiissent.* Any, even the least, sign of sorrow includes an intention and desire of salvation and its means.[125]

Unless there is absolute and certain proof to the contrary, the minimum intention is presumed in every Catholic. A Catholic who has apostatized leaves no doubt that he wants no part of the Church or its sacraments. He has retracted any intention he may once have had. A Catholic, however, who has lived a sinful life or who has neglected the duties of his Faith to a lesser or greater degree, though not completely, fits under the phrase *"verisimiliter petiissent,"* as does one who is considered in name and in fact to be a Catholic.[126]

In 1821, the Holy See was asked how priests should proceed when called to the side of a man seriously sick who during his life has been a habitual sinner, a backslider, one paying no care to the business of his salvation, who has not received the sacraments for years, who perhaps has not even made his first Communion nor been to Mass since childhood. The sick man gives some sign of repentance. The reply of the Holy Office to the Bishop of Kentucky was:

> Let the missionary consult the approved authors. He will keep in mind, however, that in danger of death any of the faithful who give signs of repentance can be absolved from any censure and sin by any priest, and no one then can be refused participation in the sacraments, namely, Extreme Unction if he is sick, and Viaticum. . . .[127]

---

salvation, but he cannot act against a man's will. God does not force His sacramental grace on any man.

[125] "Quam voluntatem Ecclesia praesumit de omnibus, qui signa poenitentiae suo tempore dederunt."—De Lugo, quoted in Cappello, *De Extrema Unctione,* n. 259; Suarez, *loc. cit.*

[126] Cappello, *op. cit.,* n. 261.

[127] S.C.S. Off. (Kentuky [sic]), 9 maii 1821: "Meminerit tamen in mortis periculo quemlibet fidèlium, qui dat signa resipiscentiaé, a quolibet sacerdote absolvi de quibusvis peccatis et censuris posse, et neminem tunc

It is presumed, says Cappello, that any unconscious Catholic would have asked for Extreme Unction if he had had the opportunity, unless this presumption is clearly disproved from solid facts.[128]

Canon 943 states that, when as much as an interpretative petition can be presumed, the recipient is to be anointed not conditionally but absolutely—*absolute praebeatur.* The earlier law did not contain the word *absolute.*[129] This is a clear indication of the sufficiency of a habitual implicit intention for the reception of Extreme Unction.

SCHOLION. THE INTENTION IN NON-CATHOLICS

If the general intention to lead a Christian life according to the dictates of conscience implicitly contains a habitual intention for the means available to do so, it seems that baptized non-Catholics also possess an intention sufficient for the reception of Extreme Unction and the other sacraments.[130]

Aertnys-Damen, Regatillo and Cappello, among others, make this distinction. If the sect to which the Protestant belongs rejects Extreme Unction as a sacrament (which most, if not all, do), he has not the habitual intention required.[131] His general intention of utilizing all the means given by God for salvation, says Cappello, is opposed by a special habitual intention, never

---

repelli a participatione sacramentorum, nempe Extremae Unctionis, si aegrotent, et SSmi Viatici, nisi quoad Viaticum obiiciatur consuetudo, qua iis qui extremo supplicio mox punientur denegatur, de qua quidem consuetudine nihil hic pronunciatur."—*Fontes,* n. 860.

128 *De Extrema Unctione,* n. 261; cf. Benedictus XIV, *De Synodo Dioecesana,* Lib. VIII, Cap. VI, n. 5.

129 *Rituale Romanum (1614 ed.),* Tit. V, Cap. V, n. 6.

130 Here, only the question of whether non-Catholics have a sufficient intention to receive the sacrament validly is considered. Whether it is licit to administer the sacrament to baptized non-Catholics will be considered in the following chapter.

131 Aertnys-Damen, *Theologia Moralis,* II, n. 337; Regatillo-Zalba, *Theologiae Moralis Summa,* III, n. 652.

retracted, of rejecting this determined rite.[132] If the Protestant belongs to a sect that recognizes the sacramentality of Extreme Unction, he does possess an adequate intention.[133]

Wouters taught that Protestants whose sect does not believe in Extreme Unction *should* not be anointed, but he chose not to condemn the priest who would anoint them conditionally.[134] This, of course, concedes the fact that such a Protestant may well have the requisite intention. Lehmkuhl, on the other hand, felt that sincere good faith in a non-Catholic, coupled with sorrow for sin, could in some way include implicitly the manifest desire to receive the means of salvation.[135]

Many authors do not take into consideration the sacramental beliefs of the various non-Catholic sects and discuss merely the licitness of administering the sacraments to non-Catholics. Genicot-Salsmans, citing LaCroix (1652-1714) and D'Annibale (1815-1892), regarded such an act as licit provided there was "probable hope that the recipient was in good faith and that he would permit the ministrations of a priest if he knew them to be necessary." [136] Iorio holds that even a formal and a public heretic can be given the sacraments when he is unconscious, and a material heretic even while he is conscious, if he is in imminent danger of death, possesses good faith (about his state of heresy) and is sorry for his sins. Iorio thinks it necessary in this case for the material heretic to be instructed about the Catholic Faith and to be led to embrace it.[137] Good faith for the authors means being

[132] "Nam huic generali voluntati, aiunt, opponitur *specialis* voluntas habitualis, numquam scil. retracta, hunc ritum determinatum reiiciendi."—*De Extrema Unctione,* n. 262. But does a Protestant who belongs to a sect that does not accept Extreme Unction as a sacrament really have "a special habitual intention of rejecting this determined rite"? Or is he simply in *intellectual* error concerning one of the sacramental means of salvation?

[133] *Loc. cit.* See also Conte a Coronata, *De Sacramentis,* I, n. 552; Kern, *De Extrema Unctione,* pp. 317, 318.

[134] Wouters, *Manuale Theologiae Moralis,* II, n. 584.

[135] *Theologia Moralis,* II, n. 515.

[136] *Institutiones Theologiae Moralis,* II, n. 264.

[137] *Theologia Moralis,* III, n. 372. In agreement with Iorio are also Ferreres, *Theologia Moralis,* II, n. 608, §§ 7, 8, and Arregui, *Summarium*

prepared to do all that God requires one to do for salvation.[138] Connell says there is good probability that non-Catholics have a sufficient intention in their general desire to make use of the means established by Christ for salvation.[139]

So far as schismatics are concerned, their intention may be looked upon in the same light as that of Catholics. There is no reason to doubt the sufficiency of their intention unless in an individual case the contrary is proved.

Theologiae Moralis, n. 589, b and c. Cf. Sabetti-Barrett, *Compendium Theologiae Moralis,* n. 753, §§ 7, 8, 9.

138 Ferreres, *loc. cit.*

139 "The Hospital Chaplain and the Administration of Extreme Unction," *AER,* CXIX (1948), 98.

CHAPTER IV

THE SPIRITUAL REQUISITES IN THE RECIPIENT

Article I. Baptism

It is impossible to speak of the sacramental nourishing, sustaining and preserving of the supernatural Christian life of grace before that life exists. Since the Christian life begins through Baptism, it is this sacrament that a person must receive before he can receive the others. Though there are three types of Baptism, the Baptisms of water, of blood and of desire, it is only the Baptism of water that constitutes a person a member in the mystical body of Christ, the Church, and that gives him the right to receive from the Church the other sacramental means of sanctification. It is for this reason that, although he may have gained the grace of justification through the baptism of desire, a prospective convert, or an unbaptized person who lives a good life in accord with the dictates of his conscience, is nevertheless not capable of receiving any of the other sacraments.

For the reason that the Baptism of water is an indispensable requisite for the valid reception of Extreme Unction, the old ritual law felt it necessary to direct that Extreme Unction be denied to the unbaptized.[1]

The Code of Canon Law specifies that Extreme Unction cannot be conferred on one who is not a *"fidelis,"* a member of the faithful.[2]

Strictly, then, since the capacity to receive the sacrament is rooted in the reception of the valid Baptism of water, all the validly baptized, Catholic and non-Catholic alike, are, on this account at least, capable of receiving Extreme Unction. It is

1 ". . . nondum baptizatis penitus denegetur."—*Ritual of 1614,* Tit. V, Cap. V, n. 8. Baruffaldo offered the following comment: "Non valet habere aditum ad alia Sacramenta qui prius per hoc non intravit, cum Baptismus sit qui hominem caeterorum Sacramentorum capacem reddit."—*Ad Rituale Romanum Commentaria,* Tit. XXVII, n. 8. Consequently theologians refer to Baptism as the *"ianua sacramentorum."*

2 "Extrema Unctio praeberi non potest nisi fideli. . . ."—Canon 940, § 1.

forbidden, however, by canon 731, § 2, to administer the sacraments, Extreme Unction included, to schismatics and heretics, even though they be in good faith and ask for them, unless these people first reject their erroneous beliefs and embrace the truths of the Faith, i.e., unless they are united to the Church.[3]

Not all the baptized, therefore, can receive Extreme Unction lawfully, but only those who are actually united to the true Church, i.e., only Catholics. The prohibition of canon 731, § 2, is not based on any factor except the baptized non-Catholic's lack of union with the Church. Even if they are in good faith—which shows that they are guiltless in their separation from the Church—and even if they ask for the sacrament—which shows both a belief in it and an adequate intention to receive it—it remains forbidden to administer the sacrament to them. They must first become in reality incorporated in the body of the faithful.[4] The sacraments, said Umberg (1875-1959), by the very institution of Christ signify a unity of faith between the minister and the subject, which unity of faith is not verified when a Catholic minister gives the sacraments to non-Catholics.[5]

When a person receives Baptism he is made a person in the Church of Christ, and becomes endowed with all the rights and duties of a Christian. His rights, however, are suspended or lost by the presence of any obstacle that separates him from actual union with the Church, or by a censure which when im-

3 "Vetitum est sacramenta Ecclesiae ministrare haereticis aut schismaticis etiam bona fide errantibus eaque petentibus, nisi prius, erroribus reiectis, Ecclesiae reconciliati fuerint."—Canon 731, § 2.

4 Canon 731, § 2, insists that they must first reject their errors and become reconciled with the Church. The simple severance of ties (if any) with the non-Catholic sect and the acceptance of the Church would fulfil this condition, at least for the internal forum.

5 "Sacramenta acatholicis nonnisi condicionate conferenda," *Periodica de Re Morali, Canonica, Liturgica,* XXXVII (1948), 101. There is a distinction, Umberg said, between the right to confer Baptism and the right to confer the other sacraments. One confers Baptism lawfully when one wishes, through it, to aggregate another to the Catholic Church; one receives Baptism according to law when one wishes to be incorporated in the Church; the other sacraments can lawfully be conferred and received only by those who are already in the Church, *de facto.—Ibid.,* p. 100.

posed by the Church deprives him of those rights.[6] One of these rights of Christians which cannot lawfully be exercised by one impeded from communion with the Church is the right to receive the sacraments.

In canon 731, § 2, the Code implies the distinction between heretics who are such in bad faith and those who are such in good faith, but it includes both of these classes under the same prohibition. The very object of the prohibition, says McCloskey, demands that all heretics be included, for "the reception of the sacraments is a prerogative of members, not of mere subjects, of the Church." [7]

Vermeersch stated that the reason for excluding these otherwise capable recipients is simply their separation from the Church which is given the sacraments to possess and use for the sanctification of its members.[8] He rightly took issue with those writers who counted non-Catholics among those who are "unworthy" to receive the sacraments. A given non-Catholic in good faith might be more worthy than a Catholic.[9]

Vermeersch insisted that there can be no exception to the positive prohibition of canon 731, § 2, in behalf of non-Catholics who are healthy and well. But in danger of death, he adds, when one must look to the eternal welfare of the soul, it is permitted to administer, at least conditionally, Penance and Extreme Unction to dying *schismatics* who are unconscious.[10] He mentioned only schismatics, not other non-Catholics. In support of this position, one may cite a reply of the Holy Office as given in 1941.

6 "Baptismate homo constituitur in Ecclesia Christi persona cum omnibus christianorum iuribus et officiis, nisi, ad iura quod attinet, obstet obex, ecclesiasticae communionis vinculum impediens, vel lata ab Ecclesia censura."—Canon 87.

7 Cf. *The Subject of Ecclesiastical Law According to Canon 12* (The Catholic University of America Canon Law Studies, No. 165, Washington, D. C.: The Catholic University of America Press, 1943), p. 132.

8 Vermeersch-Creusen, *Epitome Iuris Canonici,* II, n. 15.

9 "Nam qui bona fide errant digniores esse possunt catholicis quibus dantur."—*Loc. cit.*

10 *Loc. cit.*

The question was whether a Catholic priest could, in the absence of an Orthodox priest, minister to the spiritual needs of a dangerously sick Orthodox Christian, even conferring the sacraments if the sick man explicitly asks to receive them. The reply read:

> [after citing canon 731, § 2] Even when they are in danger of death, it is required that at least implicitly, they reject their errors, as far as this can be done (considering the circumstances and persons), and make a profession of faith.
>
> To those who are in good faith and *already deprived of consciousness,* the sacraments may be administered conditionally, especially if there is reasonable ground to conjecture that they have at least implicitly rejected their error.
>
> Care must always be taken, however, that scandal and even the suspicion of interconfessionalism be avoided. And the less danger there is in delay, the more should an explicit retractation of errors and a profession of the Catholic faith be required.[11]

What is permitted here is the conditional anointing of unconscious schismatics in good faith. On what condition are they to be anointed? Certainly not on the condition, *"si capax es,"* for of this there is usually no doubt. It is on the condition that the recipient be at least implicitly disposed to embrace the Catholic Faith. Only then does the Church feel justified in making the sacraments entrusted to it for the sanctification of its members available to other capacitated recipients not of the true fold through no fault or malice of their own.[12] If the recipient is not

[11] Bouscaren, *Digest,* III, 300. This 1941 reply is a reiteration of a similar reply made by the Holy Office in 1916: "An schismaticis *materialibus* in mortis articulo constitutis, bona fide sive absolutionem sive extremam unctionem petentibus, ea sacramenta conferri possint sine abiuratione errorum? Negative, sed requiri, ut *meliori quo fieri possit modo* errores reiiciant et professionem fidei faciant. An schismaticis in mortis articulo sensibus destitutis absolutio et extrema unctio conferri possit? *Sub conditione affirmative,* praesertim si ex adiunctis coniicere liceat, eos implicite saltem errores suos reiicere, remoto tamen efficaciter scandalo, manifestando scilicet adstantibus Ecclesiam supponere, eos in ultimo momento ad unitatem redisse."—S.C.S. Off., 17 maii, 1916—Denz., 2181a.

[12] One could well argue the point that non-Catholics in good faith, if they have never known the truth and are therefore not heretics in the strict sense of that word (someone who denies a truth or some truths of the Faith must first have known them [can. 1325]), may often fulfil this

so disposed, it is the intention of the Church that the sacraments should not be given. The condition is placed on this disposition.[13] The replies[14] of the Holy Office make the general statement that conditional Extreme Unction can be conferred on unconscious material schismatics, but with the further addition, "especially if there is reasonable ground to conjecture that they have at least implicitly rejected their error." But since the affirmative part of the answer is unrestrictive, it must be held that these schismatics can be conditionally anointed even if any positive sign of an implicit rejection is wanting.[15] Apparently the Church feels that there is enough of a reasonable presumption that all schismatics *in good faith* are habitually disposed to embrace the true Faith to warrant a conditional anointing when they are unconscious. The sacrament should never be given to a schismatic of known bad faith, nor to one in good faith under ordinary circumstances, but once a man is unconscious and dying his good faith is presumed, unless the opposite is proved from previous knowledge of him, and in such a time of extreme necessity a conditional administration to him seems lawfully permissible.

It should be remembered that these responses dealt specifically

---

minimum disposition of being united to Christ's true Church. What then prevents the Church from allowing them to receive the sacraments is what the response calls scandal and the suspicion of interconfessionalism. Christ's desire is that all be one in Faith, not merely one in the use of the same means of salvation. If the Church ever allowed the administration of the sacraments to Catholics and non-Catholics alike, it might be difficult to convince non-Catholics that "one religion is not as good as another," and some Catholics might feel that they do not necessarily have to accept all that the Church teaches if belief makes no difference.

[13] "Conditio autem sub qua in casu sacramenta etiam moribundis sensibus destitutis administranda sunt non est; Si capax es, sed; Si vis in Ecclesia catholica mori, si tuos errores saltem interne reiecisti."—Conte a Coronata, *De Sacramentis,* I, n. 72; Umberg, "art. cit.," pp. 98, 99. Whether a non-Catholic in good faith can be left in good faith while still conscious is another question.

[14] That of 1916 and that of 1941.

[15] Aertnys-Damen, *Theologia Moralis,* II, n. 337.

with one determined class of non-Catholics, the unconscious material schismatics. Authors, however, often cite these responses as warranting a conditional anointing of all non-Catholics when they are unconscious and in good faith.[16]

Woywod (1880-1941) and Iorio, adverting to the doctrine of several pre-Code authors, maintain that the prohibition contained in canon 731, § 2, applies only to those who are in good health, but not to the dying, inclusive of conscious non-Catholics who are in good faith.[17]

Jone writes that the well-founded opinion of authors holds that the Church does not urge the prohobition set in canon 731, § 2, against absolving and anointing any dying (baptized) non-Catholic who is unconscious,[18] and in good faith. Conte a Coronata claims that the prohibition suffers an exception *in articulo mortis* for non-Catholics in good faith. He does not say that they must be unconscious.[19] Regatillo allows a conditional anointing to be given to non-Catholics if they are unconscious, provided that the sect to which they adhere professes belief in the sacrament. He allows it even when they are conscious, if their good faith cannot be disturbed, and if they show signs of sorrow and a willingness to do God's will.[20]

Kilker is correct when he remarks that a priest who gives Extreme Unction to dying non-Catholics does so with much extrinsic probability that his administration is lawful,[21] and that in consequence thereof he can do so without a scruple. On the other hand, the priest who feels that it is absolutely wrong to

16 Cf. Iorio, *Theologia Moralis*, III, n. 372; Aertnys-Damen, *Theologia Moralis*, II, n. 337.

17 Woywod, *A Practical Commentary on the Code of Canon Law*, p. 365; Iorio, *op. cit.*, n. 273. The avoidance of scandal is always presupposed.

18 Jone, *Commentarium in Codicem*, II, 17; also Merkelbach, *Summa Theologia Moralis*, III, n. 705, § 5.

19 *De Sacramentis*, I, n. 72.

20 Regatillo-Zalba, *Theologiae Moralis Summa*, III, n. 652.

21 The question looks simply to lawfulness, for if he be validly baptized the non-Catholic, *servatis servandis*, receives the sacrament validly.

administer the sacraments [22] to these dying non-Catholics seems to have more intrinsic worth in his reasons for the refusal.[23]

It is certainly difficult to see, according to the present discipline, how Extreme Unction could lawfully be given to unreconciled non-Catholics in danger of death if they are still conscious. Since this sacrament is in fact to be given only in danger of death, it would not come under the prohibition set in canon 731, § 2, if danger of death constituted an exception to that canon. Yet the canon makes no exception for Extreme Unction when it says "Vetitum est Sacramenta Ecclesiae ministrare. . . ."

The prohibition against conferring the sacraments to non-Catholics is strengthened in the case of Extreme Unction as a result of the use of the word *"fidelis"* in canon 940, § 1.[24]

Article II. Grace or Attrition

Extreme Unction is essentially and primarily a sacrament of the living, and should therefore be received by one already in the state of grace.[25] For a person to receive it when he is conscious of the fact that he is in mortal sin would ordinarily be a sacrilege,[26] for the sacraments of the living, by Christ's institution are meant to augment the grace which they suppose as already possessed by the recipient.[27]

Not only would it be sacrilegious to receive the sacrament

22 This does not mean that he should not assist them to pray, or not incite them to acts of love for God and trust in His Mercy.

23 Kilker, *Extreme Unction,* p. 135.

24 Cf. *supra,* pp. 73-76.

25 Tanquerey, *Synopsis Theologiae Dogmaticae* (3 vols., Vol. III, 28. ed., quam recognovit R. De Geoffre, Paris: Desclée et Socii, 1955), III, n. 974a.

26 "Qui scienter sine debita dispositione sacramentum vivorum suscipit, gravissimum irreverentiae sacrilegium committit."—Noldin, *Summa Theologiae Moralis,* III, n. 42.

27 "Haec enim primaria sua institutione a Christo sunt ordinata (sacramenta vivorum), non ad conferendam primam gratiam, sed eius augmentum, cum primam gratiam iam in subiecto supponant. Hinc graviter peccant, qui scienter Sacramenta vivorum in statu peccati moralis suscipiunt."—Ferreres, *Compendium Theologiae Moralis,* II, n. 297.

deliberately in the state of serious sin, but it would also be sacrilegious to administer the sacrament deliberately to one who is known to be in mortal sin.[28] To be licitly anointed, then, a recipient must be, at least putatively, in the grace of God.[29]

Suarez was well aware of the intrinsic evil involved in conferring Extreme Unction on recipients who placed a hindrance to its fruitful reception, *"nam tunc constet fore peccatum grave dare sacramentum homini habenti obicem."* [30] From at least the fifth century, when Pope Innocent I forbade the administration of Extreme Unction to the *"poenitentes"* who had not yet been absolved, there has always been legislation denying the sacrament to those whom one rightfully regards as indisposed to receive it because of their sinfulness. Thus the Ritual of 1614 directed:

> Impoenitentibus vero, et qui in manifesto peccato mortali moriuntur, et excommunicatis, et nondum baptizatis, penitus denegetur.[31]

The presumption was that such people were in the state of sin until they were absolved sacramentally, at least insofar as the minister of the sacrament could know, so that for a proper ensurance against a possible sacrilegious administration and reception the sacrament was denied them.

If a sick person, then, is in the state of sin, he must be reinstated in grace, if this is possible for him, before he can receive Extreme Unction licitly as well as validly. This can be accomplished in two ways; by the reception of sacramental absolution, or through an act of perfect contrition. No positive law of the Church directs that the sacrament of Penance need be received

[28] Cf. Noldin, *op. cit.*, III, n. 42; Ferreres, *loc. cit.* There will be times, of course, when Extreme Unction must be employed also as a sacrament of the dead. In such cases its administration to a person in mortal sin, but unable to receive Penance, need not be sacrilegious.

[29] Raus, *Institutiones Canonicae*, n. 264; LaCroix, *Theologia Moralis*, II, tract. I, cap. III, dubium II, n. 185.

[30] Disp. XLII, Sect. I, n. 8—*Opera Omnia*, XXII, 850.

[31] Tit. V, Cap. I, n. 8.

by one consciously in mortal sin prior to the reception of Extreme Unction, as it does prior to the celebration of Mass or the reception of Communion.[32] The law of the old ritual as well as that of the post-Code edition states simply that, in accord with the general observance of the Church, Confession and Communion should precede the reception of Extreme Unction, if time and the condition of the sick person permit it.[33]

If the recipient is not conscious of any mortal sins unconfessed, there is no strict obligation to receive Penance before Extreme Unction.[34] But even if he is conscious of being in mortal sin the while he has the use of his reason and senses, the recipient is even then not absolutely or in principle obliged to make his confession before being anointed. This is so because an act of perfect contrition suffices to restore him to the state of grace, thus enabling him to receive the sacrament fruitfully and licitly.[35] Vermeersch stated that a serious attempt to elicit such an act suffices, if the recipient is legitimately excused from confessing here and

[32] Canons 807, 856.

[33] "In quo illud in primis ex generali Ecclesiae consuetudine observandum est, ut si tempus, et infirmi conditio permittat, ante Extremam Unctionem, Poenitentiae et Eucharistiae Sacramenta infirmis praebeantur."—*Rituale Romanum* (*1952 ed.*), Tit. VI, Cap. I, n. 2 (*1614 ed.*, Tit. V, Cap. I, n. 2). New rituals in our day witness a change in the order in which these three Sacraments are received by the dangerously sick, first Penance, then Extreme Unction, and ultimately Holy Viaticum. This order is a return to the earliest usage of the Church. But even following the Roman Ritual, it has never been considered a hard and fast rule that Penance and the Eucharist should be received before Extreme Unction. No grave reason was required for an inversion of the order. Cf. Baruffaldo, *op. cit.*, Tit. XXVII, n. 2; Kilker, *op. cit.*, p. 235.

[34] Cappello, *op. cit.*, n. 89; O'Kane, *Notes on the Rubrics of the Roman Ritual* (new edition completely revised in accordance with the latest (1925) *Editio Typica* of the *Rituale Romanum*, and Decrees of the Sacred Congregations, by Michael J. Fallon, Dublin: James Duffy & Company, Ltd., 1944), p. 445, n. 826.

[35] "Licet autem, per se loquendo, confessio non necessario praemittatur, cum per contritionem se disponere possit."—St. Alphonsus, *Theologia Moralis*, Lib. VI, n. 716. "In strictness, no doubt, it suffices that he (the recipient) elicit an act of contrition before Extreme Unction."—O'Kane, *op. cit.*, p. 444, n. 826.

now, e.g., because of the lack of suitable confessors, provided, however, he has at least attrition.[36]

The obligation to confess all mortal sins before death,[37] even those already forgiven through the use of other means, exists indeed for one who is sick and in danger of death, but this does not demand that he receive Penance before Extreme Unction is conferred, if he is otherwise properly disposed. If the case could arise wherein a sick and dying man had time for the reception of only one or the other sacrament, he would, if able, be obliged to confess his sins and receive sacramental absolution and to forego Extreme Unction, for there is in his case a strict obligation to receive Penance before death, but there is no serious obligation to receive Extreme Unction.[38]

Penance, however, is the ordinary means by which serious sin is surely forgiven and grace restored so that, unless there are causes excusing him from using that sacrament, a sick man in mortal sin is incidentally bound to receive that sacrament before being anointed if he is not certainly capable of eliciting an act of perfect contrition.[39] Causes that might excuse a sinner from confessing before receiving Extreme Unction could be the serious difficulty involved in manifesting his grave sins to a certain priest, say a relative, when no other priests are available. According to Kilker one could licitly anoint such a recipient by "preparing his soul with contrition" and the intention of confessing later.[40]

36 "Ut sacramentum hoc cum fructu recipiat, debet infirmus qui conscius sit peccati mortalis, vel confiteri ante quam ungatur vel perfecte conteri si possit. Existimata autem contritio sufficit, immo serius conatus contritionis, si copia confessionis non detur, dummodo habeatur attritio."—Vermeersch-Creusen, *Epitome Iuris Canonici,* II, n. 226.

37 Canon 901.

38 Cf. O'Kane, *Notes on the Rubrics of the Roman Ritual,* p. 445, n. 826; Cappello, *op. cit.,* n. 89.

39 ". . . porro necessaria gratiae dispositio certius per confessionem comparatur. Ergo."—Cappello, *loc. cit.*

40 Kilker, *Extreme Unction,* p. 235.

The refusal of a sick person to make a confession before being anointed cannot therefore be necessarily construed as a sign of sinfulness nor as a reason for denying Extreme Unction, just as his declining to go to confession should not deprive him of receiving Communion, unless the priest were absolutely sure and without any doubt whatsoever that he was in a state of serious sin.[41]

Although Extreme Unction is primarily a sacrament of the living, it can for incidental reasons also be a sacrament of the dead, and then is properly called the complement of Penance. "And if he be in sins, they shall be forgiven him." [42] To receive the wondrous graces of sacramental alleviation during his sickness, the patient must first be in grace, but his condition may make it physically impossible to regain the grace he has lost through sin. He may be prevented from receiving the sacrament of Penance and at the same time be unable to elicit an act of perfect contrition. He may be ignorant of the obligation to elicit an act of contrition, or such an act may be beyond his capacity. It is in this situation that Extreme Unction through the very act of its administration and application (*ex opere operato*) directly wipes out the sin, as St. James taught, so that the sacrament is at once received both validly and fruitfully. All that is necessary on the recipient's part is attrition, without which no sin can be forgiven.[43]

The person who becomes unconscious or insane in the state of sin but who possesses habitual attrition for sin—something al-

[41] Cf. *infra*, p. 150 ff.

[42] St. James, V:15.

[43] "Semper tamen requiritur attritio."—Claeys Boúúaert-Simenon, *Manuale Juris Canonici*, II, n. 179. Inasmuch as the more common opinion states that Extreme Unction can revive, it is possible, authors say, for a recipient to receive it validly even without attrition, but until attrition is aroused in the recipient the sacrament will have none of its effects. What is actually given to the subject thus anointed, say the authors, is a "*titulus exigitivus gratiae, non solum sanctificantis, sed gratiae quoque peculiariter alleviantis et confortantis.*"—Cappello, *op. cit.*, n. 310. Even if this be true, it remains a sacrilegious act knowingly to administer the anointing to one who has not attrition, and for him to receive it in such a state.

ways assumed unless the opposite is indisputably proved—can be lawfully anointed and, as Suarez put it, the sacrament will make contrite one who is attrite.[44]

A priest need have no anxiety about whether conditional absolution given to the unconscious sick who can no longer go through the judicial process of sacramental confession is a valid absolution, for when Extreme Unction is administered it infallibly produces the same effects of forgiveness and justification.[45]

St. Thomas had taught that Extreme Unction served as an antidote for the remains of original sin only in so far as they were augmented by actual sin; it served principally as an antidote for the remains of actual sin.[46] In full accord with this teaching Billuart and other theologians held that a person must

[44] "Sed quoniam diximus necessarium esse ut, quando dandum est sacramentum ei, qui tunc ratione non utitur, credatur esse dispositus ad effectum sacramenti, interrogari potest, quid faciat minister, si credit illum non esse in gratia, quia nec confessus est, nec aliud sacramentum suscipit, nec signa contritionis sufficienter exhibuit, sed cuiusdam attritionis et timoris; itaque ponamus sacerdoti constare infirmum fuisse attritum, poteritne dare hoc sacramentum licite? alter enim non potest licite accipere cum sola attritione cognita; ergo nec minister potest licite dare. Respondeo posse, quia si conferat sacramentum non carebit effectu suo. Diximus enim supra, sacramentum hoc facere de attrito contritum, quoties suscipiens de novo non peccat in illius susceptione; sed ille recipiens non peccat de novo; nam ratione talis status est incapax novi peccati et alias supponitur attritio; ergo fiet contritus virtute sacramenti; ergo digne illi tribuitur."—Suarez, Disp. XLII, Sect. I, n. 10—*Opera Omnia,* XXII, 851.

[45] This holds true provided, of course, that the subject is habitually attrite for his sins, for attrition is an element necessary for forgiveness. It seems that the only reason for the conditional absolution given before Extreme Unction to the unconscious is the slight probability that such an absolution is valid, and that therefore the priest should employ, as far as possible, the proper sacrament of the dead, namely Penance, in forgiving the sins, so that Extreme Unction, primarily a sacrament of the living, can be received in the state of grace. But if Extreme Unction were used exclusively as a sacrament of the living, when could it ever effect what St. James, The Council of Trent, and all the common teaching and tradition maintain that it can effect, namely, the direct forgiveness of sins for the sick person?

[46] *Summa Theologica,* Pars III Supp., Q. XXXII, art. 4.

actually have sinned sometime after Baptism if he was to qualify as a recipient of the sacrament of Extreme Unction.[47]

It is now the common opinion, however, that the recipient need never have actually sinned after his Baptism. It is only necessary that he have been capable of sinning after Baptism. "Ut persona absolute sit capax illius (Sacramenti)," said Suarez, "sufficit quod fuerit capax peccati actualis." [48]

In 1821 the Sacred Congregation for the Propagation of the Faith issued to missionaries in China a reply instructing them to administer Extreme Unction *immediately after* Baptism to pagan adults who were seriously ill.[49]

St. James said simply, "And if he be in sins they shall be forgiven him," which condition does not presuppose the existence of any actual sin, but at most envisages the ability to commit them, the capability of suffering temptations.[50]

SCHOLION. EXCLUSION OF THE POSITIVELY IMPENITENT

From the year 416, when Pope Innocent I in writing to Bishop Decentius instructed him that Extreme Unction could not be given to anyone who was not disposed to receive the other sacraments, there has always been ecclesiastical legislation prohibiting the anointing of the unworthy. The foundation of this prohibition is in the natural law itself. Holy things are not to be treated with reckless disrespect.—*"non mittenda canibus,"* Innocent's own words,[51] cited often by particular councils,[52] are

[47] ". . . qui habeat aut habuit usum rationis et aliquando peccavit actualiter."—Billuart, *Summa Sancti Thomae,* VII, Tract. *de Extrema Unctione,* art. VI, n. 4.

[48] Disp. XLII, Sect. I, n. 5—*Opera Omnia,* XXII, 850; "Ad Extremam Unctionem recipiendam sufficit ut in subiecto baptizato adsit capacitas peccandi, (saltem probabilius) de facto quis numquam peccaverit."—Iorio, *Theologia Moralis,* III, n. 765a; Cappello, *op. cit.,* n. 221; Regatillo-Zalba, *op. cit.,* III, n. 649.

[49] (C. P. pro Sin.), 26 sept. 1821—*Fontes,* n. 4729.

[50] Cappello, *op. cit.,* n. 222.

[51] Ep. 25, *Si instituta ecclesiastica,* 19 mart. 416, cap. 8: "Nam poenitentibus istud infundi non potest, quia genus est sacramenti. Nam quibus

quoted in the *Decretum,*[53] and are given as the source of the present law, as enacted in canon 942.[54] According to Innocent's prohibition the *"poenitentes,"* namely the unabsolved serious sinners, were excluded from the reception of Extreme Unction. They could have been worthy in so far as a perfect act of contrition might have restored them to grace while they were still *"poenitentes,"* but until sacramental absolution had been imparted to them they were barred from the reception of the sacraments.

By the time the Roman Ritual of 1614 was published, the practice of public penance before absolution had disappeared, yet the Church continued to express in law that those who are unworthy cannot be anointed.

> *Impoenitentibus vero, et qui in manifesto peccato mortali moriuntur, et excommunicatis et nondum baptizatis* PENITUS *denegetur.*[55]

Citing Gobat, Baruffaldo stated that by *"impoenitentes"* were meant those who had sinned publicly, but who had given no sign of repentance, with the result that no one could know whether they had forsaken their sin,[56] and the excommunicated were those who were burdened with a public censure which had not yet been absolved.[57]

Diana (1585-1663) and other theologians taught, however, that it would not be illicit to administer the sacrament to one unconscious and dying even if he lost consciousness in the very act of committing mortal sin, for, they said, it can be believed that the

---

reliqua sacramenta negantur, quomodo unum genus (Extrema Unctio) putatur posse concedi."—*MPL,* XX, 560; Denz., n. 99.

52 E.g., by the Council of Pavia (850)—Denz., n. 315.

53 C. 3, D. XCV—*Corpus Iuris Canonici* (editio Lipsiensis secunda post Aemelii Ludovici Richteri curas ad librorum manu scriptorum et Editionis Romanae Fidem recognovit et adnotatione critica instruxit Aemelius Friedberg, 2 vols., Lipsiae: Ex Officina Bernhardi Tauchnitz, 1922).

54 The first reference in the footnote to canon 942 is to c. 3, D. XCV.

55 *Rituale Romanum (1614 ed.)*, Tit. V, Cap. I, n. 8.

56 *Ad Rituale Romanum Commentaria,* Tit. XXVII, n. 8.

57 *Loc. cit.* Cf. also Suarez, Disp. XLII, Sect. I, n. 8—*Opera Omnia,* XXII, 851.

worst sinner, when finding himself close to death, would try to elicit at least an act of attrition in order to be saved. Others, including Clericatus (1633-1717), held these *"impoenitentes"* to be simply excluded from the reception of Extreme Unction, and Baruffaldo himself showed little regard for the lenient opinion when he wrote: "Our text speaks clearly, and it prohibits such ministration; this text sanctioned with the consent of the Universal Church is more to be followed than the opinion of even eminent doctors." [58]

It would be a grave sin, said Suarez, to give the sacrament to a man who upon having lost the use of reason in the state of sin is indisposed to receive that sacrament fruitfully. The fact that he may be capable of receiving it validly does not diminish in any way the sinfulness of giving Extreme Unction to him if he is not here and now capable of benefiting from its effects.[59]

> *Hoc sacramentum non est conferendum illis qui impoenitentes in manifesto peccato mortali contumaciter perseverant; quod si hoc dubium fuerit, conferatur sub conditione.*[60]

Although the overt meaning of the canon seems quite clear, authors are not agreed on the reason for which the Church here denies Extreme Unction to the impenitent. The problem is created by the presence of the final clause, which allows for conditional anointing in cases of doubt about impenitence.[61]

There is a generally accepted theological principle that sacraments are not to be conferred conditionally except when there is

[58] "Textus noster clare loquitur, prohibens talem administrationem, qui textus cum per consensum Ecclesiae Universalis sancitus sit, est magis attendendus, quam opinio doctorum licet classicorum."—*Loc. cit.*

[59] "Duo tamen observanda sunt; unum ut non constet illum amisisse rationis usum, in malo statu, et indispositum ad effectum sacramenti; nam tunc constat fore peccatum grave dare sacramentum homini habenti obicem, et nullo modo, id est, nec expresse nec implicite seu interpretative petenti sacramentum, et salutis suae remedium saltem per signa attritionis, aut bonae vitae."—Suarez, Disp. XLII, Sect. I, n. 8—*Opera Omnia,* XXII, 850.

[60] Canon 942.

[61] This provision for a conditional anointing is new with the Code; it did not appear in the earlier law.

doubt regarding some requirement necessary for validity, whenever there is a danger that they may be exposed to nullity.[62] According to this principle canon 942 must be treating of some element in the recipient necessary for a valid reception. The only requirements necessary to make a person capable of being anointed validly are that he be baptized, that he be sufficiently sick, that he have attained the use of reason, and that he cherish at least a habitual implicit intention to receive the sacrament. If one subscribes to the probable opinion that Extreme Unction revives, then even the present lack of grace, or even of attrition, in a serious sinner would not invalidate the unfruitful reception of the sacrament, which would later produce its effect once the hindrance to its operation has been removed.[63] Many authors conclude, therefore, that although canon 942 treats of dispositions it deals primarily with the recipient's intention to receive the sacrament as judged from his dispositions. Their position is this: if one contumaciously perseveres in manifest mortal sin it is a sure sign that he lacks the intention needed for a valid reception of Extreme Unction. He cannot be anointed. If there is doubt about these dispositions and consequently, according to them, doubt about the requisite intention, he can be anointed conditionally.

Thus Jone writes:

> In huiusmodi adiunctis dubium imprimis respicit intentionem moribundi num scilicet habeat intentionem recipiendi hoc sacramentum, num ergo sit subiectum capax.[64]

"Canon 942 must be interpreted," said Noldin, "as dealing not with disposition but with intention; and since this intention is necessary for a valid reception of the sacrament, a conditional

[62] Prümmer, *Manuale Theologiae Moralis,* III, n. 23; McCarthy, *Problems in Theology,* Vol. I, *The Sacraments* (Dublin: Browne and Nolan Limited, 1956), p. 300.

[63] If, however, the sacrament is given on condition that the subject be properly disposed, there is no possibility of reviviscence, for in the absence of these proper dispositions the sacrament is not given at all.

[64] *Commentarium in Codicem Iuris Canonici,* II, 170.

administration must be given when there is doubt whether the intention is present." [65] The same view is held by Merkelbach, Abbo-Hannan, and Iorio,[66] by Woywod, Vermeersch-Creusen and J. Genicot.[67] Espousing the same view, McCarthy writes:

> . . . but there is the other view, in our opinion the much better view, which interprets canon 942 as covering, *principally and fundamentally*, the question of the intention, and not merely the dispositions of the recipient. This latter interpretation, we submit, is preferable from every standpoint. In particular it accords perfectly with the analogy of teaching and thus escapes the difficulty . . . that canon law espouses the doctrine that Extreme Unction may be conferred conditionally on the presence of dispositions which are necessary for liceity only.[68]

Conte a Coronata sides with what he calls the milder opinion, which teaches that the canon refers principally to defective intention.[69]

There is another group of authors, however, who maintain that the text of canon 942 obviously refers primarily to the disposition of the recipient, and not to his intention. To them it is clear that when the Church describes one as contumaciously persever-

[65] "Canon 942 . . . interpretandus est agere non de dispositione sed de intentione; cum haec ad validam receptionem necessaria sit, sub conditione administrandum est sacramentum, ubi dubitatur, num intentio adsit."—*Summa Theologiae Moralis,* III, n. 446, d.

[66] Merkelbach, *Summa Theologiae Moralis,* III, n. 705, § 6; Abbo-Hannan, *The Sacred Canons,* II, 63; Iorio, *Theologia Moralis,* III, n. 766: "Cum igitur ad validam susceptionem referri debeat ex capite intentionis (de hac enim agit can. 942) ideo heic conditio esset: si capax es vel si sufficientem intentionem habes."

[67] Woywod, *A Practical Commentary on the Code of Canon Law,* n. 865; Vermeersch-Creusen, *Epitome Iuris Canonici,* II, n. 226, reversing an earlier opinion held in a previous edition that the canon dealt only with dispositions of soul; J. Genicot, "Casus," *The Clergy Monthly,* XIX (1955), 228.

[68] McCarthy, *Problems in Theology,* I, 300 (italics added).

[69] "Quae cum ita sint propendimus in mitiorem opinionem qua dicitur canonem referri praecipue ad defectum intentionis."—*De Sacramentis,* I, n. 552.

ing in manifest mortal sin it is describing his disposition of soul. Says Cappello:

> The words (of this canon 942) must be understood correctly. There is question here of impenitence, certain and indubitable, question of serious and obstinate ill will by which one knowingly and willingly perseveres in what is patently mortal sin.[70]

Doronzo unequivocally states that in canon 942 the sacrament is not denied for any want of intention, as some think, but for lack of the proper disposition required for the fruitful reception of the sacrament. He cites as proof of this the general practice of the Church of denying the sacraments to the unworthy even though they might ask for them, and the fact that the intention to receive a sacrament can exist along with a contumacious perseverance in mortal sin.[71]

Kilker granted that a person's disposition can influence his intention to receive or not to receive a sacrament, but he pointed out that it is just as possible for a man to have the will and the intention to receive even though at the time he entertains no detestation and aversion for sin. But since in every case of a contumacious perseverance in manifest mortal sin Extreme Unction is to be withheld according to canon 942, so he argued, the refusal must be ascribed to the presence of the unworthy dispositions of the recipient.[72]

[70] "Quae verba sunt rite intelligenda. Agitur quippe de impoenitentia certa atque indubitata, de voluntate obstinata graviter mala qua quis sciens et volens perseverat in culpa lethali manifesta."—*De Extrema Unctione*, n. 263, § 1.

[71] "Quoad peccatores autem seu 'qui impoenitentes in manifesto peccato mortali contumaciter perseverant (can. 942),' notandum est imprimis non ex ipso capite defectus intentionis eis sacramentum denegari, ut quidem putare videntur . . . *sed ex ipso defectu bonae dispositionis requisitae ad fructum sacramenti,* ut patet tum ex generali praxi Ecclesiae denegantis sacramenta indignis, utut petentibus, tum ex ipsa ratione, nam intentio recipiendi sacramentum potest consistere etiam cum contumaci perseverantia in aliquo peccato mortali. . . ."—*De Extrema Unctione,* II, 701 (italics added).

[72] *Extreme Unction,* p. 228.

Claeys Boúúaert writes that the rule of canon 942 exists because attrition is a disposition always required in the recipient before one can administer Extreme Unction. In doubt about this disposition the patient should be anointed with the condition *"si non es impoenitens."* If a person so anointed recuperates and regains his senses and achieves better dispositions, so Claeys Boúúaert continues, he is to be anointed again with the condition now, *"si nondum es unctus."* [73]

Blat, Cance and Raus agree that the law of canon 942 denies the sacrament strictly because of a lack of sorrow on the part of the recipient.[74]

The authors who hold that the canon refers to the recipient's intention insist that the condition placed in cases of doubt should never be *"si dispositus es,"* but always *"si capax es,"* in order to insure the possibility of future reviviscence should the impenitent subject later elicit at least an act of attrition for his sins. According to them the sacrament should always be conferred solely with the condition that the impenitent recipient have the minimum required intention of receiving the sacrament.[75]

Strangely enough, and with apparent contradiction, even some of those authors who hold that the canon has essentially to do with the recipient's dispositions also warn against the use of a condition looking to the recipient's dispositions, and accordingly recommend simply the use of *"si capax es"* as the condition. Cappello says: "In practice never use *'si dispositus es,'* for if this condition is placed and the subject is really indisposed, even *though only materially indisposed,* the sacrament is null, and if he should later correct that defect no benefit would accrue from

[73] *Manuale Juris Canonici,* II, n. 179.

[74] ". . . sed *qui impoenitentes* idest: poenitentiam cordis, qua indigent, non habentes. . . ."—Blat, *Commentarium Textus Codicis Iuris Canonici,* III, n. 286; Cance, *Le Code de Droit Canonique,* II, n. 267, note 1; Raus, *Institutiones Canonicae,* n. 264.

[75] Jone, *op. cit.,* II, 170-171; Conte a Coronata, *op. cit.,* I, n. 552; Iorio, *op. cit.,* n. 766, § 3; Vermeersch-Creusen, *op. cit.,* II, n. 226; Mahoney, "Dispositions for Receiving Extreme Unction," *The Clergy Review,* XXXV (1951), 105.

this salutary sacrament."[76] Kilker rejected outright the condition *"si dispositus es."* Though he mentioned several others, he did not clearly state what condition he favored. He concluded by advising the priest to bestow the sacrament *"ad mentem ecclesiae"* or *"ad normam iuris."*[77]

It is difficult to comprehend precisely what Cappello could mean by the expression "materially indisposed." Only one "formally indisposed" can be said to contumaciously persevere in manifest mortal sin. Only he is under the ban of canon 942. Only doubt about this formal indisposition warrants a conditional anointing. A person indisposed through no fault of his own (materially?) could only mean one not in the state of grace because Penance has not been received, or an act of perfect contrition elicited. Yet such a one does have attrition, and this suffices for him to receive Extreme Unction validly, licitly, and fruitfully under the circumstances. He does not come under the prohibition of canon 942. For him there is no question of a conditional anointing, or of a future reviviscence. In short, it does not seem that one "materially indisposed" is impenitent in the sense envisioned by the canon.

Holding that the canon denies the sacrament because of bad dispositions, Blat very logically wrote that in doubt about these dispositions the condition is to be *"si non es impoenitens in mortali."*[78] Wouters saw the condition in its obvious sense as being *"si iam non contumaciter perseveres in peccato mortali,"* but he likewise contended that the canon does not rule out the use of

[76] ". . . in praxi numquam ministrandum esse sub conditione 'si dispositus es.' Nam si haec conditio ponitur et subiectum reapse est indispositum, licet materialiter tantum, sacramentum nullum efficitur, ita ut, si postea aegrotus defectum corrigat, nullum fructum huius salutaris sacramenti consequatur."—*De Extrema Unctione*, n. 312; "Conditio apposita debet esse, 'si capax es,' non autem, 'si es dispositus.' Nam secus in casu, quo infirmus esset quidem indispositus, sed capax, sacramentum postea (obice remoto) non revivisceret."—Prümmer, *Manuale Theologiae Moralis*, III, n. 580, note 1; Raus, *Institutiones Canonicae*, n. 264.

[77] *Extreme Unction*, pp. 245-247.

[78] *Commentarium Textus Codicis Iuris Canonici*, III, n. 286.

"si capax es." [79] In doubt, says Claeys Boúúaert, the anointing is given with the condition *"si non es impoenitens."* [80]

An ecclesiastical law is interpreted first according to the proper significance of its words in their text and context.[81] Such an interpretation of canon 942 can leave no doubt that this law deals with only one specific and particular point, the sinfulness of the subject, his disposition of soul. No matter how otherwise qualified a sick person may be to receive Extreme Unction validly, it is to be refused him if he is in conscious mortal sin and deliberately remains in that sinful state, not showing any sign of sorrow for his sin—if he is *"impoenitens in manifesto peccato mortali contumaciter perseverans."*

Canon Mahoney (1888-1954), with others, insisted that "the more obvious meaning of the terms of canon 942 present the case of a person who up to the moment of losing consciousness has refused to be anointed, thus giving no probability that a minimum intention to receive the sacrament exists in him.[82] Such an interpretation simply ignores the plain meaning of the words used by the Code and reads into the canon something it just does not say or even allude to. The law in canon 942 does not advert to either the recipient's request or to his refusal of the sacrament. Such a request or refusal, in its relation to the requisite intention, is dealt with directly in the following canon, 943, which thoroughly covers the question of intention in the recipient.[83] If a

[79] *Manuale Theologiae Moralis,* II, n. 583, § 4.

[80] *Manuale Juris Canonici,* II, n. 179. Claeys Boúúaert cites Vermeersch as indicating the use of the same condition which he did at the time. Since then there has come a reversal of this opinion, so that now, in the latest edition of Vermeersch's work, it is felt that the canon refers primarily to the intention as Noldin-Schmitt taught, and the suggestion is made that the condition be *"si capax es."*—Cf. Vermeersch-Creusen, *op. cit.,* II, n. 226, which in its latest (the seventh) edition appeared in 1954.

[81] Canon 18.

[82] Mahoney, *Priests' Problems* (selected and edited by L. L. McReavy, New York: Benziger Brothers, Inc., 1958), p. 193.

[83] Cf. *supra,* pp. 126-135. When one is conscious there is no problem in verifying the intention. Canon 943 indicates how this minimum intention can be verified in one who has lost the use of his reason or his senses.

person is denied Extreme Unction because he obstinately refused the sacrament to the very moment he became unconscious, he is denied it through the ruling of canon 943—because while he was conscious he did not manifest, even implicitly, an intention to receive it, or because while he was conscious he did not act in any way indicating that he even would have wanted the sacrament.[84] If this lack of intention was the result of unrepentant sinfulness, then Extreme Unction would be denied him through the ruling of canon 942 as well, but for a different reason, namely because of the unrepentant sinfulness itself. The two canons are in their import not the same, nor does the Code look to two canons both regulating objectively one and the same case.

Merkelbach and Woywod stated apodictically that an obstinate perseverance in manifest mortal sin excludes all will and intention to receive the sacrament, and that therefore the words of canon 942 really describe circumstances in which no intention exists, which in consequence necessitates a denial of the anointing.[85] That obstinate perseverance in mortal sin *can* and, perhaps, most often does exist in one who no longer has any intention of receiving the sacrament is true. That such perseverance in sin necessarily excludes any intention to receive the sacrament is not true, however. The one can exist without the other. A man can have a desire to visit Europe and yet be deathly afraid of both air and sea travel. Because of this disposition, this fear, he cannot accomplish what he desires, but his disposition does not prevent him from wanting to visit Europe. A person living in sin and denied the sacraments of Penance and Holy Communion may want to receive these sacraments and yet not be

84 " . . . cum suae mentis compotes essent, illud saltem implicite petierunt aut verisimiliter petiissent."—Canon 943.

85 "Nec existimetur in can. 942 huic regulae poni exceptionem, quia in illis qui in manifesto peccato contumaciter perseverant, iam non potest cum aliqua probabilitate supponi intentio recipiendi sacramentum; unde si de hac contumacia dubium sit, pariter dubium erit de intentione, non de sola dispositione."—Merkelbach, *Summa Theologiae Moralis,* III, n. 703, § 1; Woywod-Smith, *A Practical Commentary on the Code of Canon Law,* n. 865: "Obstinate perseverance in open mortal sin excludes all will and intention to receive a Sacrament."

disposed to giving up his state of sin. Does his perseverance in manifest mortal sin "exclude all will and intention to receive the sacraments"? Certainly not. The excommunicate is denied the sacraments by the Church, not because he does not have a sufficient intention to receive them, but because he perseveres in mortal sin. He may not have the courage or the strength to extricate himself from the sin that prevents his reception of the sacraments, but this does not amount to a positive retractation of that minimal habitual implicit intention necessary for a valid reception of the sacraments. If he could receive them, he would. The case is not uncommon. One could contumaciously persevere in manifest mortal sin and yet have enough of an intention to be validly confirmed or ordained or even baptized. To be willing to receive something as a gift and at the same time not willing to pay a price for it are two different things, both of which can be present in the same person at the same time. To want to receive Extreme Unction, or any sacrament, and yet not be willing to give up the sin that prevents its reception, are two different things, both of which can exist in the same person, at the same time.[86]

Impenitence does not rule out a sufficient intention, but all those who are contumaciously impenitent in manifest mortal sin, whether they be with or without a sufficient intention, are nevertheless prohibited in canon 942 from receiving Extreme Unction. The refusal is based squarely on their perverse disposition of soul.

If the *"quod si hoc dubium fuerit, conferatur sub conditione"* clause had not been added in canon 942, it is safe to say that no one would have interpreted the canon as treating of anything other than the recipient's disposition. The interpretation that the canon really deals with the intention derives not from the words of canon 942, but from what Mahoney calls "the universally accepted principle that a condition should turn only upon what is required for valid reception, in order that the possibility of reviviscence should not be excluded."[87] McCarthy sub-

[86] It should be remembered that an intention need not be measured by its intensity or efficacy.

[87] *Priests' Problems*, p. 193; "Conditio apponenda est illa quae respicit validitatem sacramenti, non vero quae respicit dispositionem ad sacramenti

scribes to the "intention" interpretation as "preferable from every standpoint." It accords perfectly, he says, "with the analogy of teaching and thus *escapes the difficulty* . . . that canon law espouses the doctrine that Extreme Unction may be conferred conditionally on the presence of dispositions which are necessary for liceity only."[88]

Noldin put it very strongly. He held that it is lawful to anoint *absolutely* whenever there is a doubt about the recipient's disposition. The sacraments are for the good of men, he said, and it is therefore licit to confer Extreme Unction even with the danger that its effect may be frustrated (though the sacrament is valid), and this not only when this sacrament is the only certain means of assuring salvation but also when it is deemed greatly useful to the patient.[89] Because it would upset this reasoning, Noldin dismisses the idea that canon 942 really means to deny Extreme Unction to those who lack the proper dispositions and to call for a conditional anointing if a doubt remains regarding the requisite dispositions of the recipient. Yet the Code seems too patently to deal with the element of a sinful disposition in canon 942 to put this evident interpretation off so easily.

The law means what it says: those who are judged to be

---

fructum, quia non est impedienda sacramenti reviviscentia. . . . Nec existimetur in can. 942 huic regulae poni exceptionem. . . ."—Merkelbach, *Summa Theologiae Moralis,* III, n. 705, § 6; "The rule of the Code . . . seems at first sight to be opposed to the common teaching of theologians that a sacrament should not be given conditionally but absolutely when there is doubt about the disposition of soul of the recipient. However, some commentators explain those words of the Code as a lack of will and intention to receive the sacrament and, *when interpreted in that sense, the Code agrees* with the common teaching of theologians."—Woywod-Smith, *A Practical Commentary on the Code of Canon Law,* n. 865 (italics added).

[88] *Problems in Theology,* I, 300.

[89] "Neque illicitum putetur, extremam unctionem *absolute* conferre ubi dispositio suscipientis est *dubia* et ideo sacramentum frustratur *effectu,* si infirmus reipsa sit indispositus. Etenim quia sacramenta sunt propter homines, licet sacramentum conferre cum periculo frustrandi effectum, non solum quando sacramentum est unicum medium procurandi certam animae salutem, sed etiam quando illud infirmo magnam affert utilitatem."—*Summa Theologiae Moralis,* III, n. 446 (italics added).

consciously and unrepentantly in mortal sin cannot licitly be anointed, quite apart from any other consideration. Should there be doubt about the requisite dispositions, the sacrament is conferred with the condition that they actually exist. The basis of this denial is founded in the natural law itself. Noldin himself expressed it in an earlier section of his volume on the sacraments:

> Minister *tenetur per se sub gravi sacramenta negare indignis.* a. Duplex potissimum est ratio, ob quam indignis neganda sint sacramenta; *ex fidelitate:* cum enim minister non sit dominus sacramentorum, ea ut fidelis dispensator secundum voluntatem domini sui administrare debet; sed est contra voluntatem Christi, ut indignis dispensentur; *Nolite dare sanctum canibus, neque mittatis margaritas vestras ante porcos. Ex caritate et religione;* ipse enim minister, qui sacramentum dispensat indigno, *ad gravissimum sacrilegium cooperatur;* fideles autem grave scandalum paterentur, si viderent peccatori notorie indigno et *impoenitenti* administrari sacramenta. b. *Indigni* sunt . . . *qui cognoscuntur esse in statu peccati mortalis absque voluntate sese emendandi.*[90]
>
> Qui scienter sine debita dispositione sacramentum suscipit, *gravissimum irreverentiae sacrilegium* committit.[91]

By divine law there are excluded from the reception of the sacraments all those who lack the dispositions necessary for receiving them *fruitfully.* It is sanctifying grace that is required for the sacraments of the living, and attrition for the sacraments of the dead.[92] One who contumaciously perseveres in manifest mortal sin does not have attrition, and any administration of Extreme Unction to him in spite of this lack of disposition is inescapably sacrilegious. It does not enter into the picture at all that he may develop attrition later, or that the sacrament can possibly revive. Unless he is here and now attrite there can be no reception or

[90] *Summa Theologiae Moralis,* III, n. 36. Cf. also Ferreres, *Compendium Theologiae Moralis,* II, n. 284; ". . . sequitur in ministro obligatio ea (sacramenta) non ministrandi incapacibus *vel indignis.* Id enim per se est grave peccatum sacrilegii in quantum sacrum profanationi exponitur."—Merkelbach, *Summa Theologiae Moralis,* III, n. 88.

[91] Noldin, *op. cit.,* III, n. 42, § 2.

[92] Conte a Coronata, *De Sacramentis,* I, n. 67.

administration of Extreme Unction except a sacrilegious one,[93] and this is forbidden not by ecclesiastical law alone but by divine law as well. It is abhorrent to consider lawful the achievement of an intended possible good end through the evil means of a sacrilegious administration of a sacrament. For a priest deliberately to anoint a person whom he knows to have persevered knowingly and willingly in mortal sin on the "hope" that perhaps a future act of attrition will be elicited and the sacrament (sacrilegiously received and sacrilegiously administered) will revive is to do precisely this. Once a priest is personally convinced of the subject's impenitence—and this is what canon 942 envisions—and he nevertheless proceeds to administer Extreme Unction, he does so sacrilegiously—and this is exactly what the canon forbids.[94]

So serious is the obligation of a minister of the sacraments to administer them to only those who are properly disposed to receive them, that canon 2364 prescribes the penalty of suspension for a priest who dares administer them otherwise.

> Minister qui ausus fuerit Sacramenta administrare illis qui iure *sive divino* sive ecclesiastico *eadem recipere* prohibentur, suspendatur ab administrandis Sacramentis per tempus prudenti Ordinarii arbitrio definiendum aliisque poenis pro gravitate culpae puniatur, firmis peculiaribus poenis in aliqua huius generis delicta iure statutis.[95]

If anointing the impenitent sacrilegiously is an evil, so too is the withholding of Extreme Unction unless there is moral certitude—the highest kind of certitude a human minister of the sacraments can have—about this impenitence in mortal sin, for the basic right of a Christian to receive the sacramental aids for salvation can never be denied him unless it is known with certitude that he is not disposed for or not capable of receiving them.

93 ". . . constat fore peccatum grave dare sacramentum homini habenti obicem."—Suarez, Disp. XLII, Sect. I, n. 8—*Opera Omnia*, XXII, 850.

94 One must look to the principles which regulate the denial of the sacraments to the unworthy in order to determine when a *material* cooperation of the priest in a sacrilegious reception is permitted. The possibility of the sacrament's reviviscence is by itself not a sufficient warrant. Cf. Prümmer, *Manuale Theologiae Moralis*, III, nn. 75-80.

95 Canon 2364 (italics added).

To protect this fundamental right the Code added in canon 942 the provision that, if there is any doubt at all that one is actually contumaciously persevering in manifest mortal sin he should be anointed conditionally.[96]

The obvious sense of the condition, as Wouters and Blat pointed out,[97] is *"si non es impoenitens in peccato mortali,"* or simply, *"si es dispositus."*[98] The condition is intended by the canon to turn precisely on the disposition of the recipient in order to preclude the possibility of a sacrilegious—even if valid—administration. Even if one uses *"si capax es"* (in order not to condition the sacrament on dispositions) and in so doing intends to administer Extreme Unction as the Church directs in canon 942, he actually anoints on the condition that the recipient is disposed, for if he is not disposed then the Church wants the priest to forego the conferring of the sacrament on him.[99] In doing what the Church desires, the priest intends to administer the anointing to those who are disposed to receive it worthily, and to deny it to those who are not disposed thus to receive it.

It seems questionable to argue that a generally accepted theological principle forbids the conditional conferring of a sacrament when there is doubt about the dispositions of soul of the recipient.[100] When such a working principle is set against what derives from the divine law, that is, the obligation of a dispenser of the sacraments not to give them sacrilegiously to the positively unworthy, it is the principle (not doctrine) that must yield, and

[96] "Quod si hoc dubium fuerit, conferatur sub conditione."—Canon 942.

[97] Wouters, *Manuale Theologiae Moralis,* II, n. 583, § 4; Blat, *Commentarium Textus Codicis Iuris Canonici,* III, n. 286.

[98] The condition need not be specifically formulated or expressed in the sacramental formula.

[99] If, in using the condition *"si capax es"* the minister strictly intended to confer the sacrament validly if the subject filled all requirements for a valid reception, despite the presence of bad dispositions, the anointing might be valid, but the priest would administer the sacrament in a manner contrary to the positive will of the Church as expressed in canon 942, and his ministration would be at least materially sacrilegious.

[100] Cf. Woywod, *op. cit.,* n. 865; McCarthy, *op. cit.,* I, 300; Noldin, *op. cit.,* III, n. 446; Merkelbach, *op. cit.,* III, n. 705.

not the divine law, when it engenders an obligation that may seem incompatible with the accepted principle.

In the old Ritual, Extreme Unction was refused to the impenitent and to all persons dying in mortal sin.[101] This exclusion was absolute and outright, PENITUS *denegetur,* in order to prevent the irreverent use of the sacrament. Many theologians, however, correctly reasoning that not all those unfortunate people who seem to die in manifest mortal sin are necessarily without habitual attrition—i.e., contumaciously impenitent—regarded it as lawful to employ a conditional anointing in cases of doubt obviously centering on the recipient's sinful disposition, on the very minimum of attrition requisite for a fruitful reception of the sacrament. Others disallowed the use of such a condition.

To prevent any sacrilegious administration of Extreme Unction to the unworthy, and at the same time to insure that no one who really can receive it validly and fruitfully be deprived of this sacrament, the present Code has inserted the provision for a conditional anointing in doubt about the persistence of evil dispositions.[102] Such a provision favors the recipient by favoring

[101] "Impoenitentibus vero et qui in manifesto peccato mortali moriuntur . . . *penitus* denegetur."—*Rituale Romanum* (*1614 ed.*), Tit. V, Cap. I, n. 8.

[102] The Church is well aware of the probability of reviviscence for Extreme Unction, but again this is beside the point. The honoring of this probability does not justify a sacrilegious administration. Even if the sacrament did later revive (and this will often seem a slim possibility if it must be accomplished through the sudden repentance of an obstinately impenitent sinner who is now unconscious) the wrongful administration would thereby not be righted. It certainly seems unreasonable to believe that God intended His sacraments to be employed in such a way. He sanctifies no person against that person's will. He gives grace to those who are disposed to accept it, but they must be disposed before and not after they receive it. The sacraments are not magical, and though they produce their effects by their very operation (*ex opere operato*), they do not sanctify a man in spite of all lack of effort on his part. The first effect of Extreme Unction upon a recipient in mortal sin is to forgive that sin, so that he will be able to receive the distinctive sacramental graces of that sacrament. In this case it operates first as a sacrament of the dead, and then as a sacrament of the living. But if there is no attrition in the recipient, no sin can be forgiven, and Extreme Unction cannot effect the forgiveness of sin and thus dispose the subject to receive its particular

the administration of the sacrament rather than its denial, but it also safeguards both the sanctity of Extreme Unction and the right of Christians to receive the sacraments.

Canon 942 does not evince an isolated instance in which the Church prescribes a conditional administration of the sacraments when there is doubt about the requisite dispositions. Canon 731, § 2, forbids the conferring of the sacraments on schismatics and heretics, even though they ask for them in good faith, unless they have first become reconciled with the Church. In its replies of 1916 and 1941,[103] however, the Holy Office allowed unconscious schismatics to be anointed *conditionally,* especially if from attendant circumstances "it can be legitimately conjectured that they have, at least implicitly, rejected their errors," and provided that scandal is avoided. On what condition does the Church direct this anointing to be given? A schismatic is validly baptized, has the necessary intention (in the cases to which the Holy Office replied the schismatic had even asked for the sacrament expressly), and in this situation is sick and in danger of death. Every element necessary for *valid* reception is present, and it is evident that the schismatic is also disposed to receive the sacrament fruitfully, and yet the Holy Office allowed only conditional anointing.

According to canon 731, § 2, and these responses, what is always required to justify an administration to schismatics is reconciliation or union with the Church, and it is on the disposition to such a reconciliation that the condition is placed. There is no question here of a doubtful capacity; there is question simply of a doubtful disposition of faith in the true Church. Conte a Coronata, who later, when speaking of canon 942, says that a condition should never be centered on dispositions, holds that in the conditional anointing of schismatics according to the re-

sacramental alleviation. And if because of the recipient's impenitence the sacrament cannot achieve what would be its primary effect *in this case,* how can it be said to achieve its proper effect, the conferring of rights to special graces of alleviation during sickness, which conferral presupposes a subject to be in the state of grace? The whole question of the reviviscence of Extreme Unction is not without many unsolved difficulties.

[103] Cf. *supra,* pp. 140-141.

sponses the condition is to be, "... *si vis in Ecclesia catholica mori, si tuos errores saltem interne reiecisti, aut alia aequivalens.*"[104]

The Church, guardian and dispenser of the sacraments, feels that it is wrong to administer the sacraments to those who in their faith are not united with the Church, no matter how qualified otherwise they may be.[105] Unless it is certain that a schismatic has at least implicitly been united to the Church, he can be anointed only conditionally.

The statement that sacraments are never conditioned on requirements that look only to their licit or their worthy reception does not, in fact, seem to be true.

Canon 942, since it deals with the denial of a right, must be interpreted strictly.[106] Before Extreme Unction can be refused to an impenitent sinner, every condition contained in this canon must be fulfilled, and fulfilled with moral certainty. It must be certain that he is contumaciously persevering in manifest mortal sin. Whenever there is any doubt about any of these the sacrament is not to be denied to a subject but is to be given conditionally.[107]

MANIFEST MORTAL SIN. The recipient must be in a state that is not only objectively mortally sinful but also subjectively so, for actual, formal mortal sin is the basis of the denial of the sacrament.[108] If a man is known to be inculpably ignorant or to possess an erroneous conscience about the gravity of sins that are objectively mortal, he is not in manifest, patent, mortal sin.

104 *De Sacramentis,* I, n. 72. These are also the conditions suggested by Umberg, who excluded the use of "*si capax es*" because of the absence of all doubt about the capacity for a valid reception.—"Sacramenta Acatholicis nonnisi condicionate Conferenda," *Periodica de Re Morali, Canonica, Liturgica,* XXXVII (1948), 98-102.

105 Cf. Umberg, "art. cit.," p. 98.

106 Canon 19.

107 O'Kane, *Notes on the Rubrics,* n. 849.

108 Mahoney said that the denial enacted in canon 942 serves as a penal measure, but there is no plausible foundation for this view. Cf. Mahoney, *Priest's Problems,* p. 193.

Manifest does not mean here public or well-known; it means evident in his own particular case. It means that he himself knows that what he does is mortally sinful, that no factor exists which could diminish the moral imputability of his mortally sinful act or state.[109]

CONTUMACIOUS PERSEVERANCE. Contumacy involves deliberate intent, and deliberate intent presupposes knowledge. Perseverance means the remaining in a certain state over a period of time. If a man in manifest mortal sin, fully conscious of his situation, puts off going to confession until next week he perseveres in manifest mortal sin (unless he has elicited an act of contrition meanwhile), but his perseverance is not contumacious, for he is not averse to remedying the situation, he intends to extricate himself from sin sometime, he has attrition. If, on the other hand, he is fully conscious of his sinful condition and yet has no intention of giving up that sinful state, he perseveres in manifest mortal sin contumaciously, knowingly, and willingly. Without a purpose of amendment there is no attrition, so that as long as a man remains in this state he falls under the definition of an impenitent sinner, to whom Extreme Unction is denied.

As long as the sick man is conscious it is not difficult to learn from him whether he is in fact penitent and wishes to amend his life. If his sinfulness involves living in a sinful situation, like an irremediably invalid marriage, some declaration must be had of his intention to rectify matters if and when he recovers, says Connell, and if he gives no assurance of this at all the sacrament cannot be given.[110]

In 1892 the Holy Office declared that those who order their bodies to be cremated and persist in their intention, even after being admonished of its prohibition along with the consequent denial of the sacraments and Christian burial, cannot be given the sacraments. The reply added, however, that whether the admonition was to be given must be decided by the priest—mindful always that all scandal be avoided—in each individual case

[109] Cf. Kilker, *Extreme Unction*, p. 230.

[110] Connell, "Ministration to a Divorced Man," *AER*, CXLII (1960), 345.

according to the principles given by theologians for leaving good faith undisturbed.[111]

In 1898 The Sacred Congregation for the Propagation of the Faith issued a response declaring that Catholics who had joined condemned societies and whose membership in them was well known could not be given the sacraments before they were absolved and became reconciled with the Church. If they were unable to make a formal retractation, because of weakness or unconsciousness, then it sufficed if they had shown some sign of repentance and devotion while still able to do so.[112]

Extreme Unction is to be denied to those conscious patients, said Kern, who obstinately refuse to satisfy a serious obligation, e.g., restitution, or the removal of an unnecessary proximate danger of sin or scandal. The non-fulfillment of such an obligation is incompatible with repentance, since it spells out a complete absence of a genuine sorrow for sin.

The rule for dealing with the unconscious, said Kern, is that they are never to be considered positively unworthy unless this fact has been proved *with moral certitude.*[113]

The only judgment that can be made about the dispositions of a man who is now unconscious must rest upon what was known about him before he became unconscious. If a sinner really perseveres impenitent in mortal sin to the moment he loses consciousness, there is *moral* certitude that he perseveres in that state after losing consciousness.[114] Lynch feels that there is both intrinsic reason as well as extrinsic authority to justify the conclusion that Extreme Unction, as well as Baptism and Penance, "may be given conditionally to the unconscious, *whatever their*

[111] S.C.S. Off., 27 iul. 1892—*Fontes,* n. 1158. This reply is indicated as a source for canon 942 in the Code.

[112] S.C. de Prop. Fide, 10 maii. 1898—*Fontes,* n. 4937. Also a source for canon 942 in the Code.

[113] Kern, *De Extrema Unctione,* p. 321; "Ad hoc autem ut indignus quis habeatur, de ipsa indignitate moraliter certo constare debet."—Conte a Coronata, *De Sacramentis,* I, n. 67; Cappello, *De Extrema Unctione,* n. 264; Suarez, Disp. XLII, Sect. I, n. 6—*Opera Omnia,* XXII, 850.

[114] Cf. *supra,* pp. 131-133.

previous disposition may have been, provided always that scandal be avoided." [115]

The writer cannot see the intrinsic reason that could support this doctrine, which either limits the scope of canon 942 to those who are conscious, or renders its prohibition totally meaningless as soon as an impenitent sinner loses consciousness. One always begins with the presumption that an unconscious recipient's dispositions are good, *if nothing is known about them before he loses consciousness*. But if from what is known of his disposition before he lost consciousness there looms up a grave suspicion that he did not have even attrition for his sin, he should be anointed conditionally. If from his deportment during the moments of consciousness he was definitely known to be inexcusably unrepentant of his manifest mortal sin—rare as one hopes this might be—he cannot be anointed even conditionally. That state of impenitence cannot reasonably be presumed to change upon the loss of consciousness. It does matter what his previous dispositions were. These are the only dispositions on which one can act when administering to the unconscious.[116]

Canon 942 makes no distinction between the conscious and the unconscious who persevere in mortal sin. It includes both, for what makes it evil to confer the sacrament to these non-disposed subjects when they are conscious remains the same when they are unconscious.[117] The possibility that the sinner's interior dispositions could change in consequence of a special grace does not alter matters, for such a change could be known only to God. It is beyond the scope of a human minister and his sacramental ministrations.

When a priest must deal with the impenitent sinner mentioned in canon 942, it is important to ask those close to him whether the patient at any time demonstrated any devotion, or furnished any sign of sorrow for sin or love of God, even the slightest. It

[115] *Theological Studies*, XVII (1956), 196 (italics added).

[116] Cf. Suarez, Disp. XLII, Sect. I, n. 8 and n. 10—*Opera Omnia*, XXII, 851; Laymann, *Theologia Moralis*, II, Lib. V, tract. VIII, cap. IV, n. 3.

[117] Cf. Cappello, *De Extrema Unctione*, n. 263, where he says that this canon refers to the unconscious.

is on such indications that a priest can base at least a doubt about the sinner's continued contumacious impenitence. The presence of such a doubt would justify the priest in anointing conditionally, for he must remember that before he can deny the sacrament outright he must be certain beyond doubt about the sinner's contumacious perseverance in manifest mortal sin. Cappello believes that such certitude will be rarely attained.[118]

But man is capable of anything, and so there can be times when a priest has to deal with one who contumaciously perseveres in manifest mortal sin. The minister of the sacraments must with a human approach (*modo humano*) make his judgment about the recipient to whom he ministers. If the priest is convinced beyond all doubt that the recipient has no sorrow for sin at all, he can do nothing but withhold the sacrament completely. If he doubts whether the patient has any sorrow, he should anoint conditionally on the *condition that he be really disposed,* for only to one so disposed does Christ wish to confer his grace.

A person who loses consciousness and is dying in the very act of committing a mortal sin is not thereby necessarily excluded by canon 942 from being a recipient of Extreme Unction.[119] The fact of this sin alone does not give any certitude that attrition is lacking in this sinner. Even a habitual sinner can have an habitual attrition for his sinfulness. Contumacious perserver-

[118] "Si agitur de aegroto sensibus destituto, regula generalis haec est; quoties prudenter praesumitur, infirmum habere debitam intentionem, licite ei confertur extrema unctio, nisi *plena certitudine* constet eum esse *positive* indignum. Quae certitudo in praxi vix habetur. Quare ad sacramentum licite ministrandum sufficit quaelibet probabilis etiam levis coniectura de existentia requisitae conditionis ex parte suscipientis; quae practice semper aut fere semper adesse merito praesumitur."—*De Extrema Unctione,* n. 264, § 2.

[119] The earlier law did, however, exclude "*qui in manifesto peccato mortali moriuntur*" (*Rituale Romanum of 1614,* Tit. V, Cap. I, n. 8), and authors taught that one stricken unconscious in the very act of sin, in fornication, blasphemy, theft, etc., was in a state of manifest mortal sin. In consequence he lacked the needed disposition and accordingly had to be denied Extreme Unction. Cf. Baruffaldo, *Ad Rituale Romanum Commentaria,* Tit. XXVII, n. 8.

ance in manifest mortal sin means more than being in the state of sin. In the former condition there cannot exist the needed disposition for being forgiven, in the latter there can be such a disposition, that is, sorrow in the form of attrition. The Code is very precise in canon 942, clearly indicating that it is the sinner who has not even attrition, and not simply one who is in mortal sin, who is excluded from what would be a sacrilegious reception.[120]

[120] "Nec deneganda (extrema unctio) . . . iis, qui in statu vel ipso actu peccati, signo poenitentiae non manifestato, sensibus privantur."—Cappello, *op. cit.*, n. 264, § 3; Genicot-Salsmans, *Institutiones Theologiae Moralis,* II, n. 427.

CONCLUSIONS

1. Neither the Epistle of St. James nor the Council of Trent taught that any danger of death in an illness is an intrinsically necessary requisite in the recipient of Extreme Unction. The practice of the Church for at least the first nine centuries gives no indication that the anointing was limited to only those sick persons who were considered in danger. Although, in fact, the administration of this sacrament has for perhaps ten centuries been reserved for the sick whose life is endangered, the degree of the danger in which one is is allowed to become anointed has lessened notably during that time. The imminent (in articulo) danger as postulated in the twelfth, thirteenth and fourteenth centuries gave way to a proximate danger, and this in turn to even a remote danger. (Cf. pp. 14-51.)

In fulfilment of the condition stated in canon 940, § 1, regarding the presence of a danger of death it suffices that, from the attendant circumstances, some interested person reasonably judge that the sickness in the patient raises a real probability that death *could* follow from it. (Cf. pp. 54-67.)

Canon 940, § 1, does not imply that this danger is a condition postulated for the valid administration and reception of the anointing. The writer believes that this canon sets but a norm which governs the discipline of the administration of the sacrament—a requisite binding *sub gravi,* indeed, but affecting only the lawful or licit, not the valid, use of Extreme Unction. (Cf. pp. 67-81.)

2. The new danger postulated for a reanointing in the same illness is not of the same character as the danger postulated for an initial anointing. The expressions *periculum mortis* in canon 940, § 1, and *discrimen vitae* in canon 940, § 2, are not synonymous or interchangeable. New danger in the same illness means a new crisis, a new imminent struggle for life, a new proximate danger. *Convaluerit* in canon 940, § 2, implies, not a recovery from *all* danger, but a recovery from the crisis that attended the danger, i.e., from a *discrimen vitae.* (Cf. pp. 81-100.)

3. Canon 943 deals, not directly with the intention to receive

the sacrament, but immediately with the petition, actual or interpretative, by which the minimum habitual implicit intention can be judged to exist in an unconscious recipient. A *positive and morally inexcusable* refusal to receive Extreme Unction up to the very time when one loses consciousness puts one outside the terms of canon 943, and thus excludes him from the reception of the sacrament. (Cf. pp. 126-134.)

4. Children, as soon as they are considered capable of distinguishing right from wrong in any degree, even though they are not yet seven years old, and may not yet have received first Holy Communion, or ever have approached the sacrament of Penance, should be anointed when they become seriously ill. In doubt about their attainment of the use of reason, they should be anointed conditionally. (Cf. pp. 101-104.)

5. Canon 942 denies Extreme Unction to those serious sinners who lack even attrition for their sins. The refusal is based on the natural divine law which forbids all sacrilegious administration of the sacraments. In order to forestall all possible sacrilegious administration and reception on the one hand, and to protect the right of a Catholic to receive the sacrament unless he is certainly and positively excluded on the other hand, the law calls for the use of a conditional administration when there exists some doubt regarding the cessation of impenitence. The condition turns on the presence or absence of this disposition and not on the presence or absence of an intention to receive the sacrament. The writer believes that an intention to receive the sacrament could co-exist with a recipient's lack of attrition for his sins. (Cf. pp. 150-172.)

BIBLIOGRAPHY

Sources and Encyclopedias

Acta Apostolicae Sedis, Commentarium Officiale, Romae, 1909-1928; Civitate Vaticana, 1929-

Acta Ecclesiae Mediolanensis, Mediolani, 1599.

Acta Genuina SS. Oecumenici Concilii Tridentini, edita ab Augustino Theiner, 2 vols., Zagabriae (in Croatia): Typis et Sumptibus Societatis Bibliophilae, 1874.

Canon Law Digest, The, 4 vols. and supplement, Milwaukee: Bruce, Vol. I, 1934, Vol. II, 1943, Vol. III, 1954, edited by T Lincoln Bouscaren; Vol. IV, 1958, and supplement, edited by T. Lincoln Bouscaren and James I. O'Connor.

Codex Iuris Canonici, Pii X Pontificis Maximi iussu digestus Benedicti Papae XV auctoritate promulgatus, Romae, 1917; Reprint, Westminster, Md.: The Newman Press, 1951.

Codicis Iuris Canonici Fontes, cura Emi Petri Card. Gasparri editi, 9 vols., Romae (postea Civitate Vaticana): Typis Polyglottis Vaticanis, 1923-1939 (Vols. VII-IX, ed. cura et studio Emi Iustiniani Card. Serédi).

Catechismus Romanus ex decreto Concilii Tridentini ad Parochos Pii V Pontificis Maximi iussu editus, editio quarta, Ratisbonae: Pustet, 1907.

Concilium Tridentinum Diariorum, Actorum, Epistolarum, Tractatuum, Nova Collectio, edidit Societas Goerresiana, Vol. VI, Actorum Pars III Volumen I, ex collectionibus Sebastiani Merkle, auxit, edidit, illustravit Theobaldus Freudenberger, Friburgi Brisgoviae: Herder, 1950.

Collectio Rituum, Milwaukee: Ex Typographia Bruce, 1954.

Corpus Iuris Canonici, editio Lipsiensis secunda post Aemelii Ludovici Richteri curas ad librorum manu scriptorum et Editionis Romanae fidem recognovit et adnotatione critica instruxit Aemilius Friedberg, 2 vols., Lipsiae: Ex Officina Bernhardi Tauschnitz, 1922.

Dictionnaire de Théologie Catholique, 15 vols. in 30, Paris: Letouzey et Ané, 1903-

Enchiridion Symbolorum, Definitionum et Declarationum de Rebus Fidei et Morum, Henrici Denzinger, quod post Clementem Bannwart et Ioannem B. Umberg, S.I., denuo edidit Carolus Rahner, 30. ed., Friburgi Brisgoviae: Herder, 1955.

Enciclopedia Cattolica, 12 vols., Città del Vaticano: Ente per L'Enciclopedia Cattolica e per Il Libra Cattolico, 1948-1954.

Encyclopedia Americana, The, 30 vols., 1957 edition, Chicago: Americana Corporation, 1957.

Hardouin, Jean, *Acta Conciliorum et Epistolae Decretales ac Constitutiones Summorum Pontificum,* 11 vols. in 12, Parisiis, 1714-1715.

Mansi, Ioannes, *Sacrorum Conciliorum Nova et Amplissima Collectio,* 53 vols. in 60; Vols. I-XXXV, Florentiae, 1758-1798; Vols. XXXVI-LIII, Parisiis, 1901-1927.

Martène, Edmundus, *De Antiquis Ecclesiae Ritibus,* nova ed., 3 vols., Venetiis, 1783.

Morin, Germanus, *Sancti Caesarii Arelatensis Sermones,* 2 vols. (*Corpus Christianorum, Series Latina,* Vols. CIII-CIV), Turnholti: Typographia Brepols, 1953.

Muratori, Ludovicus Antonius, *Liturgia Romana Vetus,* 2 vols., Venetiis, 1748.

Patriarchalis Ecclesiae Venetiarum Synodus XXXI, Venetiis, 1957.

Prima Romana Synodus MDCCCCLX, Città del Vaticano: Typis Polyglottis Vaticanis, 1960.

Rituale Romanum Pauli V Pont. Max. iussu editum, Antverpiae: Ex Architypographia Plantiniana, 1744.

Rituale Romanum Pauli V Pont. Max. iussu editum aliorumque Pontificum cura recognitum atque ad normam Codicis Iuris Canonici accommodatum Ssmi D.N. Pii Papae XII auctoritate ordinatum et auctum, New York: Benziger, 1953.

Schroeder, Henry J., *Canons and Decrees of the Council of Trent,* St. Louis: Herder, 1941.

Schema Codicis Iuris Canonici, cum notis Petri Card. Gasparri, 4 vols. in 2, Romae: Typis Polyglottis Vaticanis, 1912-1914.

Synodus Dioecesana Aprutina et Hatriensis, Teramo: Cooperativa Tipografica "Ars et Labor," 1956.

Synodus Dioecesana Bergomensis XXXVI, Bergamo: Editrice S.E.S.A., 1952.

Synodus Dioecesana Novariensis XIX (1955), Novara, 1955.

Synodus Pistoriensis et Pratensis (1892), Pistorii: Ex Typographia Episcopali Fratrum Bracalium, 1893.

Synodus Dioecesana I Ravennatensis et Cerviensis (1955), Faenza: Stabilimento Grafico F.lli Lega, 1956.

Synodus Dioecesana Regiensis, Reggio Emilia: Societate Editrice Age, 1956.

Reference Works

Abbo, John A.–Hannan, Jerome D., *The Sacred Canons,* 2 vols., revised ed., St. Louis: Herder, 1957.

Aertnys, J.–Damen, C. A., *Theologia Moralis,* 2 vols., 15. ed., 7. ed. post Codicem, Taurini: Marietti, 1947.

Alphonsus Liguori, St., *Theologia Moralis,* editio nova, cura P. Leonardo Gaudé, 4 vols., Romae: Typographia Vaticana, 1905-1912.

Arndt, William F.–Gingrich, F. Wilbur, *A Greek-English Lexicon of the New Testament and Other Early Christian Literature,* a translation and adaptation of Walter Bauer's *griechisch-deutsches Wörterbuch zu den Schriften des neuen Testaments und der übrigen urchristlichen*

Literatur, 4th revised and augmented edition, 1952, London: Cambridge University Press, 1957.

Arregui, Antonius M., *Summarium Theologiae Moralis,* 20. ed., (17. ed. Latina), Bilbao: Editorial El Mensajero del Corazón de Jesús, 1952.

Augustine, Charles, *A Commentary on The New Code of Canon Law,* 8 vols., St. Louis: Herder, 1918-1922.

Ballerini, Antonius, *Opus Theologicum Morale,* absolvit et edidit Dominicus Palmieri, 7 vols., Prati: Ex Officina Libraria Giachetti, Filii et Soc., 1889-1893.

Baruffaldo, Hieronymus, *Ad Rituale Romanum Commentaria,* editio tertia Veneta, Venetiis: Typographia Balleoniana, 1792.

Benedictus XIV, *De Synodo Dioecesana,* 3 vols., novissima editio auctior et castigatior, Romae: Ex Typographia I. Baptistae Cannetti, 1783.

Beste, Udalricus, *Introductio in Codicem,* editio quarta, Neapoli: M. D'Auria, 1956.

Billuart, Charles René, *Summa Sancti Thomae,* editio nova, 8 vols., Paris: Apud Victor Palmé, 1874-1886.

Blat, Albertus, *Commentarium Textus Codicis Iuris Canonici,* 5 vols. in 6, Vol. III, Pars I, 2. ed., Romae: Ex Typographia Pontificia in Instituto Pii IX, 1924.

Bonaventura, St., *Opera Omnia,* 10 vols., Quaracchi (Florentiae), 1882-1902.

Bord, J. B., *L'Extrême-Onction, d'après l'Epître de Saint Jacques,* Examinée dans la tradition, Bruges: Charles Beyaert, 1923.

Brzana, Stanislaus J., *Remains of Sin and Extreme Unction According to Theologians after Trent,* Rome: Catholic Book Agency, 1953.

Bucceroni, Ianuarius, *Institutiones Theologiae Moralis,* 6. ed., 4 vols., Romae: Ex Typographia Pontificia in Instituto Pii IX, 1914-1915.

Cance, Adrien, *Le Code de Droit Canonique,* 3 vols., Vol. II, 8. ed., Paris: Librairie Lecoffre, 1951.

Cappello, Felix M., *Tractatus Canonico-Moralis de Sacramentis,* 5 vols., Vol. III, *De Extrema Unctione,* 4. ed., Taurini: Marietti, 1958.

Chaine, Joseph, *L'Epître de Saint Jacques,* Paris: J. Gabalda et Fils, 1927.

Chavasse, A., *Étude sur l'Onction des Infirmes dans l'Eglise Latine* du III au XIe Siècle, Tôme I, *De Troisième Siècle à la Réforme Carolingienne,* Lyons: Librairie du Sacré-Coeur, 1942.

Claeys Boúúaert, Ferdinandus–Simenon, G., *Manuale Juris Canonici,* 3 vols., Vol. II, 3. ed., Leodii: Dessain, 1947.

Clericatus, Ioannes, *De Sacramentis Baptismi Confirmationis atque Extremae Unctionis Decisiones,* Venetiis, 1703.

Conte a Coronata, Matthaeus, *Institutiones Iuris Canonici, De Sacramentis Tractatus Canonicus,* 3 vols., Vol. I, editio altera emendata et aucta, Taurini: Marietti, 1951.

Cornelius a Lapide, *Commentarium in Sacram Scripturam,* 21 vols., Neapoli, 1859.

Cuttaz, F., *Remède Divin pour les Chrétiens Malades,* Paris: Desclée & Cie., 1950.

D'Angelo, Sosio, *La Morte Reale ed Apparente e l'Amministrazione dei Sacramenti,* Torino: Lega Italiana Cattolica Editrice, 1927.

Davis, Henry, *Moral and Pastoral Theology,* 5. ed. revised and enlarged, 4 vols., New York: Sheed and Ward, 1946.

DeClercq, Charles, *Traité de Droit Canonique,* publié sous la direction de Raoul Naz, 4 vols., 2. ed., Vol. II, Paris: Letouzey et Ané, Editeurs, 1947.

Dionysius Carthusianus, *Opera Omnia,* 42 vols. and index, Montreuil sur Mer, 1896-1913.

Doronzo, Emmanuel, *De Extrema Unctione,* 2 vols., Milwaukee: Bruce, 1954-1955.

Elbel, Benjamin, *Theologia Moralis,* novis curis edidit P. F. Irenaeus Bierbaum, 9 vols. in 3, Paderbornae, 1891-1892.

Fanfani, Ludovicus J., *Manuale Theorico-Practicum Theologiae Moralis,* 4 vols., Romae: Libraria Ferrari, 1949-1951.

Ferreres, Ioannes B., *Compendium Theologiae Moralis,* 13. ed., 7. ed. post Codicem, 2 vols., Barcinone: Eugenius Subirana, 1928.

Genicot, E.-Salsmans, I., *Institutiones Theologiae Moralis,* 17. ed., quam paravit A. Gortebecke, 2 vols., Bruxellis: L'Edition Universelle, 1951.

Gerson, Jean, *Summa Theologica et Canonica in Sex Libros Digesta,* Venetiis, 1587.

Gotti, Vincentius Ludovicus, *Theologia Scholastico-Dogmatica,* 3 vols., Vol. III, Venetiis, 1763.

Healy, Edwin F., *Medical Ethics,* Chicago: Loyola University Press, 1956.

Iorio, Thomas A., *Theologia Moralis,* 3. ed., recognita et emendata, 3 vols., Neapoli: M. D'Auria, 1946-1947.

Jone, Heribertus, *Commentarium in Codicem Iuris Canonici,* 3 vols., Paderbornae: Officina Libraria F. Schöningh, 1950-1955.

Kern, Josephus, *De Sacramento Extremae Unctionis Tractatus Dogmaticus,* Ratisbonae: Sumptibus et Typis Friderici Pustet, 1907.

Kilker, Adrian, *Extreme Unction,* The Catholic University of America Canon Law Studies, No. 32, Washington, D. C.: The Catholic University of America, 1926.

King, Lester S., *The Medical World of the Eighteenth Century,* Chicago: University of Chicago Press, 1958.

Koch, Anthony, *A Handbook of Moral Theology,* adapted and edited by Arthur Preuss, 5 vols., St. Louis: Herder, 1918-1924.

Kryger, Henry S., *The Doctrine of the Effects of Extreme Unction in Its Historical Development,* The Catholic University of America Studies in Sacred Theology, Second Series, No. 13, Washington, D. C.: The Catholic University of America Press, 1949.

LaCroix, Claudius, *Theologia Moralis,* 2 vols., Coloniae, 1719.

Lanza, A.-Palazzini, P., *Principi di Teologia Morale,* 3 vols., Roma: Editrice Studium, 1952-1956.

Laymann, Paulus, *Theologia Moralis,* 2 vols., Bambergae, 1669.

Lehmkuhl, Augustinus, *Theologia Moralis,* 9. ed., 2 vols., Friburgi Brisgoviae: Herder, 1898.

Leeming, Bernard, *Principles of Sacramental Theology,* Westminster, Md.: The Newman Press, 1956.

Mahoney, E. J., *Questions and Answers,* 2 vols., Vol. I, *The Sacraments,* London: Burns Oates & Washbourne Ltd., 1950.

McCarthy, John, *Problems in Theology,* 2 vols., Vol. I, *The Sacraments,* Dublin: Browne and Nolan Ltd., 1956.

McFadden, Charles J., *Medical Ethics,* 3. ed., Philadelphia: F. A. Davis Company, 1953.

Merkelbach, Benedictus Henricus, *Summa Theologiae Moralis,* 10. ed. aucta et emendata, 3 vols., Brugis: Desclée de Brouwer, 1956.

Migne, J. P., *Patrologiae Cursus Completus, Series Latina,* 221 vols., Parisiis, 1844-1855.

Mothon, Joseph, *Institutions Canoniques,* 3 vols., Vol. II, Bruges: Société Saint-Augustin, Desclée de Brouwer, 1924.

Noldin, H.-Schmitt, A., *Summa Theologiae Moralis,* 27. ed., 3 vols., Barcelona: Herder, 1951.

O'Malley, Austin, *The Ethics of Medical Homicide and Mutilation,* New York: Devin-Adair, 1922.

O'Kane, James, *Notes on the Rubrics of The Roman Ritual,* New edition completely revised in accordance with the latest (1925) *Editio Typica* of the *Rituale Romanum* and decrees of the Sacred Congregations, by Michael J. Fallon, Dublin: James Duffy & Co., 1943.

Palazzini, P.-DeJorio, A., *Casus Conscientiae,* 2 vols., Taurini: Marietti, 1958.

Palmer, Paul F., *Sources of Christian Theology,* 2 vols., Westminster, Md.: The Newman Press, 1955-1959.

Piscetta, A.-Gennaro, A., *Elementa Theologiae Moralis,* 7 vols., Vol. 5, 6. ed., Torino: Società Editrice Internazionale, 1938.

Pourrat, P., *Theology of the Sacraments,* translated from the 3rd French Edition, St. Louis: Herder, 1910.

Prümmer, Dominicus M., *Manuale Theologiae Moralis,* 12. ed., recognita a P. Engelberto M. Münch, Friburgi Brisgoviae: Herder, 1955.

Raus, J. B., *Institutiones Canonicae,* altera editio, Paris: Typis Emmanuelis Vitte, 1931.

Regatillo, Eduardo, *Casos Canonico-Morales,* 2 vols., Vol. II, Santander: Sal Terrae, 1959.

———, *Ius Sacramentarium,* 2 vols., Santander: Sal Terrae, 1945.

Regatillo, E.-Zalba, M., *Theologiae Moralis Summa,* 3 vols., Matriti: Biblioteca de Autores Cristianos, 1952-1954.

Righetti, Mario, *Manuale di Storia Liturgica,* 4 vols., Milano: Ancora, 1950-1956.

Roberti, Francesco, *Dizionario di Teologia Morale,* Roma: Editrice Studium, 1954.

Romani, Sylvius, *Institutiones Iuris Canonici,* 2 vols., Romae: Editrice "Iustitia," 1941-1944.

Sabetti, Aloysius, *Compendium Theologiae Moralis,* 33. ed., 7. ed post Codicem, concinnata a Timotheo Barrett, Neo Eboraci: Pustet, 1931.

Sainte-Beuve, Jacobus, *Tractatus de Sacramentis Confirmationis et Unctionis Extremae,* Parisiis, 1686.

Scotus, Duns, *Summa Theologica,* 6 vols., Romae, 1903.

Scheeben, Matthew J., *The Mysteries of Christianity,* translated by Cyril Vollert, St. Louis: Herder, 1954.

Suarez, Franciscus, *Opera Omnia,* 28 vols., Parisiis, 1856-1861.

Tanquerey, Ad., *Synopsis Theologiae Dogmaticae,* 3 vols., Vol. III, 28. ed., quam recognovit R. De Geoffre, Paris: Desclée et Socii, 1955.

———, *Synopsis Theologiae Moralis et Pastoralis,* 3 vols., Vol. III, 24. ed., quam quarto post Codicem recognovit F. Cimetier, Paris: Desclée et Socii, 1955.

Thomas, Aquinas, St., *Summa Theologica,* 5 vols., Romae: Forzani, 1894.

Tournely, Honoratus, *Praelectiones Theologicae,* 10 vols. in 13, Venetiis: Pezzana, 1755-1765.

Vermeersch, A.-Creusen, J., *Epitome Iuris Canonici,* 3 vols., Vol. II, 7. ed., Bruxellis: L'Edition Universelle, 1954.

Wouters, Ludovicus, *Manuale Theologiae Moralis,* 2 vols., Vol. II, Brugis: Beyaert, 1932.

Woywod, Stanislaus, *A Practical Commentary on the Code of Canon Law,* revised by Callistus Smith, revised and enlarged edition of Combined Volumes I and II, New York: Joseph F. Wagner, 1957.

Zorell, Franciscus, *Lexicon Graecum Novi Testamenti,* Paris: P. Lethielleux, 1931.

Articles

Alszeghy, A., "L'effetto corporale dell'Estrema Unzione," *Gregorianum,* XXXVIII (1957), 385-405.

Anciaux, P., "L'Onction des Malades," *Collectanea Mechliniensia,* Nova Series, XXIX (1959), 7-12.

Charue, A., "Epître de St. Jacques," *La Sainte Bible,* Vol. XII, Paris: Letouzey et Ané, Editeurs, 1946, 380-433.

Condon, Kevin, "Sacrament of Healing," *Scripture,* XI (1959), 33-42.

Connell, Francis J., "Case for the apparently dead," *The American Ecclesiastical Review,* CXXXVII (1957), 345-346.

———, "The Hospital Chaplain and the Administration of Extreme Unction," *The American Ecclesiastical Review,* CXIX (1948), 95-104.

———, "Ministrations to a divorced man," *The American Ecclesiastical Review,* CXLII (1960), 345-346.

———, "Repetition of Extreme Unction," *The American Ecclesiastical Review,* CXXVIII (1953), 145-146.

Danagher, John J., "Extreme Unction in Doubtful Danger of Death," *The Homiletic and Pastoral Review*, LVII (1957), 655-656.

Davis, Charles, "The Sacrament of the Sick," *The Clergy Review*, XLIII (1958), 726-746.

De Ninno, Giuseppe, "Morte," *Enciclopedia Cattolica*, VIII, col. 1427-1435.

Didier, J. C., "Faut-il donner facilement l'Extrême-Onction sous condition, ou vaut-il mieux s'abstiner?" *L'Ami du Clergé*, 7th Series, LXIX (1959), 239-250.

Genicot, Joseph, "Casus (Canon 942)," *The Clergy Review*, XIX (1955), 225-230.

Kelly, Gerald, "Notes on Moral Theology," *Theological Studies*, XIII (1952), 94-97.

Lesage, Germain, "Sources textuaires de canons relatifs à l'Extrême-Onction," *Revue de l'Université d'Ottawa*, XXIX (1959), 65-87.

Lynch, John J., "Autopsy—How soon after death?" *The Linacre Quarterly*, XXVII (1960), 98-101.

———, "Notes on Moral Theology," *Theological Studies*, XX (1959), 260-263.

McCarthy, J., "Anointing after Apparent Death," *The Irish Ecclesiastical Record*, 5th series, LVIII (1941), 369-371.

McReavy, Lawrence, "Extreme Unction—How Near to Death?" *The Clergy Review*, XL (1955), 489-492.

———, "Ministering to Dying Non-Catholics," *The Clergy Review*, XL (1955), 79-90.

Madden, James, "Repetition of Extreme Unction," *The Australasian Catholic Record*, XXIX (1952), 144-150.

Mahoney, E. J., "Dispositions for Receiving Extreme Unction," *The Clergy Review*, XXXV (1951), 104-106.

———, "Extreme Unction—Monthly Repetition," *The Clergy Review*, XXXII (1949), 201-202.

———, "The Position of Extreme Unction," *The Clergy Review*, XXXIV (1950), 268-269.

Maroto, Philippus, "Dubia circa canones Extremae Unctionis applicandos casibus mortis apparentis," *Apollinaris*, I (1928), 176-180.

Meurant, F., "L'Extrême-Onction, Est-elle le sacrement de la dernière maladie?" *La Vie Spirituelle*, XCII (1955), 242-251.

Michaud, H. "La Mort Apparente et l'Administration des Sacrements," *Revue Apologétique*, LXIII (1936), 280-297.

Montague, G. F., "Extreme Unction: Sacrament of the Sick or of the Dying," *The Irish Ecclesiastical Record*, 5. series, XCIII (1960), 190-194.

Murray, Placid, "The Liturgical History of Extreme Unction," *The Furrow*, XI (1960), 572-593.

Palmer, Paul F., "The Purpose of Anointing the Sick: a Reappraisal," *Theological Studies*, XIX (1958), 309-344.

Parres, Cecil L., "Repetition of Extreme Unction in the Same Illness," *The Homiletic and Pastoral Review*, LVIII (1958), 1165-1168.

Pickar, Charles, "Is anyone sick among you?" *The Catholic Biblical Quarterly*, VII (1945), 165-174.

Quinn, J. Richard, "The Time of Administration of Extreme Unction," *The American Ecclesiastical Review*, CXXXV (1956), 292-299.

Ruch, C., "Extrême-Onction du Ier au IXe siècle," *Dictionnaire de Théologie Catholique*, V, col. 1927-1985.

Tesson, Eugène, "Réanimation et Casuistique," *Etudes*, CCXCVI (1958), 96-98.

Umberg, I. B., "Sacramenta Acatholicis nonnisi conditionate Conferenda," *Periodica de Re Morali Canonica Liturgica*, XXXVII (1948), 97-102.

Periodicals

American Ecclesiastical Review, The, Vols. I-XXXII, Philadelphia, 1889-1905; from 1905, *Ecclesiastical Review, The*, Vols. XXXIII-CIX, Philadelphia, 1905-1943; from 1944, *American Ecclesiastical Review, The*, Vol. CX-, Washington, D. C., 1944-

L'Ami du Clergé, Langres, 1879-

Apollinaris, Romae, 1928-

Australasian Catholic Record, The, Sidney, 1924-

Clergy Monthly, The, Ranchi, 1936-

Clergy Review, The, London, 1931-

Etudes, Paris, 1856-

Furrow, The, Maynooth, 1950-

Homiletic and Pastoral Review, The, New York, 1900-

Irish Ecclesiastical Record, The, Dublin, 1864-

Linacre Quarterly, The, New York, 1932-

Periodica de Re Canonica et Morali, Brugis, 1905-1926; from 1927, *Periodica de Re Morali, Canonica, Liturgica*, Brugis, 1927-

Revue Apologétique, Bruxelles, 1900-

Revue de l'Université d'Ottawa, Ottawa, 1931-

Theological Studies, Woodstock, Md., 1940-

La Vie Spirituelle, Paris, 1919-

ALPHABETICAL INDEX

BIOGRAPHICAL NOTE

Charles George Renati was born in San Francisco, California, on April 23, 1931. After attending public and Star of the Sea parochial elementary schools in San Francisco, he entered St. Joseph's Minor Seminary, Mountain View, in 1945, and was graduated from there in 1951. The same year he entered St. Patrick's Major Seminary, Menlo Park, where he received the Bachelor of Arts Degree in 1953. On June 15, 1957, he was ordained to the priesthood in St. Mary's Cathedral, San Francisco, and was assigned by Archbishop John J. Mitty as an assistant to Mission Dolores Basilica in the same city. A year later he was sent to undertake postgraduate work in Canon Law at The Catholic University of America, where he received the degree of Bachelor in Canon Law in June of 1959, and the degree of Licentiate in Canon Law in June of 1960.

CANON LAW STUDIES *

416. Cunningham, Rev. Thomas M., O.S.M., J.C.L., The Canonical Suppression of Religious Houses.
417. McGough, Rev. James P., J.C.L., The Laws of the State of Mississippi Affecting Church Property.
418. Nace, Rev. Arthur J., A.B., M.A., J.C.L., The Right to Accuse a Marriage of Invalidity.
419. Renati, Rev. Charles G., A.B., J.C.L., The Recipient of Extreme Unction.
420. Song, Rev. Raphael H., M.A., J.C.L., The Sacred Congregation for the Propagation of the Faith.

* For a complete list of the available numbers of this series apply to the Catholic University of America Press, 620 Michigan Avenue, N.E., Washington (17), D. C., for a general catalogue.

www.ingramcontent.com/pod-product-compliance
Lightning Source LLC
LaVergne TN
LVHW050236080826
844660LV00012B/540

* 9 7 8 0 8 1 3 2 2 5 7 6 0 *